D0001364

PROGRESS IN
PENAL REFORM

Progress in
Penal Reform

edited by

LOUIS BLOM-COOPER

CLARENDON PRESS · OXFORD
1974

Oxford University Press, Ely House, London W.1

GLASGOW NEW YORK TORONTO MELBOURNE WELLINGTON
CAPE TOWN IBADAN NAIROBI DAR ES SALAAM LUSAKA ADDIS ABABA
DELHI BOMBAY CALCUTTA MADRAS KARACHI LAHORE DACCA
KUALA LUMPUR SINGAPORE HONG KONG TOKYO

ISBN 0 19 825325 7

© *Oxford University Press 1974*

Printed in Great Britain by
William Clowes & Sons, Limited, London, Beccles and Colchester

CONTENTS

INTRODUCTION   vii

1. Penal reform and penal history: some reflections
                              NOEL MCLACHLAN   1

2. The Constitutional framework of the English penal
   system   LOUIS BLOM-COOPER   25

3. Parliament and penal policy   GAVIN DREWRY   35

4. Policy and administration in penal establishments
                              J. E. THOMAS   54

5. The evaluation of penal systems   PETER NOKES   68

6. Aspects of European penal systems   NORMAN BISHOP 83

7. The ideology of imprisonment   GORDON HAWKINS   101

8. The contribution of prison medicine   R. R. PREWER 116

9. The role of psychologists in the penal system
                              GORDON TRASLER   129

10. The role of education in the penal system
                              W. R. STIRLING   142

11. The woman offender   ANN D. SMITH   155

12. The sentencing process: present practice and future policy
                              SIR ARTHUR JAMES   165

13. Sentencing structure: a paradigm for the future
                              LOUIS BLOM-COOPER   174

14. General deterrence   SIR BRIAN MACKENNA   182

15. Winners and losers: a perspective on penal change
                              JOHN P. CONRAD   196

16. A prisoner's perspective   HANUS HERMANN   209

Contents

17. CAUTION: some thoughts on the penal involvement
    rate   NIGEL WALKER   221

18. Intermediate treatment   NICHOLAS HINTON   238

19. The Community Service Order   JEF SMITH   245

20. Non-custodial supervision   PETER MCNEAL   254

    BIOGRAPHICAL NOTES   268

    SELECT BIBLIOGRAPHY   273

    INDEX   281

INTRODUCTION

PRISON is the core of our penal system, and not just in the eyes of the general public. Even though in 1972 only 197 offenders per 1,000 convicted of indictable offences—compared with 440 in 1953—were sent to prison, courts often, if not invariably, start by considering whether a prison sentence is appropriate.[1] We inherit from the nineteenth century the view that imprisonment is the natural penalty for crime, from which offenders can be spared only if one can show that some other method of dealing with them is likely to be effective. Underlying even current thinking on the topic, there is a pre-supposition that sending an offender away from his community is the natural course to fall back on if one cannot show convincingly that some other form of penal sanction is appropriate, even when custodial treatment may itself be ineffective and harmful to the individual, as well as being expensive. Thus central and crucial to the process of sentencing is the ultimate sanction of imprisonment, the more so since the final disappearance in 1965 of the death penalty.

While more and more sentencers are beginning to learn that prison imposes moral, psychological, and physical degradation upon prisoners, others still comfort themselves, when passing prison sentences, with the thought that the avowed primary function of the prison system, spelt out in the words of Rule 1 of the Prison Rules 1964, is to encourage and assist prisoners to lead a useful and industrious life—a belief which is at best sanguine, at worst self-deceiving. (How often one hears or reads of a judge justifying a sentence of imprisonment by saying that the treatment the offender needs will be provided in prison.) In practice, Rule 1 is not even given its supposed priority. Containment of prisoners within the prison walls and trouble-free administration come first, rehabilitation follows as a struggling third. Until a few years ago, thoughtful and humane scholars, prison administrators, and penal reformers preached that it was the duty of a civilized prison service to rehabilitate offenders. Much commendable effort has been expended towards that end in

[1] R. M. Jackson, *Enforcing the Law*, Revised Edition, Pelican Books (1972), p. 307.

the face of the appalling odds of overcrowding, the preoccupation with security, and lack of resources. This belief in reformative influences grew out of the reaction to the prison conditions of the last century, as the antidote to the brutality of the separate and silent system. It was given official blessing in the Gladstone Committee's oft-quoted dictum that the purpose of imprisonment is deterrence and reformation. Those twin, and probably incompatible aims have remained obstinately with us.

The weight of opinion among the *cognoscenti* about the rehabilitation of prisoners has, however, perceptibly shifted. The Americans have led the field in putting a large question mark over the reformative effects of treatment in custody; indeed, they are questioning all penal measures by asking, do any of them do any good?[1] The most striking observation comes from an unexpected quarter. The Wisconsin Citizens' Study Committee on Offender Rehabilitation—composed of ordinary people as well as professionals—stated in July 1972, in its final report to the Governor of Wisconsin, that 'no amount of resources, however great, can enhance a convicted citizen's chances for productive re-entry to a democratic society when that citizen has been confined in an institution too large to provide individual services, too geographically remote to provide vital life-contacts, and too regimented to foster self-esteem. In short, current Wisconsin institutions cannot rehabilitate.'

The English prison system has continually throughout this century failed to rehabilitate offenders. It is undoubtedly true, however, that some offenders have been helped towards a life free from further crime by their experiences in prison; it is no reflection on the prison service to say that the same help could probably have been provided as effectively outside prison. This is testified to in the altogether more cautious language of the report of the Advisory Council on the Penal System on Young Adult Offenders in May 1974; 'such research as there has been has cast doubt on the effectiveness of custodial treatment as opposed to treatment in the community.'

It is a matter for no little wonderment that this transparently obvious fact has only now dawned upon a society that professes to care for its prisoners, and has genuinely tried to deal with them humanely and sensibly. But we have to ask how any of us would

[1] John P. Conrad, *Corrections and Simple Justice*, The Journal of Criminal Law and Criminology, June 1973.

react if we were required to live for any length of time in a cell containing few of the modern conveniences of life (indeed, to have to undergo the revolting practice of 'slopping-out'), with few social facilities, little privacy, limited mobility, highly restricted contact with families and friends, sparse access to gainful employment, and a high degree of authoritarian regimentation in which personal choice is almost non-existent. How might we fare upon our return to society, where competition with our fellow man is a prerequisite for life, and in circumstances where we would be greeted with the social disadvantage (not to say, stigma) of 'having done time'? The inherently dehumanizing influence of penal institutions has been (and is) only too plain for those who wish to see. Only the blinkered could tolerate such a system. The very least we can do is to stop that to every extent possible.

To be fair, the story of our modern penal system has been the gradual whittling away of the harsh penalties of the past, and the attempt, however ineffective and crude, to cure offenders of their criminal propensities, both within and outside prison walls. We have struggled to dismantle at least some of the monuments to an outmoded penal philosophy. However, most of the nineteenth-century penitentiaries remain, supplemented since the last war by a growing number of penal establishments adapted from military needs or purpose-built to cater for the almost continuous growth in the prison population. These institutions are the living embodiment of a penal policy that has not shaken off its commitment to the incarceration of criminals. Only in recent years has there been any concerted effort to move away, on anything but a small scale, from custodial to non-custodial treatment. How we became entrapped by the legacy of our Victorian forebears is a matter of history.

Public discussion—in contrast to professional debate—about crime and punishment is conducted against the background of the pervasive criminal code. The great range of the criminal law, with its long list of imprisonable offences, disguises the simple fact that there are troublesome people who, quite apart from any specific misdeeds, ought to be coped with by the social services. Prison becomes a social dustbin to which society too readily consigns those offenders for whom community resources are either unavailable or inadequate.

Alternatively, the argument is conducted on the over-simplified assumption that people who are found guilty of crimes are just plain wicked, and deserve to be punished; courts that inflict imprisonment upon criminals must (so the argument runs) be acting both correctly and in the public interest.

Neither view assists in the framing of a future penal policy which aims at treating offenders within the community, because they both omit to ask the vital question: what are the real effects of the measures imposed? (As a cautionary note, it is jumping to conclusions in the other direction to take it for granted that community treatment will always be more effective; but it is no more ineffective, and probably has less harmful side-effects.)

The task that lies ahead is to discover how we can, with public support, escape the trap we have fallen into. The way out is tolerably plain. We must turn the system inside out. Prison (by whatever name we call it) should be reserved for the dangerous and for use, sparingly, as an aid to the control and supervision of offenders within the community. The object of treatment should be to persuade and enable the offender to lead a good and useful life within the community. This should become the core of the penal system. Custody would be a relevant consideration only as part of a continuing programme of adjustment; the real-life environment of the offender is infinitely to be preferred to the artificial atmosphere of the closed institution. Rule 1 would read, not that the purpose of *prison* is to encourage and assist the offender to lead a useful and industrious life, but that the *sentencing process* and the treatment that follows it has that aim; and that the better way of achieving this is almost always not by imprisonment at all.

Where removal from ordinary social intercourse is deemed essential, either in support of community-based treatment or in response to public demand for protection from the depredations of armed robbers or large-scale fraudsters, the physical conditions of captivity do not need to obtrude or impinge so starkly upon the lifestyle of the inmate. If prisons are not to be shapeless communities of social rejects, the methods of custody must be transformed. Ostentatious key-jingling must be replaced by less obtrusive surveillance; the close-circuit television has gone some way towards that aim, although, obnoxiously, Alsatian dogs still patrol the inner perimeters. There are still far too many restrictions on internal movement. The fence-variety perimeter should relieve much of the internal locking and unlocking of gates. It also provides a less forbidding outlook for the inmate who can see more than just the sky above him.

Modern prisons for the greatly reduced prison population need also to be much smaller units, geared to individualized treatment, and centrally sited so that the social, educational, and medical services of the community are readily available for institutional and extra-mural use. Prisons within urban centres of population facilitate access for visitors, both families and legal representatives. Above all, the regimes, while infinitely variable in their range of facilities, should be soundly based on the principle of justice for prisoners.

A prisoner does not, in theory at least, lose his basic human rights because he is imprisoned—save for the right to personal liberty during his sentence. Consistent with the duty of containment, the prison service should strive to preserve and develop the prisoner's personality and his links with the community outside. Prison should be within the community and not a place apart. And it should be committed fundamentally to returning its inmates to their communities as soon as this can be done without undue risk to the public.

Justice, John Rawls wrote,[1] is the first virtue of social institutions. If justice is not more ruthlessly pursued as an instrument of penal policy, treatment programmes (both custodial and non-custodial) will continue to be frustrated. The rhetoric of rehabilitation, so redolent of our past and present penal philosophy, must be re-examined. It must be translated so as to enhance the requirement of restoring to prisoners the sense of dignity of which the physical fact of incarceration deprives them. Stripped of any potential for reform—at least, if they are not used as part of a longer-term programme of non-custodial treatment—prisons would be in real danger of becoming dumping grounds for social outcasts, where neither justice nor care played any significant part in the life of the institutions. And that would hardly represent progress in penal reform. As Dr. McLachlan sharply reminds us in the leading essay in this volume, not all penal reform has led to progress.

The purpose of this collection of essays is two-fold. First, to demonstrate, by the near-unanimity of the contributors, that the rehabilitation of offenders in prison has proved so far unattainable. The first half of the book is devoted to an explanation of how and why the English prison system has failed to reform. But even meritorious iconoclasm must never be the sole task of the reformer. The book's complementary aim is to point the way to a new penal philosophy in which imprisonment ceases to occupy the central

[1] *A Theory of Justice*, Clarendon Press (1972), p. 3.

position, and in which responsibility for offenders rests primarily with the communities of which delinquency is a product.

This book of essays was initiated by a generous grant from the I.T.T. Executive Association in the United Kingdom Charitable Trust to the National Association for the Care and Resettlement of Offenders, with a view to the publication of a book dedicated to the theme of penal reform. N.A.C.R.O. in turn invited me to organize and edit the book. I have been both sensitive to, and privileged by, the honour of being asked to act as editor of essays by distinguished authors, the more so since the invitation came before my elevation to the chairmanship of the Howard League for Penal Reform, when occupation of that prestigious office might in itself have attracted such an invitation regardless of the occupant.

The editorial task was made easier by the willing response of essayists to entreaties to contribute and to harassment for the supply of the essays. Given the time scale from drawing-board to publication, it was possible for each contributor to have a sight of the contributions of his co-authors at some stage of production, so that the essays could be dovetailed, and overlapping avoided. This considerably lightened the editor's burden.

This is my opportunity to thank all those who responded so readily to the invitation to contribute. Any merit that this symposium of essays has is due entirely to the quality of the individual essays. The editor's task has largely been an administrative one; the editorial pen has hardly been in evidence. It is, I hope, consistent with a proper sense of modesty that I venture to think that the volume will be a major contribution to thinking, in and out of official circles, on penal affairs.

1. Penal Reform and Penal History: Some Reflections

NOEL MCLACHLAN

Such then are the lessons of history. Penal reform will have its expectations fulfilled only when it can rely on personal reformative efforts, differentiation of treatment, and the support by an enlightened public conscience.[1]

SURPRISINGLY little stock has been taken of the happy coincidence that all three European founding fathers of modern British criminology—Max Grünhut, Hermann Mannheim, and Sir Leon Radzinowicz—have shared an intense interest in penal history, though I have heard at least one of them described (unfairly) as more an historian than a criminologist. That interest has given a valuable historical dimension to criminological study in Britain less evident elsewhere.[2] Grünhut's essay on 'Historical Experience' (1948) remains the classic short statement of what penal history can apparently teach us, and the homily quoted above from it provides an appropriate springboard for a discussion of some aspects of the historical background to the penal system of the last quarter of this century.

But in the quarter century since they were written these words have acquired an unmistakable patina of innocence. Confronted with ever-rising (official) crime rates, dwindling detection rates, and intractable recidivism, criminologists these days are a good deal more sophisticated—or cynical—about their 'expectations'. Criminological research has never looked quite the same since Barbara Wootton's cruelly deflating *Social Science and Social Pathology* (1959), and not long ago two Assistant Directors of Research at the Cambridge Institute of Criminology, while reporting substantial progress with some 'key issues', referred cryptically to 'idealists (*if there are any left*) in the fields of correctional administration and

[1] M. Grünhut, *Penal Reform* (Oxford, 1948), p. 134. I am grateful to David Biles, Senior Criminologist, Australian Institute of Criminology, Canberra, for helpful advice concerning this essay.
[2] For example, the United States.

research'.[3] Evidently healthy cautiousness and concentration on concrete penological problems are likely to characterize such research during the rest of this century.

Grünhut's interpretation of penal history, however, has never been seriously challenged. One almost has the impression that criminologists believe there is nothing much left to be said on the subject, except perhaps to fill in a few passing details or occasionally provide brief, pious, historical prefaces to their own published research.[4] What I want to suggest is that, in fact, what we *don't* know about British penal history is even now much more impressive than what we do know—there are, indeed, few more under-researched aspects of modern British social history—and that, meanwhile, though acknowledging the wisdom of many of Grünhut's pioneering insights, important other 'lessons' can be drawn from the past. Perhaps the most important is the need always to distinguish clearly between penal reform and penal progress.

1. PENAL REFORM AND PENAL PROGRESS

Grünhut's prejudices were natural enough. Like other social scientists he turned to the past mainly to learn how the present state of his subject had been reached.[5] This inevitably involved a search for origins. The classification of prisoners, for example, could be traced remotely to Peel's Gaol Act of 1823; the notion of progressive stages of imprisonment to the Australian transportation system; the Prison Commission beyond its creation in 1877 to the provision of a prison inspectorate in 1835; the 'separate' and 'silent' systems of prison discipline to American penitentiary practice; probation to the Acts of 1887 and 1907 and beyond; approved schools to Parkhurst youth prison (1838) and to both reformatory and industrial schools; Borstal to Ruggles–Brise's innovation of 1902 partly derived, like probation, from U.S. precedent; preventive detention to the 1908 Act, payment of prison labour to the experimental earnings scheme at Wakefield and, earlier, to the princely traditional gratuity of up to

[3] R. Hood and R. Sparks, *Key Issues in Criminology* (London, 1970), p. 214. My emphasis. The fiasco over the Royal Commission proudly announced by the 1964 White Paper could hardly have encouraged idealism either. Cf. R. Cross, *Punishment, Prison and the Public* (London, 1971), pp. 188–90.

[4] The only substantial modern survey is G. Rose, *The Struggle for Penal Reform* (London, 1961), but there is also R. S. E. Hinde's sketch, *The British Penal System 1773–1950* (London, 1951), and the Webb's *English Prisons under Local Government* (London, 1922), remains invaluable, perhaps their best book.

[5] Cf. H. Mannheim (ed.), *Pioneers in Criminology* (London, 1960).

10*s*. per six months endorsed by the Gladstone Committee in 1895.[6] Some of his attributions have been refined since, but, set in the context of overseas practice, they have been a valuable guide to penal origins.

But Grünhut did not confine himself to lists of sources of current ideas about punishment. He was also concerned to *explain* the transition. In doing so he was too intelligent to swallow whole the naïve Whiggish view of history common among social scientists. He did not mistake penal history for the simple history of 'progress' to the present. At first sight, he confessed, 'historical experience' did not seem very encouraging. Indeed, he described prison history as 'a history of "ideals and errors"': 'Separate confinement, the Progressive Stages idea, the reformatory—each "system" was hailed as a panacea and subsequently rejected as a disappointing failure.' All the same, each step was necessary to the next. For example:

From an historical point of view solitary confinement was a necessary step on the way to progress. Under the exciting influence of a forceful idea the chaotic state of the old gaols was definitely removed . . . the new order introduced a wholesome atmosphere of earnestness and dignity into prisons.

So it was still the history of 'progress' and apparently a deterministic view of history:

Social reformers cannot be expected to exhibit the objectivity of unbiased historians. They work hard to overcome prevailing evils which they ascribe to the deficiencies and omissions of the past, whilst they often owe their advanced standards to the ill-rewarded achievements of the former generation. Capital punishment had to be drastically reduced before a major problem of imprisonment could arise. The period of transportation had to be closed before the mother country felt full responsibility for the readjustment of criminals. Separate confinement offered the first opportunity for studying the prisoner's personality, but not before further unnatural and oppressive elements of prison discipline had been removed could such observation lead to an understanding of the prisoner's mind. It was one thing to acknowledge reformative principles of prison discipline and another to provide special facilities for pursuing this object and to try to develop appropriate methods of treatment. Each new task became necessary—and possible—by the preceding stage of reform.

And, despite the successive 'failures', the total achievement at the end was remarkable:

Even in the face of such modest progress prison history shows one remarkable result. In little more than one century mankind made the extraordinary step from considering imprisonment as a mere substitute for the

[6] Grünhut, op. cit., pp. 53, 83, 56, 43 ff., 300, 370–3, 381, 392, 212–13.

death penalty and a mortification closely allied to other forms of bodily
punishment to considering it as something which, by its underlying principles, is an appeal to the moral personality of the prisoner.[7]

Now this interpretation is admittedly attractive—especially the
generational factor in penal reform—and it is precisely because I
suspect many readers will find themselves in general agreement with
it that I feel disposed to quarrel with it here. For it seems to me to
imply a profound misconception of the process of historical change,
which must seriously affect a proper understanding of the relevance
of the past to the present—and to the future. Let me try to explain
what I find so unsatisfactory about it.

In the first place, rather than emphasize the 'inevitability' of the
last hundred years or so of 'prison history', it seems to me important
in 1974 to recognize that they were very largely (though not entirely)
a mistake, a blind alley into which the British Government wandered
as much through short-sighted financial and political expediency as
from any considered penal philosophy.[8] An interpretation in terms of
'all for the best' does less than justice to the hard fact that it was
sometimes 'for the worst' and that we are still suffering from disastrous policy decisions made more than a century ago. These
included the ambitious programme of cellular prison building[9]
launched by Lt.-Col. Joshua Jebb, architect of Pentonville model
prison (1842) and from 1837 Surveyor-General of Prisons, and the
1865 Prisons Act which, following the Carnarvon Committee recommendations two years earlier, imposed a strictly separate system of
discipline.[10]

---

[7] Ibid., pp. 131, 133, 62, 132.   [8] Cf. Cross, op. cit., pp. 84–6.

[9] The preposterous statement of Du Cane (*The Punishment and Prevention of
Crime* (London, 1885; p. 56) that: 'In six years after Pentonville was built
fifty-four new prisons were built after its model, affording 11,000 separate cells'
has been uncritically accepted (see, for example, L. W. Fox, *The English Prison
and Borstal Systems* (London, 1952), p. 38; D. L. Howard, *The English Prisons*
(London, 1960), p. 63; and J. E. Thomas, *The English Prison Officer since 1850*
(London, 1972), p. 16). Admittedly Jebb himself tended to be vague about
prison-building statistics, but in his evidence to the Select Committee on Prison
Discipline in 1850 he produced a table which listed fifty-four prisons 'which have
been erected *or Improved* on the Pentonville Plan during the last few Years' with a
'probable accommodation' of 8,770 cells. Du Cane evidently got 11,000 by
adding in six other 'prisons in progress' with a probable accommodation of
2,537 cells, but forgetting to add six to the fifty-four (Minutes of Evidence, p. 4).
Cf. Appendix to Jebb's Second Report as Surveyor-General of Prisons, 1847, p. 39.

[10] S. and B. Webb, op. cit., pp. 188–92. At the same time, a version of the
'mark system' was introduced to regulate remission and progress to less stringent
discipline, but it was far from a fair test of Maconochie's principles.

Though D. L. Howard's 1960 estimate that only four (closed) prisons had been built since 1877 is happily no longer quite true, most prisoners are still housed in institutions built at least a century ago.[11] True, the regimes have been transformed, but even now one prisoner to a cell remains general Home Office policy even if honoured almost as much in the breach, since a still rapidly rising prison population has belied the confidence of the 1964 White Paper that new prisons then under construction would relieve the overcrowding.[12] Whether single cells are really essential, even in closed prisons, remains virtually unargued, presumably for the practical reason that no alternative accommodation is in sight.[13]

This dead hand of the architectural past still seriously obstructs, if it does not, in fact, destroy, recent emphases on training and preparation for return to the outside world. Even the 'prevention of deterioration' which Rupert Cross proposes[14] as the main aim of prison reform must be hard to achieve in such an environment. If long-term hospitalization commonly induces 'institutional neurosis',[15] what must be its incidence in our prisons?

All this reflects what is almost the only constant in the history of British prisons (apart perhaps from Millbank (1816–21) and the 1840s): the very low priority accorded public spending on erecting and maintaining them, even when crime is allegedly stirring serious public concern. After World War II the replacement of hopelessly obsolete school buildings understandably took top priority, and more recently vestiges of antiquated Poor Law hospitals and other Poor Law institutions have been steadily disappearing, but the anachronism of prison buildings has until recently been relieved less by rebuilding

[11] Howard, op. cit., p. 86. The centenary of Wormwood Scrubs is due this year (1974). Howard's estimate (p. 146) that complete rebuilding of English prisons would cost at least £100 m. now looks overly modest in the light of the £100 m. or more to be spent on prison building over a five-year period.

[12] *The War against Crime in England and Wales 1959–1964*, p. 12. On the other hand, it has to be recognized that sexual freedom is probably the deprivation most prisoners feel most keenly and that, as long as three to a cell remains common, courts in sentencing a man to prison are often also sentencing him to sodomy.

[13] New secure prisons indicate a cautious desire to experiment: Blundeston, for instance, was built with predominantly cellular, but some dormitory, accommodation.

[14] Cross, op. cit., p. 85.

[15] R. Barton, *Institutional Neurosis* (Bristol, 1959). Cf. T. and P. Morris, *Pentonville* (London, 1963), p. 171. The 'inadequate', dependent, petty criminal who commits an offence soon after release in order to return to the psychological security of prison is not a figment of prison officers' imagination, but hardly an argument for 'less eligibility'.

6 *Noel McLachlan*

than by small open prisons usually housed in old country mansions or Nissen huts and by devising new alternatives to imprisonment.

As with so much of government in the nineteenth century and since, whatever the Home Office proposed, it was the Treasury that disposed, and that department was under constant pressure from Parliament for economy.[16] At the same time, the old Poor Law principle of 'less eligibility', the penal implications of which Mannheim drew attention to long ago,[17] clearly still applies, though some recognition that standards of living outside have changed drastically during the past century has penetrated prison cells—and diets. The lesson here is surely that only a major assault on public opinion, though alien to Howard League tradition, for example,[18] is likely to transform this depressing situation.

What then of the 'extraordinary' metamorphosis of imprisonment in little more than a century admired by Grünhut? Despite the welcome reforms in prison life since 1948, the valiant if forlorn efforts to reconcile 'deterrence' and 'reform' and the proliferation of alternatives to prison like probation, parole, suspended sentences, attendance centres, and the day-training centres and community service orders provided by the 1972 Criminal Justice Act, the more extraordinary fact, if one takes a long view, is surely *how little* the penal system has changed. Not only in respect of buildings has the pace of reform been depressingly slow. The reasons are obvious enough. In keeping with nineteenth-century administrative trends prisons came under increasingly centralized control, from the establishment in 1850 of the Directors of Convict Prisons who administered a uniform, 'separate' system of convict prisons from 1865, to the wholly centralized control under Du Cane, the first chairman of the Prison Commission, in 1877. But uniformity did not make for adventurousness, least of all under Du Cane who secured the reduction of the number of local prisons from 113 to sixty in the name of 'economy' in a decade.[19] Like Jebb and

[16] Cf. the argument of Henry Parris that 'Treasury control was a symptom not a disease' (*Constitutional Bureaucracy* (London, 1969), p. 257). His study usefully places prisons within the general development of British central administration.

[17] H. Mannheim, *The Dilemma of Penal Reform* (London, 1939), Chapter II, III, and IV.

[18] Cf. Rose, op. cit., pp. 266–71.

[19] See Cross, op. cit., pp. 7–42, for a brief discussion of Du Cane and his successors. Thomas, op. cit., p. 28, argues that 'he is the greatest figure in the history of the English prison system'. Certainly the suggestion that 'a proper

Du Cane governors and prison officers frequently came from military service and infused military notions of discipline and frugality more often than imaginative new ideas or humanitarian concern.[20]

It was the unique achievement of the Gladstone Committee of 1895 that it managed to overthrow the whole philosophy of uniformity and severity so carefully nurtured by Du Cane, advanced 'deterrence and reform' as 'the primary *and concurrent* objects' of prison treatment, and attracted statutory endorsement of its major recommendations within three years. Although the Home Secretary, in introducing the 1898 Bill, insisted that it was 'not a revolution in prison government',[21] the implications of the second clause giving him power to make rules for the government of all prisons, including hard labour and the classification of prisoners, were not much less than revolutionary. Herbert Gladstone, who had chaired the committee, described this clause (which had *not* been one of their recommendations) as 'the most valuable provision in the Bill', and Sir Lionel Fox, the second-last chairman of the Prison Commission, later testified that, under this more elastic procedure, 'the natural development of fifty years was able to proceed without further intervention of parliament'.[22]

Certainly there is a more or less straight line from the 1899 Rules to Rule 1 of the hundred and one 1964 Rules[23] and emancipation from the need to legislate every change in policy may well have accelerated penal reform since the 1898 Act. But it is arguable that, with a less enlightened Prison Commission, this reform need not

evaluation of his achievements is long overdue' is sound. On prison closures see Appendix in Thomas, pp. 232–4. Jebb likewise emphasized that the separate system made prison building cheaper: see minutes of evidence, Select Committee on Prison Discipline, 1850, pp. 5–7.

[20] Thomas, op. cit., pp. 40–50, explains and defends the para-military structure, and on p. 113 tabulates the ex-service component in the prison services. His book appeared after this essay was drafted. By challenging major premises of penal reform he has made one of the most stimulating contributions to penal history since the war, even if his special pleading inevitably distorts.

[21] Sir M. W. Ridley, 24 Mar. 1898, *Parliamentary Debates*, 4th series, vol. lv, 1898, col. 837. My emphasis. Thomas (op. cit., p. 118) argues that the Gladstone Committee 'with its contradictory proposals, sowed the seeds of organisational confusion which has dogged the twentieth-century prison service'. An authoritative study of these events is urgently needed.

[22] Ibid., col. 854; Gladstone calculated the number of his committee's recommendations in the Bill (col. 859). Fox, op. cit., p. 58.

[23] The 1899 Code of Rules was consolidated and simplified in 1933; these in turn lasted until the 1949 Rules made under the 1948 Act. The 1899 Rules (190 for convict and 312 for local prisons) did not state the objects of prison discipline.

have been beneficial and, in any case, that more parliamentary
attention to prisons need not have been obstructive. Duncan Fairn,
head of the Prison Department from 1964 to 1968, has described the
Gladstone Committee Report as 'until the publication of *Penal
Practice in a Changing Society* in 1959, the most considered statement of penal policy ever enunciated in this country', but Professor
Cross has commented that there have, after all, been few such
statements made.[24] This reflects, among other things, the scant
attention that governments have given to prisons in both the nineteenth and twentieth centuries and their much greater accessibility
to Treasury arguments than to those of penal reformers. All things
considered, it is too much to conclude that the rate of prison building, for example, during the fifty years after 1898 was a 'natural'
one. And was not the persistence of almost meaningless distinctions
between penal servitude, imprisonment, and imprisonment with hard
labour, until 1948 another illustration, as Cross says, of 'the snail's
pace with which penal reform proceeds'?[25] Was the refusal to permit
prison officers to form a staff association until 1939 really inevitable
and excusable?[26] And has the abolition of the Prison Commission
in 1963 and its absorption by the Home Office, the culmination of
some 140 years of growing centralization, raised or lowered the
status of prisons in the consciousness of Government and public?[27]

Certainly atavistic features persist in prison administration.
Consider, for example the role of the prison chaplain. Just as the
emphasis on separate cells reflected religious prejudice about the
value of isolation and contemplation, the regimes adopted at Millbank and other new penitentiaries were strongly imbued with
religious zeal. The importance of religion as a reformatory influence
in prisons is common to the reports of all parliamentary committees
that investigated them between 1831 and 1863. As Elizabeth Fry
told the 1835 committee, 'if any one wants a Confirmation of the
Truth of Christianity, let him go and read the Scriptures in Prisons
to poor Sinners; you see there how the Gospel is exactly adapted to

[24] R. D. Fairn, 'Prisons 1866–1966', in H. J. Klare (ed.), *Changing Concepts of
Crime and its Treatment* (Oxford, 1966), p. 160; Cross, op. cit., p. 3.

[25] Ibid., p. 11.

[26] Thomas, op. cit., pp. 171–2.

[27] Since I took an active if anonymous part in the campaign against abolition
and have been out of England during most of the period since, I venture no
opinion on this matter, but Thomas (op. cit., p. 196) argues that the administrative and psychological effects of the change were 'disastrous'.

the Fallen Condition of Man'.[28] Arthur Griffiths, who was deputy governor of Millbank later on, reflected that 'the general tone of public opinion' in the 1830s 'turned towards entrusting the ministers of religion with full powers to preach prisoners out of their evil courses', but was sceptical of the effect: 'The incessant religious exercises—the prayers, expositions, and genuflexions, were more in keeping with a monastery of monks than a gaol full of criminals.'[29]

At this time the chaplain ranked second only to the governor in status and salary if not authority.[30] One of the first prison inspectors appointed was the former chaplain of Millbank, and in 1837 his successor there, the Revd. Daniel Nihil, was permitted to combine the offices of chaplain and governor. His attempt to imbue the prison with high moral fervour was not a success, and his rigorous preference for solitary confinement allegedly led to an embarrassing rise in the suicide rate.[31] During the rest of the century, as the Prison Ministers Act of 1863 testifies,[32] the chaplain's status remained high —at least in official eyes. So it has in this century. Though Ruggles-Brise called himself a pagan, Alexander Paterson, easily the most influential Prison Commissioner of the 1930s, noted with approval

[28] Minutes of Evidence, 2nd Report of Select Committee of House of Lords on the Present State of the Gaols, 1835, p. 328: 'it has strongly confirmed my Faith,' she went on, 'and I feel it the bounden duty of the Government and the Country that those Truths should be administered to Sinners in the Manner most likely to conduce to the real Reformation of the Prisoner; you then go to the Root of the Matter . . .' Cf. U.R.Q. Henriques, 'The Rise and Decline of the Separate System of Prison Discipline', *Past and Present*, 54 (Feb. 1972), 61–93.

[29] A. Griffiths, *Memorials of Millbank* (London, 1875), vol. i, pp. 205, 195. He quoted (p. 196) the case of Joseph Wells, an old offender, who was reported for writing on his pint cup:

Yor order is	but mine is
for me to go	that I'll go to
to chapel,	Hell first.

When remonstrated with, Wells 'merely laughed in the governor's face'. Cf. G. Ives, *A History of Penal Methods* (London, 1914), Chapter XIII, and the evidence of Capt. Donatus O'Brien, chairman of Visiting Justices of Westminster House of Correction and active in prison administration since 1847, to the Select Committee on Prison Ministers Acts, 1870 (p. 21): 'I question much the reformation of any prisoner of any sort, or either sex, being effected by any kind of religious teaching in prison.'

[30] For chaplains' duties and salaries see Appendix No. 21 to Report of Select Committee on Gaols 1835, pp. 563 ff. The Millbank chaplain's myriad duties are described on p. 579.

[31] Griffiths, op. cit., pp. 200–1, 290–308. Cf. H. Mayhew and J. Binny, *The Criminal Prisons of London* (London, 1862), pp. 236, 106–7.

[32] The Act provided for the appointment and remuneration of ministers who were not members of the Established church.

that 'the extent to which provision is made by setting aside places of worship and by appointing chaplains is some indication of the importance which the State attaches to religion as a necessary part of prison administration'.[33] The accession of education and welfare officers (and later psychologists) rendered parts of the chaplain's function redundant, but the annual report of the Prison Department continues to include a chapter on 'Religion'.[34]

What is most remarkable here is the failure to take account of changes in religious attitudes in the outside world. In the nineteenth century, religion touched the new industrial proletariat only marginally.[35] Even the Revd. John Clay, the indefatigable chaplain of Preston gaol, almost admitted as much when he claimed 'the poor home heathen, whom neither the parish minister nor the town missionary could reach, is, at last, brought into contact with the religious teacher, and may be prepared to receive the message of salvation'.[36] More commonly, to be compelled to attend church must have given many prisoners a healthy hatred of religion, whatever pious façade discretion made politic.[37]

The depiction of the chaplain in the film *A Clockwork Orange* was no doubt grossly unfair to existing chaplains, but it did catch something of the alienating effect such a role must have, even though attendance at services is no longer compulsory. After all, regular church-going is now the practice of a minority of the population, as is apparently belief in an after-life.[38] In such circumstances, the fact

[33] Cross, op. cit., p. 28; S. K. Ruck (ed.), *Paterson on Prisons* (London, 1951), p. 124. Cf. Fox, op. cit., Chapter 12 and pp. 89–90, and Grünhut, op. cit., pp. 252–60.

[34] The 1970 Report, for example, observed (p. 34) that 'Open-minded adult enquiry' is encouraged to help Borstal trainees 'find a philosophy which is their own rather than one imposed upon them by others to which they have to conform on pain of rejection'.

[35] See K. S. Inglis, *Churches and the Working Classes in Victorian England* (London, 1963). Cf. 'Popular Attitudes to Religion', in H. Pelling, *Popular Politics and Society in Late Victorian Britain* (London, 1968), pp. 19–36; O. Chadwick, *The Victorian Church*, Part I, 3rd ed. (London, 1971), Chapter V, and Part II (London, 1970), pp. 262 ff.; D. Bowen, *The Idea of the Victorian Church* (Montreal, 1968), pp. viii–ix, 255.

[36] Report for 1853–4, quoted in W. L. Clay, *The Prison Chaplain* (Cambridge and London, 1861), p. 335.

[37] For a spectacular instance of a death-cell conversion and its ironical sequel see my 'Edward Eagar (1787–1866): A Colonial Spokesman in Sydney and London', *Historical Studies*, Melbourne, x, 40 (May 1963), 431–56.

[38] See G. Gorer, *Exploring English Character* (London, 1955), pp. 241 ff., 253. More recent opinion polls suggest a further decline in religious faith and observance.

that there is still an Established church is less relevant than the legal decision in 1917 that Christianity does not form part of the law of England. At Pentonville the Morrises found that, once a man opted to attend church, he had to continue to do so regularly, and changes of religion could only be granted by the visiting justices. 'For the most part', they concluded, 'the impact of religion upon the prison community, in the sense of being an influence from outside, is small.'[39]

Is it unfair to detect in all this the persistence of atavistic, bureaucratic habits, uneasiness about what moral instruction, if any, should exist (group therapy?) and what it might cost, and deference to religious groups as some of the few pressure groups actively interested in prisons? Has the Prison Department ever made a realistic, long-term assessment of the future of religious activity in prisons?

This is not, of course, to disparage the contribution that devout Christians from John Howard and Elizabeth Fry on have made to penal reform. One need only consider the roles of the Police Court Mission and of the Canadian-born Wandsworth chaplain, W. D. Morrison, to establish how important they have been.[40] But it is precisely the strongly Christian colouring of the penal reform movement in England that has made its approach to such issues as religion in prison less than objective.[41] Might not evangelical–Christian bias also have predisposed reformers in the nineteenth century to emphasize the moral aspects of crime and to believe in the instant practicability of prison conversion and reform—as well as the beneficence of isolation? Might not the same prejudice help to account for the conspicuous reluctance of government to do more than play a supporting role in after-care?[42]

Instead, therefore, of accepting each stage in penal reform as a

[39] Morris, op. cit., pp. 39, 64, 297–8.

[40] In reality Elizabeth Fry was by no means the sedate Quaker matron depicted in iconography and pious biography. On Morrison see G. D. Robin, 'Pioneers in Criminology: William Douglas Morrison (1852–1943)', *Journal of Criminal Law, Criminology, and Police Science*, lv (1964), 48–58.

[41] Cf. E. R. Glover, *Probation and Re-education*, 2nd ed. (London, 1956), p. 247: 'For all these reasons probation officers who hope to help their probationers to find God should go humbly and gently, only venturing on a direct approach by invitation, whether this be given by word or implication.'

[42] The Act of 1862 authorized the payment of up to £2 per prisoner to voluntary discharged prisoners' aid societies, though according to Rose (op. cit., p. 183) the actual sum paid per head was nearer 6*d*.

Noel McLachlan

necessary instalment of 'progress' it is essential, I suggest, to appreciate that often it has been nothing of the sort. Even Grünhut's depiction of some of these stages is dubious. There was a major problem of imprisonment, for example, long before capital crimes (not the same as capital punishment) were drastically reduced in number. The resumption of transportation in 1787 certainly enabled the Government to postpone a thorough appraisal, but there were plenty of ideas about penitentiaries in circulation, not only Bentham's, and useful indigenous precedents were at hand in the bridewells. Separate and solitary confinement, in the context of prevailing ideas, *obstructed* rather than facilitated the study of prisoners' personalities and the development of sophisticated classification systems.[43] It proliferated not dignity but a heartless form of torture throughout the penal system. 'Progress' has no place in describing these last 'reforms'.

By the same token, though no one who studies the history of the Howard League and its predecessors can fail to admire the skill and perseverance they have displayed, it must be remembered that William Tallack, a founder of the Howard Association and its secretary from 1866 to 1901 (and another devout Quaker), was a lifelong apologist of the separate system and bitterly opposed to associated labour. Yet he was also actively opposed to capital punishment and in favour of reformatories.[44] In other words, not all penal reform is enlightened, nor penal reformers invariably wise.

Whether Grünhut's view of penal history was really deterministic or not is less important than his failure to evaluate penal reform in terms other than as the apparently necessary route to the present. Hindsight need not obstruct historical understanding if it helps us to distinguish wrong turnings from right, but it is also important to discern what real alternatives were open to policy makers. Consider, for example, a critical event in British penal history: the end of the Australian transportation system. Criminologists have commonly dismissed that system as an utter aberration, even as 'one of the most repulsive phases of human activity in dealing with criminals' and 'a ghastly failure wherever it has been tried'.[45]

[43] Jebb proudly told the Select Committee on Prison Discipline in 1850 (minutes of evidence, p. 3) that 'no classification of prisoners is necessary under the separate system'.
[44] See Rose, op. cit., pp. 66, 27, 28–30.
[45] H. E. Barnes and N. K. Teeters, *New Horizons in Criminology*, 3rd ed. (Englewood Cliffs, N.J., 1959), p. 305.

Alan Shaw has, however, demonstrated that, while it is difficult to generalize about a system which underwent major amendments and was never free from abuses, it was probably more humane and progressive than the penitentiary system which eventually replaced it.[46] In introducing the 1853 Transportation Bill which substantially substituted penal servitude for it the Lord Chancellor, Lord Cranworth, testified to his admiration for the old system:

... the experience I have obtained while presiding in criminal courts has impressed most strongly on my mind the conviction that transportation answers more effectively the ends of secondary punishment than any other that can be devised. It appeared to me to possess all the main ingredients of what was desirable in punishment; it created the *maximum* of apprehension, and the *minimum* of endurance; it excited great terror, without, perhaps, eventually inflicting great pain; and I do not know how we can expect to obtain so desirable a secondary punishment.[47]

Judicial opinion of this sort may be suspect, but it is worth noting that he was joined in his 'requiem of transportation' by Brougham and Grey and the Duke of Newcastle.

Why then was it abandoned? The short answer is not 'progress', but a combination of an almost uniquely influential parliamentary pressure group and the prejudices of some free colonists. The Molesworth Committee of 1837–8, which condemned transportation, was dominated by Wakefieldians for whom transportation represented a serious threat to their schemes of free colonization. The wild distortions of their report were widely broadcast, and traces remain in the conceptions of modern criminologists, like those quoted above. 'The ultimate judgment of history', Grünhut observed, 'confirms the verdict by the Select Committee of 1837.'[48] Nothing of the sort.

Though there were other critics of transportation[49] it was the

[46] A. G. L. Shaw, *Convicts and the Colonies* (London, 1966); 'Reformatory Aspects of the Transportation of Convicts to Australia', in N. Morris and M. Perlman (eds.), *Law and Crime* (New York, 1972), pp. 135–54. Shaw, and L. L. Robson in *The Convict Settlers of Australia* (Melbourne, 1965), have also authoritatively answered a question Grünhut considered unanswerable: 'Who were the transported convicts?' George Rudé's latest essay in this field is 'Early Irish rebels in Australia', *Historical Studies*, Melbourne, xvi, 62 (April 1974), 17–35.

[47] *Parliamentary Debates*, 3rd ser., vol. cxxix (1853), col. 7. Emphasis in original.   [48] Grünhut, op. cit., p. 81.

[49] See R. Whately, *Thoughts on Secondary Punishments* (London, 1832). Like Wakefield, Whately, the Archbishop of Dublin, attended sessions of the 1837–8 Committee, and both apparently prompted the chairman, Molesworth, to ask witnesses particular questions. See *Sydney Monitor*, 5 Jan. 1838. Whately was also a witness.

complementing of Wakefieldian criticism by an increasingly articulate group of colonists, many of them assisted immigrants with economic interests directly opposed to convict labour, which sealed the fate of the system. In this connection it is worth indulging in the exercise recommended by Hugh Stretton of devising 'imagined alternatives to reality'—subtracting some cause of an event and substituting another feature in order to help measure the subtracted cause and perhaps understand how much needs to be explained.[50] In this case, let us suppose in place of the anti-transportation colonists a much more powerful group than actually existed of colonial employers concerned to maintain this source of cheap labour. Then what would have happened? There can be little doubt that the British Government would have been very relieved and happy to continue transportation on a substantial scale as long as any Australian colonies were prepared to receive them.[51] And the programme of local and other prison building would have been reduced accordingly. In other words, the Government was far from disposed to abandon a system that had served its predecessors well, and the recourse that was subsequently made to penitentiaries at home was simply a response to the *fait accompli* that no alternative was available any longer.

If this is borne in mind it puts a rather different complexion on the new policy implicit in the Transportation and Penal Servitude Acts of 1853 and 1857. Neither the Wakefieldians nor Whately had any very precise conception of the secondary punishments that should replace transportation. Neither, it seems, had the British Government. The idea of introducing a 'ticket of leave' system like that applied to transportees was not originally in the 1853 Bill, but was suggested by Earl Grey during the second reading debate:

Men with sudden and unrestricted freedom were much more likely to relapse into crime than men who enjoyed a restricted degree of freedom by means of tickets of leave. He thought, then, that when we were doing away with the system of transportation, it might not have been impossible to establish something of the same kind in this country.

He also criticized Cranworth for failing to describe in detail how the new penitentiary system would work.[52] Probably Cranworth did not

[50] H. Stretton, *The Political Sciences* (London, 1969), pp. 238–40.
[51] The last convict ship sailed for Australia on 12 Oct. 1867. See Shaw, *op. cit.*, p. 358.
[52] *Parliamentary Debates*, 3rd ser. vol. cxxix, cols. 18, 14.

know. The whole Bill was clearly very makeshift. If a coherent and progressive penal policy had been born in such vexed political circumstances it would have been a miracle.[53]

For the same reason, it was hardly surprising that the 'ticket of leave' experiment, when tried in England, failed. This seems to have reflected lack of both care and conviction on the part of the Home Office as well as the hysterical state of public opinion during the 'garrotting' outcry of the 1860s.[54] If, finally, the extension in time of transportation had permitted a reduction in prison building and more careful study of overseas experience, including some features of convict discipline in Australia and America, perhaps the worst rigours of the separate system could have been avoided.[55] What, for example, if the Select Committee on Prison Discipline in 1850 had heeded the radical principle enunciated to it by Captain Maconochie that 'the life to which you subject the men in prison should very closely resemble the life they will lead out of prison'?[56] To describe what actually happened simply as 'necessary' progress to the present is to miss both the tragic limitations of policy-making and the dimensions of the lost opportunities.

One hard lesson this history has for the future. It is that what is regarded as 'progress' and desirable reform today *may* turn out to be the opposite tomorrow. For that reason, reforms, even when won, are not necessarily irreversible. For instance, though the post-war

[53] On the background cf. Shaw, op. cit., pp. 348 ff.

[54] See Rose, op. cit., pp. 11–12; J. J. Tobias, *Crime and Industrial Society in the 19th Century* (London, 1967) (now available in Pelican), pp. 139 ff., 213–14.

[55] Apart from tickets of leave and progressive stages it is not too fanciful to see roots of both parole and probation in Australian transportation, not to mention experiments in associated labour, the rehabilitation of ex-convicts (including establishing them as farmers), and the Point Puer boys' prison established in 1834. It is interesting that America and Australia should have provided the most influential penal ideas in Britain at this time. In virtually no other areas of government, I think, despite some interest in its democracy and social legislation later, has Australian experience been followed in Westminster. Another legacy of transportation was the 'tariff' maxima penalties of 7 and 14 years' penal servitude definitively legislated in 1861. On the separate and silent systems, see Philip Collins's excellent *Dickens and Crime* (London, 1962), Chapters 3, 5 and 6, and Henriques, loc. cit.

[56] Minutes of evidence, p. 424. It was no accident that Alexander Maconochie, who had been superintendent of the Norfolk Island penal settlement and invented the mark system of convict discipline, was opposed to both the silent and the separate system. In 1850 he told the same committee that he had found the silent system 'very demoralising' and that the separate system 'seeks to exclude the possibility of vice, but is not calculated, as I think, to teach virtue' (p. 460). Cf. J. V. Barry, *Alexander Maconochie of Norfolk Island* (Melbourne, 1958), p. 181.

campaigns against capital and corporal punishment have triumphed, that does not mean, alas, that they may not have to be fought all over again, especially if murder statistics are sufficiently disturbing. The arguments against preventive detention and life imprisonment, and the problem of what to do with unconditional homicidal 'psychopaths', could all be turned in this direction.[57] Penal reform, because of its strongly emotive and subjective elements, is more vulnerable to upheavals of this kind than other areas of social policy. It is now unthinkable, for example, that the Poor Law should ever be revived. But J. E. Thomas has recently challenged the whole recent course of penal reform by arguing forcefully that it has failed to give adequate attention to problems of security in prisons and the role and morale of prison officers.[58] Revaluations of this kind are bound to continue during the rest of this century.

2. STATISTICS AND THE CAUSES OF CRIME

Another lesson from historical research since the war concerns the application of statistics to the understanding of the causes of crime in the nineteenth century. This has direct implications for the discussion of the penal system required during the next quarter century. There are continuous series of criminal statistics relating to England and Wales from 1805 on, but their interpretation presents all the problems posed by contemporary criminal statistics plus others inherent in less sophisticated statistical methods and our ignorance of early statisticians' assumptions, which they never committed to paper.[59] In this respect the celebrated controversy of Morrison and Du Cane in *Nineteenth Century* at the end of the century as to whether crime was increasing or decreasing relative to population remains a highly relevant cautionary tale. Drawing on a common stock of statistics Morrison argued that it was, Du Cane that it was not.

[57] Cf. H. J. Eysenck, 'Little Albert, the Rats and the Psychologists', *Twentieth Century*, clxxi (Winter 1962/3), 26: 'What I have said is not to be interpreted as advocating the return to such barbarous methods of correction as flogging and capital punishment *for all and sundry*' (my emphasis).

[58] Thomas, op. cit., pp. 217 ff.

[59] On nineteenth-century criminal statistics see T. P. Morris, *The Criminal Area* (London, 1957), Chapter III, and V. A. C. Gatrell and T. B. Hadden, 'Criminal Statistics and their Interpretation', in E. A. Wrigley (ed.), *Nineteenth Century Society* (Cambridge, 1972). On twentieth-century statistics see F. H. McClintock and N. H. Avison, *Crime in England and Wales* (London, 1968), N. Walker, *Crimes, Courts and Figures* (Harmondsworth, 1971).

Neither argument was free of dubious inference obvious to our eyes.[60]

Does it follow that such statistics are an insignificant tool for elucidating the penal history of the past century? Dr. J. J. Tobias evidently thinks so. At any rate he concludes from a study of the Leeds police statistics for 1857–75 that 'the statistics of crime in the nineteenth century are of very little use' for the study of the social history of crime. Accordingly in his study of *Crime and Industrial Society in the 19th Century* he prefers to rely on literary sources. Unfortunately these too have inherent shortcomings, notably that one is forced to rely, however discriminatingly, on the often prejudiced views of contemporaries about the 'causes' of crime for example. Although a valuable collection of such evidence his study consequently leaves one dissatisfied with such findings as that 'crime was not as a rule the result of want'.[61]

It is, moreover, unfortunate that Tobias's study, based on a London Ph.D. thesis submitted in 1965, should have been published, while K. K. Macnab's Sussex doctoral thesis of the same year, 'Aspects of the History of Crime in England and Wales between 1805–60', has not. For Macnab's attitude to statistics is very different, as are his findings, and though few of Tobias's readers would realize this, *his* criticism of crime statistics amounts to a criticism of Macnab. Using the records of detected crime as a guide to trends in actual crime Macnab discerns a close correlation between peaks of crime and W. W. Rostow's 'index of social tension' caused by economic pressures (unemployment, high food prices) on the working classes.[62] This suggests that the economic contribution to criminality was much more substantial than Tobias with his emphasis on a 'criminal class' had supposed. Admittedly the assumption that the relation of detected to actual crime was constant is questionable, in the nineteenth

[60] W. D. Morrison, 'The Increase of Crime', *Nineteenth Century*, xxxi (June 1892), 950–7; E. F. Du Cane, 'The Decrease of Crime', *Nineteenth Century*, xxxiii (March 1893), 480–92.

[61] Tobias, *Crime and Industrial Society in the 19th Century*, pp. 267, 21, 152. But he does not disdain the use of criminal statistics altogether. Cf. his collection of documents, *Nineteenth-century Crime: Prevention and Punishment* (Newton Abbot, 1972), Part Three.

[62] See pp. 312 ff., for example. I am grateful to Dr. Macnab for lending me a copy of his thesis which he is preparing for publication. He also modifies conventional views about the effects of the criminal law and police reforms on detected crime—and criminal migration. The disagreement between Tobias and Macnab is a little reminiscent of the Hobsbawm–Hartwell debate over standard of living trends in the Industrial Revolution, but the statistics in that case are, if anything, even more dubious.

century no less than in the twentieth,[63] but the exercise is clearly a worthwhile one, especially as it has recently been repeated for the entire century by Vic Gatrell and Tom Hadden. They confirm Macnab's pioneering picture of increasing crime rates closely related to economic conditions in the first half of the century and also Tobias's conclusion that prevailing prosperity was associated with decreasing crime rates during the second half. They judge there was then 'a real decline in criminal activity, and quite a spectacular one'.[64]

But they also suggest that the incidence of property offences ceased to be positively associated with economic depression as the century advanced, and that it was in this period that the gradual change from 'poverty-based' offences to 'prosperity-based' offences of the kind familiar to our generation apparently began,[65] a change unaccompanied by any corresponding transformation of the penal system. Clearly all this is only the beginning of a promising application of 'quantification' to penal history.[66] Much remains to be investigated.[67] What is needed is a more rigorous appraisal of a number of possible relevant factors including the spread of primary education and the creation of special corrective institutions for children. It is even possible—perish the thought—that the decline, if it occurred, had something to do with the emphasis on a severe, deterrent criminal law for adults. It is a possibility that penal reformers need to face. Unfortunately it is not only in respect of the present[68] that research into deterrents is still slight.

But already one implication of this research for the present—and

[63] Cf. Hood and Sparks, op. cit., pp. 43–5.

[64] Gatrell and Hadden, loc. cit., pp. 368–74.

[65] Ibid., pp. 368–9, 378–9. *Relative* poverty could still, of course, lie behind much contemporary crime.

[66] Now that the way has been cleared for further statistical study one looks forward to intensive regional studies like that of D. J. Philips into crime and law enforcement in the Black Country, 1835–60. See his interesting contribution to J. Stevenson and R. Quinault (eds.), *Popular Protest and Public Order in the Nineteenth Century*, (Allen & Unwin), forthcoming. These should throw much light on the precise association of crime with industrialization and urbanization which H. Perkin, *The Origins of Modern English Society 1780–1880* (London, 1969) takes for granted on the basis of Macnab's figures. Such inquiries need to be carried back well into the eighteenth century, but the limited statistics make this difficult.

[67] For example, Gatrell and Hadden argue that 'the overall decline in the male criminal rates must be accounted for either in terms of the deterrent effect of the new police efficiency, or else in terms of the increasing general prosperity of the later nineteenth century'. This is clearly very vague. Loc. cit., p. 374.

[68] Cf. Hood and Sparks, op. cit., pp. 172 ff.

future—may be spelt out. It is that extreme caution is called for against supposing that criminogenic factors apparently dominant in one period will necessarily be so in another. As we have seen, the correlation between property offences and economic depression apparently declined in the last century and, despite the continued predominance of property crime among indictable offences since, different explanations are clearly needed for more recent trends. For example, Hermann Mannheim concluded from his study of *Social Aspects of Crime in England between the Wars* (1940) that 'unemployment pay and other welfare work seemed to have an important crime-preventing effect, interfering with the simple chain of cause and effect'.[69]

If such considerations had been borne in mind by the authors of *Penal Practice in a Changing Society* (1959) they might not have been so disappointed when, after the dip in crime in the early 1950s, prosperity later in that decade did not produce declining crime rates.[70] Similarly the correlations noted between juvenile delinquency on the one hand and both childhood in the last world war and rapid post-war industrialization may well be temporary.[71] In other words, historical research probably undermines all attempts to produce eternal blueprints of the causes of crime or the effects of certain punishments. That in itself is pertinent to speculation about the future of the penal system. It may seem to deny the relevance of the past, but the implication that criminological research needs to be continuous, and repeated, in the face of changing generations and a changing society, is surely very much to the point.

It also suggests that, given the artificiality of any definition of crime and the persistence of venerable argument about the relative contributions of heredity and environment to criminality,[72] such

[69] 'The conclusion was that unemployment seemed to play a widely varying role in different areas and also for different age groups, and that subtle psychological factors had to be taken into account which did not become easily visible in statistical investigations.' Mannheim, *Comparative Criminology*, vol. ii, pp. 587–8, summarizing the earlier findings. [70] p. 1.
[71] See L. T. Wilkins, *Delinquent Generations* (London, 1960); H. Mannheim, *War and Crime* (London, 1941), and *Comparative Criminology*, vol. ii, pp. 597–8; *Juvenile Delinquency in Post-war Europe* (Strasbourg, 1960). Cf. H. Jones, *Crime in a Changing Society* (Harmondsworth, 1965). McClintock and Avison, op. cit., p. 271, point out that the delinquency-prone war-generation theory cannot account for the high incidence of crime among young males in the 1960's'.
[72] See, for example, H. J. Eysenck, *Crime and Personality* (London, 1964), pp. 53–4, and Mannheim, *Comparative Criminology*, vol. i, pp. 229–36.

research should concentrate on the aetiology of particular offences in particular societies at particular times and on aids to sentencing particular offenders to particular treatments. Prediction studies of the kind summarized by Hood and Sparks seems more relevant than a search for the general 'roots' of crime, especially when English criminal law is likely to undergo further reform as well, even if not in quite the drastic fashion prescribed for the United States by Norval Morris and Gordon Hawkins.[73]

3. CRIME IS NORMAL

Easily the most ambitious programme in British penal history since the war is Sir Leon Radzinowicz's great *History of English Criminal Law and its Administration from 1750*.[74] It is remarkably rich in material relating to the social history of both crime and punishment, but the fourth volume, the latest, only reaches the abolition of public hanging in 1868 and, since the author is carefully unpolemical, the relevance of the enterprise to the present may not be at once obvious. Yet two major implications if not themes which emerge from the volumes published so far are worth noticing. One is the importance of regarding crime as more or less 'normal' and the imposition of 'law and order' with a modern, national police force as a relatively recent, unusual, gradually evolving and highly imperfect phenomenon.[75]

'What we think of as characteristics of human nature such as compassion and honesty', Terence Morris has remarked, 'have in fact been socialized into us through the learning process.'[76] That much can be learnt from history as well as from educational psychology. It squares not only with the embarrassing fact that we all, even the most 'socialized' of egos, lapse into 'crime' when we think

---

[73] Hood and Sparks, op. cit., Chapters 6 and 7; N. Morris and G. Hawkins, *The Honest Politician's Guide to Crime Control* (Chicago, 1969). The opportunities for crime have also greatly changed over the past century. One of the most depressing courtroom spectacles today is the queues of people prosecuted at the taxpayer's expense for shoplifting, especially when self-service stores apparently often operate on the principle of maximum temptation and minimum security. Pocket-picking at the beginning of the nineteenth century perhaps presents the closest historical analogy, but that was not a distinctively feminine offence.

[74] 4 vols (London, 1948–68).

[75] See especially vol. iv, *Grappling for Control*, Chapters 4, 6, and 7.

[76] T. Morris, 'The Social Toleration of Crime', in Klare (ed.), op. cit., p. 18.

we can get away with it (especially on the road),[77] but with crowd
behaviour during police strikes and the history of colonization where
the creation of relative 'law and order' often followed a dangerously
long way behind the frontier of settlement.[78] The fragility of both
social controls and conditioning is also demonstrated by the persistence of extensive 'criminality' even in so-called police states.

Radzinowicz demonstrates that the precariousness of 'public order'
was an enduring characteristic of English society throughout the first
half of the nineteenth century.[79] G. Kitson Clark has likewise
emphasized that survivals from 'the old harsh wild world of the
eighteenth century' lingered on well into the Victorian age.[80] It was
not until about 1890, Gatrell and Hadden suggest, that Britain
became 'what may properly be called a "policed" society'.[81] It is
only by bearing in mind how relatively recent are our conceptions of
'law and order' that present trends in crime and punishment can be
placed in their true perspective. By the same token the level of law
and order achieved by the end of the nineteenth century may one day
seem phenomenal, ephemeral, and unrepeatable if present trends in
crime rates and detection persist.[82]

Radzinowicz's 'informed guess' in 1964 that only about 15 per
cent of crimes committed in England and Wales are officially
recorded may well under- rather than over-state the proportion. He

[77] To an historian it seems highly likely that the present situation in which we
can all with only a little trouble acquire a licence to drive a highly lethal vehicle,
in which we shall from time to time jeopardize other people's lives and our own,
will look to posterity as irrational a phenomenon as, say, the gin-drinking craze
of late-eighteenth-century London—and a shocking instance of the almost
'criminal' failure of government.

[78] See, for example, G. W. Reynolds and A. Judge, *The Night the Police went on
Strike* (London, 1968); J. Templeton, 'Rebel Guardians: The Melbourne Police
Strike of 1923' in J. Iremonger, J. Merritt, and G. Osborne (eds.), *Strikes*
(Sydney, 1973), pp. 104–5, and H. C. Allen, *Bush and Backwoods* (London, 1959).

[79] See, for example, *A History of the English Criminal Law*, vol. iv, pp. 153 ff.,
232 ff.

[80] G. Kitson Clark, *The Making of Victorian England* (London, 1962), p. 62.
Cf. F. C. Mather, *Public Order in the Age of the Chartists* (Manchester, 1959); E.
Hobsbawm and G. Rudé, *Captain Swing* (London, 1969); E. J. Hobsbawm,
Bandits (Penguin ed., 1972).

[81] Gatrell and Hadden, loc. cit., p. 377. The somewhat ambiguous phrase 'the
policed society' is derived from A. Silver, 'The Demand for Order in Civil
Society: A Review of Some Themes in the History of Urban Crime, Police, and
Riot', in D. J. Bordua (ed.), *The Police* (New York, 1967), pp. 1–24.

[82] Gatrell and Hadden also point out that the number of indictable offences
per 100,000 population known to the police in England and Wales in 1890—
about 300—was a considerably lower crime rate than that prevalent today.

also pointed out that nearly one in three males is likely to be convicted of an indictable offence some time in his lifetime.[83] If one
throws in non-indictable, as well as undetected, offences it seems
highly probable that the majority of the population engage in
'crime' sometimes. In the 1963 sample of the Government survey 84
per cent of youths aged between 18 and 22 admitted to traffic
offences at least.[84] Given the density of offences in modern law it is,
in fact, unthinkable for anyone to go through life without breaking
the law, even if his offence comprises merely leaving his car at a
meter for a few minutes after the rental period has expired, failing
to pay a bus fare on a short ride when the conductor is upstairs or
accidentally exceeding the speed limit by 2 m.p.h.[85]

Such considerations certainly reinforce the notion of crime as
relatively 'normal' rather than as an eradicable aberration or
'disease'. Mannheim's concept of the 'criminogenic society' supports
it too.[86] The importance of this lesson for penal policy-makers is
that it suggests a more realistic approach to crime prevention and
'suppression'. By encouraging the confusion of 'crime' and 'sin'
and the idea that both could be 'cured' by a simple act of 'conversion'
or 'reformation' administrators and reformers alike in the nineteenth
century bequeathed a legacy which has been both embarrassing and
dangerous.

But, despite escalating crime rates and immunity from detection,
the future is not unrelievedly grim. Though often highly professionalized[87] the fact that crime can no longer be characterized as
confined substantially to a 'criminal class' or subculture and its
punishment is being disentangled from class prejudices means that,
perhaps for the first time in British history, a civilized, relatively
realistic penal system should now at least be feasible. And that is not
negligible compensation.

4. IDEOLOGY AND THE PENAL SYSTEM

Another lesson which emerges from Radzinowicz's splendidly

[83] L. Radzinowicz, 'The Criminal in Society', *Journal of Royal Society of Arts*,
cxii (1964), 917, 921, 925. Cf. Hood and Sparks, op. cit., pp. 15–18.

[84] See the discussion in N. Walker, *Sentencing in a Rational Society* (Harmondsworth, 1972 ed.), p. 85.

[85] I well remember the reluctance of Sir William Haley, when editor of *The
Times*, to accept that traffic offences could be 'crimes'.

[86] H. Mannheim, *Comparative Criminology* (London, 1965), vol. ii, Part 4.

[87] See M. McIntosh, 'Changes in the Organization of Thieving', in S. Cohen
(ed.), *Images of Deviance* (Harmondsworth, 1971), pp. 98–133.

idiosyncratic history of English criminal law, as well as from the discussion so far, is the importance of taking careful stock of contemporary ideology.[88] 'The action possible to each generation', Fox wisely observed, 'is conditioned by the climate of opinion of its time.'[89] Although the issue has been hotly disputed by historians[90] the evidence that attitudes to administrative, including penal, reform—the so-called nineteenth-century revolution in government— were profoundly affected by ideological factors, notably Benthamism, humanitarianism, and classical political economy, is impressive and instructive. Penal reform certainly displays such factors very clearly. Religious influences have already been touched on. Maconochie's 'mark system' which envisaged sentencing to set amounts of labour rather than time in prison smacks strongly of Benthamite thinking, though its precursors include two clergymen, Archbishop Whately, a political economist, and Archdeacon Paley, a non-Benthamite utilitarian.[91] More recently, to take a very different example, Borstal regimes have been modelled on the public-school house system.[92]

Penal reform has, in fact, never been wholly empirical. Accordingly simple generalizations like 'As people in the growing towns found that the problem of crime was getting worse, they naturally felt that they had better do something about it'[93] are unsatisfactory historical explanations even—or rather *especially*—in a text for students. They beg too many questions. Social reform is not in this sense 'inevitable' either; otherwise, abuses which now look flagrant would be legislated against as soon as they appeared. Full account, as Fox says, has to be taken of the changing climate of opinion, and that will go for the next quarter of a century no less than for the past.

Grünhut's emphasis on 'an enlightened public conscience' has, in fact, been vindicated by the years since he wrote and, though one may admire how much has been achieved by discreet pressures in the face of an apathetic and sometimes hostile public, the truth probably is that this last circumstance has severely retarded or dis- torted reform in the past. If the further reform of the penal system

[88] See, for example, vol. i, Parts III, IV, and V, and vol. ii, Part VI.
[89] Fox, op. cit., p. 57.
[90] See, for example, O. MacDonagh, 'The Nineteenth-century Revolution in Government: A Reappraisal', *Historical Journal*, i (1958), 52–67, and H. Parris, 'The Nineteenth-Century Revolution in Government: A Reappraisal Re- appraised', ibid., iii (1960), 17–37. Cf. Parris, op. cit., Chapter IX.
[91] See Barry, op. cit., pp. 75–9.
[92] See Thomas, op. cit., pp. 165–8.
[93] J. J. Tobias, *Against the Peace* (London, 1970), p. 62.

is to be accelerated in the future one suspects that more careful attention to prevailing public sensibilities, prejudices, and ignorance will be indispensable.[94] Though traditional public deference and concentration on influencing what Dicey called 'law-making opinion' has served pressure groups like the Howard League well in the past neither of these habits can be relied on indefinitely. The whole climate of opinion is in fact still changing and new tactics are probably needed.

In any case, while penal reformers continue to confuse change with progress, while, even for particular offences, certainty about causes still seems a long way off and the causes may well change within a generation or less, while governments are more sensitive to rising crime rates and defective security than about scientific sentencing and treatment in custom-built institutions and the community, and while public ignorance and apathy are often mistaken for consensus, and prejudice is still as evident as open-mindedness among our legislators, it can hardly be surprising if penal reform continues to be 'a history of "ideals and errors"'. Perhaps the best that one can hope for is that the 'errors' as well as the 'ideals' are more modest than in the past, and here the contribution of historical understanding should not be disregarded.

[94] It is quite possible, for example, that a reaction will set in against the present degree of centralized administration, and more encouragement will be given to governors of local prisons to experiment with new forms of treatment. But that will only be carried through harmoniously if more serious attention is given to the nurturing of good relations with local communities.

2. The Constitutional Framework of the English Penal System

LOUIS BLOM-COOPER

THE Prison Service is unique among the social services providing residential accommodation, in that it can control neither the volume nor the flow of the intake of the prison population. Subject to certain minor qualifications, local prisons must receive into custody every person sentenced to imprisonment at the moment sentence is passed, and must keep him in lawful custody for the period specified in the sentence. A prison can never put up a sign 'No room at the inn'.[1] The courts determine the daily average prison population. The Prison Service may only marginally *influence* the flow of the prisoners out of the system by a liberal use of the powers of pre-release and parole.

This reflects the British constitutional doctrine of the separation of powers: the independence of the judiciary demands that the criminal process—including that part devoted to the sentencing of convicted persons—should not be interfered with by penal administrators. The judges are empowered to select the appropriate sentence; the penal administrators in executing that sentence have only very limited statutory powers to remit a part of it. Each thus has his separate function. A judge who exceeds the amount of an appropriate sentence intrudes upon the power to remit, while the administrator who remits an excessive part of the sentence usurps the judicial role.

The clear division of functions is more often blurred at the sentencing stage. There have been occasions in the recent past when courts

---

[1] The number of people in custody in England and Wales reached a new record figure in 1971. The average population of prison establishments was then 39,708—*Report on the Work of the Prison Department 1971* (Cmnd. 5037), p. 1. On 31 Dec. 1972 there were 37,692 prisoners. Plans for the prison population are currently being made on the assumption that the figure will be 47,500 in 1976, and somewhere between 55,000 to 60,000 at the beginning of the 1980s. *Hansard*, vol. 849, col. *312*, 29 Jan. 1973; cf. Holland whose rate is 22 per 100,000 of the population compared with ours of 72 per 100,0000. (See Bishop, *Aspects of European Penal Systems*, p. 87, below). The point was alluded to by the Home Secretary in his address to the Annual Conference of NACRO held at the University of East Anglia, 31 Mar. 1973.

have passed sentences which, in their apparent excessiveness, take
on the appearance of judicial manoeuvres in order to shackle the
release powers of penal administrators.[2] To the extent that any
sentence is inappropriate, it is not unreasonable for the public to
criticize the judiciary for impinging upon the role of the penal
administrator. By parity of reasoning, any exercise by the Executive
of release powers that exceeds, or appears to exceed, the norm of
legislative authority may be seen by the judiciary as an unwarranted
intrusion upon its exclusive power of sentencing. The early release
of a 'lifer', or the decision to place a prisoner on an open hostel
scheme could be seen as an excess of Executive power.

The constitutional doctrine of the separation of powers finds its
purest expression in the sporadic statements of Home Secretaries
when faced with the public demand to alter an apparently over-
severe sentence on a particular offender.[3] The formula used is that
unless there are some relevant and highly pertinent facts available
to the Secretary of State that were not revealed to the sentencing
court or the Court of Appeal, the Executive cannot, and will not act
as court of appeal from the sentences of judges. Whenever such cases
happen, one is tempted to ask for whose benefit the independence
of the judiciary is maintained—is it for the offender who has suffered
the excesses of the sentencing court, for the public (a section of
which at least clamours for mercy from whatever source), or for the
benefit of the Executive, which can constitutionally shuffle off the
blame for unwarranted punitiveness on the part of the judiciary,
which by tradition does not answer publicly the criticism levelled at
it?

It is Parliament, and Parliament alone, that can shift the boundary
line that marks off the judicial from the Executive function in the
task of determining periods of custody to be served by offenders.

[2] The two classic examples were respectively the sentence of forty-two years'
imprisonment (three consecutive sentences of fourteen years' imprisonment—the
maximum— to run consecutively) on George Blake: *R.* v. *Blake* [1962] 2 Q.B.
377 and the sentences of thirty years' imprisonment on the mail-train robbers: *R.*
v. *Wilson and others* [1965] 1 Q.B. 402. In the latter case Mr. Justice Fenton
Atkinson said, at p. 410, that the maximum sentence was imprisonment for life,
'and such a sentence might well have been imposed'. More recently a detention
order for twenty years on a sixteen-year-old for 'mugging' under s. 53 (2), Children
and Young Persons Act 1933, reflects the continuing drive on the part of some
of the judges to exert an influence against any early release: *R.* v. *Storey* [1973] 1
W.L.R. 1045.

[3] See the case of Pauline Jones, Dec. 1971.

There are broadly two categories of parliamentary restrictions upon the power of the courts:

a. the limitation upon the sentencing function of the court; and
b. the extent to which the offender may be released by the prison authorities before the lapse of the period of custody prescribed by the court.

The issue is how far, if at all, the shifting of the boundary line has up till now preserved or altered the basic constitutional doctrine.

The supremacy of Parliament in law-making, untouched in the penal field by anything that emanates from the European Communities Act 1972, is crucial. It is only by legislation that the penal administrators can hope to put a brake upon the numbers of persons committed to penal establishments by the courts. Anything less than legislative change of penal sanctions (and their mode of imposition) is likely to be ineffective, or at most only marginally effective. It is vital, therefore, to consider how far Parliament desires, and is able, to fetter both the courts' power at the level of sentencing and the effect of such powers at any point after the courts have handed the miscreant over to the Prison Service. With the notable exceptions of the mandatory sentence of life imprisonment for murder[4] and of the partial indeterminacy of the sentence of Borstal training,[5] the courts are free to pass any sentence within the maxima prescribed. (Such a tariff as may exist in practice is wholly of judicial origin.)[6] Ever since the ending of the death penalty for all but a very few crimes, and of transportation in the second half of the nineteenth century, the fixing by the legislature of maximum sentences has been the only statutory limitation on the sentencing power. There are no minimum sentences—the minimum forty hours of community service is a rare departure from a time-honoured practice.[7] There are only maximum sentences, sufficiently long to provide for the greatest degree of flexibility in sentencing. There have, however, been stringent limitations placed on the lowest rung of the judicial ladder: magistrates' courts cannot, as a rule, pass a sentence of more than six months' imprisonment (or, cumulatively, twelve months on two or

[4] The law is helpfully stated in the Twelfth Report (*Penalty for Murder*) of the Criminal Law Revision Committee (Cmnd. 5184), Jan. 1973, pp. 6–9.
[5] s. 1, Criminal Justice Act 1961.
[6] Thomas, *Principles of Sentencing*, Heinemann Educational Books (1970), pp. 3 and 33 ff.
[7] s. 15, Criminal Justice Act 1972.

more offences), but if they feel their powers of imprisonment are inadequate they can invite a higher court to use its more ample powers, by committing the offender for sentence. Even statutory limitations upon these sentencers, who possess little or no legal training, are stoutly resisted as an unwarranted interference with judicial discretion in sentencing. When in 1967 Parliament provided that, in general, sentences of not more than six months should be mandatorily suspended[8] there was no small perturbation among sentencers of this fettering of the court's powers, which was then reflected in parliamentary opposition to the provision. When that opposition became the Government in 1970, a previous commitment to remove the mandatory element, coupled with a powerful lobby from the Magistrates' Association, secured the repeal of the provision.[9]

Other examples of restrictions abound, although they do not add up to very much. The restriction on the imprisonment of young offenders between the age of seventeen and twenty-one (imprisonment is proscribed in favour of borstal training for the middle range of custodial penalties) is one instance.[10] The limited indeterminate sentence of Borstal training has been denounced by the higher judiciary which has actively campaigned in the corridors of power for this fetter to be removed. The Advisory Council on the Penal System, in its report on the young adult offender has responded to this demand by restoring the element of determinacy to all custodial sentences for young adult offenders.[11]

The restriction upon imprisonment for first offenders by magistrates' courts[12] has been accepted generally by the higher judiciary. The extension of this principle in 1972 to all first prison sentences[13] (i.e. not just first offenders but all offenders who have not actually served a term of imprisonment) strikes a responsive chord in the heart of even the most punitive sentencer. More pertinent to the theme advanced here, that the legislature has been circumspect in reducing the courts' sentencing powers, is the reaction to the Children and Young Persons Act 1969. That Act gave expression to the phil-

---

[8] s. 37 (3), Criminal Justice Act 1972.   [9] s. 11, Criminal Justice Act 1972.
[10] s. 17, Criminal Justice Act 1948, and s. 3, Criminal Justice Act 1961.
[11] *The Young Adult Offender*, H.M.S.O. (1974).
[12] First Offenders Act 1958.
[13] s. 14, Criminal Justice Act 1972. Some arguments were advanced against the removal of the mandatory position by Mr. Edmund Dell, M.P., during the Committee stage of the Bill.

osophy that decisions as to guilt or innocence are exclusively the province of the courts of law, but that treatment decisions are for the authorities which have the day-to-day care of the delinquents committed to them by the courts. If that philosophy is being questioned in certain influential quarters, it is still gaining widespread acceptance as the proper basis for dealing with children in trouble with the law. So far there has been little or no attempt to extend the philosophy to the young adult offender or to adults.

Legislation thus not merely sets out the limits of the courts' powers; it also steers the judicial course of action. But legislation is neither complete nor sufficiently responsive to changing social attitudes to crime and punishment. By its general disinclination to impose fixed penalties or minimum sentences it leaves room for interpretation and execution by sentencers and takes no account of changes in both judicial and public attitude to crime and criminals. It is static and cannot move with the times. It speaks only for the moment of time at which it is enacted.[14] And to the extent that legislation appears to state unequivocally the limits of judicial powers courts are not a little astute in negotiating the minefields of legislative prohibitions.[15] There is the additional factor of the delay in passing remedial legislation. Unlike the mandarins in the Inland Revenue, the administrators of criminal justice and of the penal systems do not have ready to hand an annual vehicle to legislate away the contrivances of the courts. Major Criminal Justice Bills have been coming through every twenty years since the turn of the century.[16] (The 1972 Act was exceptional in following hard on the heels of the 1967 Act.)

Apart from legislation, there are a number of ways in which sentencing policy and practice can be, and is, influenced in any particular direction. The reports of the Advisory Council on the Penal System, quite apart from stimulating legislation, have an educative purpose. Their influence on changes in penal treatment is testified to by the penal authorities in and out of penal establishments; what influence they have on sentencers however, is altogether more

[14] The classic instance of change in judicial sentencing as a result of penal practice is reflected in attitudes to corrective training and preventive detentions: see *Practice Direction* (*Corrective Training: Preventive Detention*) [1962] 1 W.L.R. 402.

[15] *R.* v. *Newsome: R.* v. *Browne* [1970] 2 Q.B. 711, 712 H, 713 H.

[16] In 1908, 1925, 1948, and 1967. The 1961 Criminal Justice Act dealt exclusively with young offenders.

Louis Blom-Cooper

problematic. Many sentencers read little more than a précis of, or commentaries on the reports, which no doubt have some effect. Home Office circulars, couched in cautious language so as, nominally at least, to conform to the constitutional propriety of non-interference, are influential. The well-known circular urging courts to rely on social inquiry reports before imposing any custodial sentence[17] has had some impact, although it would be altogether too sanguine to conclude that there is sufficient observance of the circular to make it unnecessary for the matter to be statutorily enforced.[18] Practice of the courts varies infinitely in this respect. And the publication, *The Sentence of the Court*,[19] setting out the precise powers of sentencing, has had its impact upon sentencers. More ambitious was the recent pamphlet, *Criminal Justice Act 1972: A Guide for the Courts*. And, finally, there were the numerous sentencing conferences in the 1960s, initiated imaginatively by the late Lord Chief Justice, Lord Parker. Most sentencers in the higher courts have attended more than one such gathering; a few have served, since its inception in 1967, on the Parole Board; and magistrates appointed after 1965 have been subjected to a compulsory training course during the first year of appointment. An evaluation of these gatherings is hard to make. But at least sentencers will have become better informed about the penal system even if they have been made no wiser about the effects of particular sentences passed on offenders. The laymen among them have acquired, albeit vicariously, a degree of professionalism which can only improve the quality of the justice they are likely to dispense.

All this, however, has had little impact on our penal jurisprudence. The fact is that, in spite of legislative command and extra-parliamentary advice and information amounting to official cajoling, the courts are largely free to choose what they deem the appropriate penalty to inflict. Where the offence is imprisonable, the only guides are the statutory maxima and the remote control of the Court of Appeal (Criminal Division). Non-imprisonable offences, by definition, inhibit the courts' sentencing powers drastically, but the range of offences for which non-custodial penalties alone are prescribed is within the narrow compass (although numerically large) of adminis-

[17] Home Office Circulars No. 28–31/1971, see the *Report of the Work of the Probation and After-Care Dept. 1969 to 1971* (Cmnd. 5158), Nov. 1972, para. 72.
[18] s. 57, Criminal Justice Act 1967 gives the Home Secretary the power to make statutory rules imposing the use of social inquiry reports.
[19] The latest edition was published in 1969.

trative infringements. They do not, other than formally, correspond to crimes. Of those found guilty of indictable offences tried in the Crown Courts, custodial sentences are imposed in approximately 70 per cent of cases. In magistrates' courts the over-all rate of imprisonment is about 10 per cent of those convicted of imprisonable offences. The constitutional doctrine of non-interference is thus substantially observed, even by the one institution—Parliament— which can, consistent with the doctrine, nevertheless drastically and dramatically alter the courts' sentencing powers in such a way as to restrict their areas of choice of penalty.

If the legislature has done no more than supply the legal framework in which the courts can operate a flexible sentencing policy and practice, equally it has observed the constitutional properties when defining the scope of Executive power to alter the effects of a court sentence. Except in the case of the Children and Young Persons Act 1969 (in relation to offenders under seventeen), Parliament has repeatedly declined to adopt the principle that penal treatment is a matter solely for penal administrators, or to deprive the courts of differential sentencing which predetermines the kind of treatment to which the offender will be subjected. The Prison Service may select the type of prison in which the offender shall serve his sentence, or order that part at least of the sentence shall be in open conditions, or decree that at the tail end of his sentence a prisoner may be assigned to the hostel scheme. But what it may not do is to alter by a single day the length of sentence passed by the court, even to the extent of maintaining supervision of the offender in the community. The court decrees a period of imprisonment. The Prison Service must execute that sentence, subject only to well-defined and limited statutory qualifications.

Remission is the longest established method of mitigating the full execution of a court sentence. Rule 5 of the Prison Rules 1964 (the current Rules)[20] provides that a prisoner serving a sentence of imprisonment for a term of more than one month may 'on the grounds of his industry and good conduct' be granted remission. Ostensibly discretionary,[21] remission of one-third of the sentence is in practice automatic, subject only to periods of remission lost for

[20] Amended as a result of the Criminal Justice Act 1972 to provide that time spent in custody awaiting trial should count in the calculation of remission.
[21] *R.* v. *Governor of Leeds Prison: ex parte Stafford* [1964] 2 Q.B. 625, 630. And see *In Re Savundra* [1973] 1 W. L. R. 1147, 1149, where the Divisional Court discounted a possible argument that remission is in fact discretionary.

prison disciplinary offences. This one-third, so long as the prisoner keeps out of trouble while in prison, is only a marginal encroachment upon judicial sentencing. Moreover, courts, not unmindful of the existence of automatic remission, do sometimes consciously or unconsciously calculate the length of sentences with that element in mind, although such practice has been judicially frowned upon.[22] But clearly remission, which started out as a carrot held out by the penal authorities to sustain discipline in prison, remains a stick. (There is a powerful case for abolishing automatic remission and for deploying parole more extensively. Prisoners who commit disciplinary offences could have periods of time added to their sentence or lose periods of time for which they are eligible for parole.)

Parole is a more recent innovation on the British penal scene. Here again both Parliament and the Parole Board have shown excessive caution lest there be a judicial or public outcry against apparent interference with the courts' sentences. The Criminal Justice Act 1967, setting up the Parole Board, provided for eligibility of offenders only after they have served either one-third of a fixed-term sentence or one year, whichever is the longer. This stipulation means that parole applies only to prisoners with sentences of eighteen months or more. In practice parole recommendations have followed the cautious, highly selective policy designated by the Home Office, and adopted independently by the Board itself.[23]

Like remission, parole can hardly constitute a threat to judicial sentencing powers. At best it represents a modest inroad upon the full impact of a term of imprisonment imposed by the courts. It is not too tendentious to assert that the parole system simply shores up the existing sentencing structure.

As a long stop there remains the prerogative power of mercy—a kind of special remission.[24] This power is used very sparingly, the more so since the advent of parole and the departure of the death

---

[22] Lord Parker said in *R. v. Assa Singh* [1965] 2 Q.B. 312: 'It is the practice of this court to treat matters of remission as matter for the Home Secretary alone and in particular the court has never in sentencing a man taken into consideration that he may be released for good conduct and for that reason increased the sentence.'

[23] In his speech to the NACRO Conference held at the University of East Anglia in Mar. 1973 the Home Secretary did portend a reversal of that cautious policy when he advocated that greater risks be taken with the release of parolees.

[24] Table XVI, *Criminal Statistics (England and Wales) 1971*, Cmnd. 5020, shows a total of 109 free pardons and 121 remissions on imprisonment, 12 for Borstal training, 4 for Detention Centre Orders, and 41 fines.

penalty. Apart from its use to pardon those found to have been wrongly convicted, 'it is reserved for cases deserving reward for assistance to the authorities' and occasionally used 'on medical or other compassionate grounds'. These and a miscellany of grounds provide an opportunity to remit sentences. But even in these cases the effect is only to anticipate by a few weeks or months the end of an offender's time in prison. The prerogative power of mercy similarly represents no substantial incursion into the judicial preserve of determining how long a prisoner must stay locked away from the community.

The daily average prison population is thus a reflection of the activities of the courts. Given the increasing numbers committed by the courts, the judiciary, by sending more people to prison for longer periods of time, still bears responsibility for the sharp increase in prison figures. (The general effect of the suspended sentence provision has been to keep down the number of prisoners received into prison on sentence of imprisonment, and to increase the effective length of sentence per reception, i.e. the total length of sentence to be served, including consecutive sentence).[25] The instinctive response of successive Home Secretaries has been to provide more accommodation to overcome the inevitable overcrowding of prisons. But even ambitious prison-building programmes have so far not made much impact upon the situation whereby nearly a third of all prisoners share a cell constructed to house one only.[26] Simultaneously Government has contrived to encourage a greater use of non-custodial penalties for offenders.

The main provisions of the Criminal Justice Acts of 1967 and 1972 were prompted by a desire to keep offenders out of prison, and both contain penal sanctions directed exclusively to that end, but neither Act compels courts to opt for non-custodial penalties.[27] Courts are merely invited to give urgent consideration to the appalling consequences of rejecting new penal measures outside prison walls.

The constitutional position which preserves the two domains of judicial sentencing and penal treatment in their separate compartments reflects the public desire both that the courts, independent of the Executive, should alone be the arbiters of inflicting punishment,

[25] Report of the work of the Prison Dept 1971, pp. 2–3.
[26] Roughly 12,000 in shared cells—8,000 'twoed', 4,000 'threed' at the end of Jan. 1973.
[27] s. 14 (restrictions on first prison sentences) and s. 37 (suspended sentence).

and that no bureaucrat should be able to keep a person in prison one day longer than has been prescribed by the judiciary. The question we might reasonably ask ourselves is: can we resolve the crisis of our prison population without abandoning our valuable principles? Or can we persist in regarding the effect of the penal sanctions as unconnected with the criminal process, and hence detached and remote from the judiciary which merely imposes the sanctions.

Mr. Justice Fitzjames Stephen's aphorism that 'the sentence is to the trial what the bullet is to the powder'[28] has been faintly observed, and then only in the recent past. Penal sanctions are an essential part of the continuum of the criminal process. Direct judicial involvement in penal administration might make sentencers more acutely aware of penal problems without necessarily endangering the independence of the judges; alternatively, the Executive may have to be given discretionary powers over the release of prisoners altogether more sweeping than those conferred by the present system of remission and parole. The solution might simply be to require the court to fix the maximum sentence, the administrator the minimum.

[28] 'The Punishment of Convicts', *Cornhill Magazine*, 7 (1863), 189.

3. Parliament and Penal Policy

GAVIN DREWRY

THAT there is a link between social *mores* and penal policy remains a truism even if the precise nature of that link cannot readily be identified. Refuting the view of John Stuart Mill that punishment should not be related to the moral guilt of the offender, Lord Devlin points out that:

This is not in fact how the law is administered. The degree of moral guilt is not the only determinant of the severity of the sentence but it is universally regarded as a very important one. It manifests itself in two ways. Firstly, in the gradation of offences in the criminal calendar: in order of gravity they are not arranged simply according to the harm done. Secondly, by taking into account the wickedness in the way the crime is committed . . .[1]

But how do *mores* become translated into policy? How can the essentially subjective concept of 'wickedness' find a place amid the objective rigour of legal rules? Even if Lord Devlin's famous 'man on the Clapham omnibus' were to be accepted as a proper arbiter of matters of crime and punishment there remains the problem of how his views become known to policy-makers, and how far the latter can properly be expected to subordinate their own judgment to the homespun wisdom of the man in the street. Jurymen play no direct part in determining punishment;[2] judges tend to be both professionally and socially isolated and seldom travel on buses or mix with those who do. The political system is notoriously ill equipped to transmit grass-roots opinion to the insulated inner sanctum of the power élite. So what possibilities remain?

Even Jean-Jacques Rousseau, staunch advocate of the embodiment of the 'general will' in the governmental process, admitted that

[1] *The Enforcement of Morals* (Oxford University Press, 1965), p. 129.
[2] Though during the era of capital punishment jurors sometimes made recommendations to mercy: see *Report of the Royal Commission on Capital Punishment*, Cmnd. 8932 of 1953, paras. 30, 35, 36, 44, 210, 576–9. The related issue of whether jurors are (or should be) aware of the punishment likely to be imposed if the accused is convicted is discussed in W. R. Cornish, *The Jury* (Pelican edn., 1971), pp. 181–5.

his conception of democracy was utopian.[3] A modern pluralist society admits of no universal morality. In Western democracies the popular will, if such it may be called, is sublimated into imperfectly representative forms of parliamentary government. The extent to which any area of public policy reflects a corresponding element of public opinion depends upon the personal characteristics of decision-makers as well as upon the efficacy of channels of political communications such as parties, pressure groups, and the mass media and upon the role of elected legislatures *vis-à-vis* other governmental institutions.

Nigel Walker in his *Crime and Punishment in Britain* sums up the impact of public opinion on penal policy as follows:

An important influence in the shaping and modification of penal measures is undoubtedly public sentiment . . . Its main impact is upon legislators, especially elected legislators, and upon lay sentencers in the lower courts. Although few legislators would concede that to satisfy the public was one of the aims of a penal system, they would probably point out at the same time that an electorate which thinks in terms of retribution, deterrence and permanent or temporary elimination sets a limit to innovations which are primarily reformative or supervisory in their aim . . . Few legislators would deny that they foresee the satisfaction or dissatisfaction that is caused by the removal, introduction or modification of a penalty, or that there are tactical considerations which affect the timing or presentation of the legislation.[4]

It would be wholly unreal to pretend that more than a tiny minority of the public takes very much interest in the minutiae of official policy, and in the field of punishment the only issues to have prompted much public concern in recent years have been the series of proposals to abolish capital punishment and the more recent debate about whether it should be restored. Even in the latter case the public furore seems to have been generated at least as much by the clash of rival pressure groups and fomented by the mass media, as by the spontaneous uprising of grass-roots opinion.

Even if the political process is characterized by a low level of civic awareness on the part of the general public the tenous link between government and public opinion provided by an elected legislature remains the cornerstone of parliamentary democracy. It is instructive, therefore, to examine how Parliament applies itself to matters of penal policy where *mores* might be expected to be an important

---

[3] *The Social Contract* (Oxford University Press, World Classics edn.), p. 331.
[4] (Edinburgh University Press, revised edn., 1968), pp. 139–40.

ingredient. But first it is necessary to make some more general observations about the role of Parliament in the policy-making process and to suggest some hypotheses which can be tested against empirical data.

PARLIAMENT AND PENAL POLICY-MAKING: A MODEL

Walter Bagehot's evergreen classic, *The English Constitution*, first published in 1867, drew a distinction between the 'dignified' and the 'efficient' parts of the machinery of government. The former he saw as 'theatrical' devices to impress the ignorant and apathetic masses; the real job of governing (the 'efficient' part) is entrusted to an Executive linked to Parliament by the all-important Cabinet.

In its details Bagehot's analysis was rapidly overtaken by the constitutional developments of the latter part of the nineteenth century and *The English Constitution* is no longer a Baedeker of British government. Nevertheless, translated into the modern idiom of functional analysis, his emphasis upon the realities behind the façade of the political process remains completely valid to this day.

It is not possible to devise (other than in terms so broad as to be practically useless) a model of governmental policy-making which can accommodate every facet of these complex processes. An analysis of, for example, foreign policy, requires different techniques from those employed in an analysis of domestic policy, though important insights may be gained from comparing the two. Similarly penal policy must be distinguished from other areas like social policy and criminal-law reform, even though subject areas of this kind obviously overlap and all can be reduced to a conceptual lowest common denominator—in terms, for example, of the structural–functionalist concepts of inputs, conversions, and outputs. But the latter, though of importance to the political theorist, are of little immediate assistance to the penologist.

Political scientists tend to regard Parliament somewhat ambivalently. A recent spate of literature stressing the 'decline' of parliamentary government implicitly relegates the House of Commons and *a fortiori* the House of Lords to Bagehot's 'dignified' category. One commentator has suggested that 'the House of Commons has the right which Bagehot attributed to the monarchy, the right to be consulted, the right to encourage and the right to warn.'[5]

But no academic analyst has yet dismissed Parliament altogether,

[5] Henry Fairlie, *The Life of Politics* (Methuen, 1968), p. 20.

and the existence of a large and ever-growing literature on the subject bears witness to the continuing scholarly preoccupation, either with Parliament's continuing significance in the processes of government or with regret at, and apologia for, its 'decline'. And it cannot be denied that Parliament lives on as an invaluable 'visible' link in a long chain of political activity, much of which is concealed from public view. There is no logical inconsistency in acknowledging that nine-tenths of the iceberg is hidden from view while admitting at the same time that it is a considerable blessing to shipping that the remaining one-tenth is not.

If there exists a 'middle of the road' academic attitude to Parliament—between the Scylla of outright cynicism and the Charybdis of naïve encomium—it is probably best epitomized in S. A. Walkland's *The Legislative Process in Great Britain*, where it is argued that:

The legislative process in Britain is now complex: it comprises deliberative, parliamentary and administrative stages, over all of which executive political influence is dominant. Legislation is now an almost exclusively executive function, modified, sometimes heavily, by practices of group and parliamentary consultation ... The process is not one which occurs entirely along a chain of command and assent ... [it] could equally well be termed a continuous process of consultation, reconciling group and party interests to its objects and acting as a powerful legitimating and integrating influence within the constitution.[6]

This view of the legislative process can be applied without difficulty to the making of penal policy. Executive responsibility is vested in the Home Office, a department whose essential task has been described, rather idealistically, by one distinguished mandarin, as maintaining 'the widest possible liberty consistent with law and order'.[7] Close contact is maintained with the legal departments of government, with the Advisory Council on the Penal System, and with interest groups mostly representing State functions such as the police, the Prison Service, and the lay magistracy (though outside bodies like NACRO and the Howard League for Penal Reform are also listened to with respect). But where does Parliament fit into the scheme of things?

Here the subject of crime and punishment presents peculiar problems to the would-be policy analyst. For one thing, crime and the

---

[6] (George Allen and Unwin, 1968), p. 20.
[7] Sir Frank Newsam, *The Home Office* (George Allen and Unwin, 1954), p. 18.

punishment of crime have always been two distinct issues (though in practice the distinction is not always recognized—see below). Certainly Parliament has been responsible for the enactment of a large body of criminal-law statutes and these enactments invariably say something about punishment, usually confined to stipulating maximum sentences.[8] Statutes concerned solely with penal policy are much rarer although there have been two Criminal Justice Acts in the last seven years. Many aspects of penal practice are not initiated by Parliament at all but are either dealt with 'administratively' or grow, Topsy-fashion, through the on-going practices of penal administrators. Nowhere is there a greater blurring of the distinction between 'legislation' (supposedly the prerogative of Parliament) and 'administration' (traditionally the province of the civil servant or the professional administrator).

Thus penal policy-cum-administration is evolved at several levels and it is not surprising to discover that Parliament's role varies from one level to another:

Level 1: Broad legislative specification of the type (or range) of punishment appropriate to a particular crime. Here it is Parliament that sets the upper limits; but in practice it must have some regard for precedents set in existing penal practice and in any event the decision is almost invariably an executive one.

Level 2: Introduction, modification, or abolition of particular types or regimes of punishment—e.g. the decision whether to retain or abolish hanging or imprisonment with hard labour, or to introduce variations on the theme of suspended sentences and community service orders. Such matters may be subject to full-dress parliamentary debate on periodic Criminal Justice Bills or in other legislative contexts; but it is very difficult to delineate this level of activity from level 3 where Parliament has little or no part to play.

Level 3: 'Details' of penal administration. While Parliament can address itself to broad questions of whether to hang murderers or to flog rapists, or to more specific ones like whether the maximum

---

[8] There are exceptions, e.g. minimum of forty hours under community service orders provided by s. 15 of the Criminal Justice Act 1972; also Borstal training and life sentences. There was an interesting discussion about the possibility of introducing minimum sentences for firearms offences during the Commons committee stage of the Criminal Justice Bill; *H.C. Committee Hansard*, Standing Committee G, 14th sitting (15 Feb. 1972), cols. 584 ff.

term of imprisonment for possessing cannabis should be five years or seven, there exists within the framework of penal policy laid down by Parliament considerable room for variation. The concept of a 'prison sentence', for example, is by no means monolithic. Parliament decrees that there shall be prisons, it innovates particular variations on the theme of a prison sentence and it votes money for prison buildings and administration; yet the *kinds* of prison—open, closed, maximum security, etc.—and the *nature* of prison regimes vary with the lengths of successive Home Secretaries', senior prison administrators', and even (or perhaps especially) prison governors' reach. It is open to Members of Parliament to raise particular aspects—for example, to question ministers about allegations of harsh conditions or, more generally, to debate the efficacy of the parole system or the pros and cons of maximum-security detention; but the means open to Members to publicize, let alone to control, penal policy-making by the prison authorities and other administrative agencies suffer from serious drawbacks. The same is true *a fortiori* of level 4.

Level 4: Sentencing policy and the application of principles of penal policy to particular cases. This particular lawn is, by hallowed tradition, the exclusive preserve of the judiciary, and 'keep off the grass' notices are all too visible. Occasional hard cases may be ventilated in Parliament (subject to the *sub-judice* convention[9] which stipulates, in effect, that Members can only talk about sentences when it is too late for their intervention to be effective); a few cases of allegedly wrongful conviction (viz. Stafford and Luvaglio, Hanratty, Evans) are the subject of sustained campaigns by parliamentarians to secure pardons or retrials, the daily half-hour adjournment debate being a medium which is peculiarly suited to such matters.

Even in the broad areas where Parliament is called upon to make a contribution to the development of penal policy, there is no guarantee that its contribution will be particularly useful or effective, still less that it will in any real sense enable public attitudes to punishment to be embodied in legislation. For one thing there is the perennial problem of lack of expertise. All too often debates are dominated by ministers who have mastered (with varying degrees of success) their departmental briefs; by Opposition front-bench spokesmen who do

[9] See Gavin Drewry 'Parliament and the Sub-Judice Convention', 122 *New Law Journal*, 1158.

at least specialize in the subject area concerned, though they are denied detailed and up-to-date briefing by officials; and by a few back-benchers with an interest (occasionally backed by special expertise) in the subject. One consequence of the blurring of the line between 'criminal law' and 'penal policy' is that lawyers (who inhabit Parliament in large numbers) lay claim, not always supportable in fact, to an expertise in penology and play a disproportionate part in parliamentary proceedings in this field: this is a theme to which we shall return in the following sections.

Then there is the problem of Executive control. This is not so much a matter of party discipline exercised by the whips as of all legislation being drafted as an integrated package deal, often embodying the product of a delicately balanced process of give-and-take between the department responsible and influential pressure groups. Bills are presented to Parliament as *faits accomplis*, and it may not be easy for ministers to make concessions, other than of a token kind, even if they are half persuaded of the desirability of doing so. Finally, the M.P. faces a perennial and insuperable problem of identifying any mainstream of 'public opinion' in a pluralist society with a huge 'silent majority'.

The foregoing sketch of some of the features of parliamentary involvement in penal policy-making provides some points of reference for the study of actual events. It is proposed, first of all briefly to examine certain features of one well-documented case study, the events leading up to the abolition of capital punishment in 1969, and then to examine the penological content of a single complete session of Parliament.

THE ABOLITION OF CAPITAL PUNISHMENT

To discuss the part played by Parliament and by public opinion in the formation of penal policy without saying something about the modern debate on capital punishment would be to ignore ungratefully a rich vein of evidence; but it must be stressed that the lessons to be learned from this case study cannot readily be applied in other aspects of Parliament's dealings with issues of punishment. It is not necessary to trace the history of relevant events in any detail, since this is already well documented (at least up to the early 1960s) notably by the American scholar, James B. Christoph.[10]

[10] *Capital Punishment and British Politics* (George Allen & Unwin, 1962); see also Peter G. Richards, *Parliament and Conscience* (George Allen & Unwin, 1970), Chapter 3.

Parliamentary discussion of capital punishment dates back to the early-nineteenth century and the campaign led inside Parliament by Sir Samuel Romilly and Sir James Mackintosh to abolish hanging for minor offences. The modern debate, confined almost exclusively to application of the extreme penalty to the crime of murder, dates back to well before the Second World War, but the lineage of the Murder (Abolition of the Death Penalty) Act 1965, reaffirmed by parliamentary resolution in 1969, can be traced back via the debates of the mid-1950s and the Report of the Gowers Commission, to the overwhelming defeat by the House of Lords of a back-bench abolitionist clause inserted in the Government's Criminal Justice Bill in 1948.

Although this particular subject must be considered in the wider context of penal policy, capital punishment has in many respects been an issue *sui generis*. To quote from the concluding pages of Christoph's account:

> Questions like capital punishment, embodying as they do moral as well as legal considerations, are likely to call forth strong emotions . . . Emotional issues are likely to be 'popular' issues in the sense that the layman feels at home with them and competent to pronounce upon them. They evoke widespread public interest of a sort not present when technical or mundane issues are raised in politics . . . On the Second Reading and Report Stages of bills before Parliament . . . as many laymen expressed their views as did barristers or former Home Secretaries, and most of them were willing to match their knowledge of foreign statistics or their acquaintance with the criminal elements with those of their Learned Friends . . . So long as the issue remained moral and emotional, as well as legal and statistical, there could be few acknowledged experts in the usual sense. And if experts were allowed a smaller place than is generally the case, public opinion occupied a larger one.[11]

And, on another aspect: '. . . the important decisions on this subject differed from many others in that they could not very well be taken at the administrative level or through informal agreement between interest group spokesmen and their counterparts in the officialdom.'[12]

Here was an issue where Home Office responsibility was clearly involved but where successive governments (and the political parties) chose to maintain an unsatisfactory pose of neutrality. One Labour Government got into a tangle over its free vote[13] on the abolitionist

---

[11] Christoph, op. cit., pp. 171–2.   [12] Ibid., p. 173.
[13] The luxury of a free vote was denied to government office-holders.

clause in 1948; a Conservative Government suffered similar embarrassment when it gave the Commons an opportunity to vote for abolition in 1956; another Labour administration strained the definition of governmental responsibility by promising in the 1964 Queen's Speech, not to legislate, but to provide special facilities for back-bench legislation.

Successive Home Secretaries let their personal views be known but the initiative on both sides of the capital-punishment campaign emerged, if not from that nebulous and media-synthesized entity 'public opinion' then at least from a public debate between opposing pressure groups and from parliamentarians unusually free of party (though not always of constituency)[14] constraints. For once Parliament played an active role at the stage of policy formation instead of being called in at an advanced stage to sandpaper the administrative edges of a ministerial *fait accompli*. This fact alone distinguishes the capital-punishment debates from most parliamentary involvement in penal policy. And here the policy-making model outlined in the last section requires extensive modification, though the exception serves to underline the more usual rule.

In the extract quoted above Christoph points out that as many laymen as lawyers took part in the debates; that this fact is thought worthy of comment is itself symptomatic of the widespread belief that lawyers and (particularly judges) have, by virtue respectively of their forensic and sentencing experience, a near monopoly of expertise relevant to debates on punishment. That many lawyers do take part in parliamentary debate on penal issues is hardly surprising, if only because so many politicians are members of the legal professions; ninety-six barristers were elected to the House of Commons in 1970. In the House of Lords, moreover, there are the Law Lords, currently numbering about twenty, many of whom, having served previously as trial judges and gained long experience of sentencing, are not slow to express opinions on penal matters. But their influence in this field is out of proportion to their numbers.

In the capital-punishment debates there can be no doubt about the degree of influence exercised upon the House of Lords by the formidable personality of Lord Chief Justice Goddard, epitomizing the retributive viewpoint. The conversion of a House of Lords which in

---

[14] viz. the clash between Nigel Nicholson, a Conservative abolitionist, and his constituency organization during the 1950s, Christoph, op. cit., pp. 153–4. See also N. Nicholson, *People and Parliament* (Weidenfeld & Nicolson, 1958).

1956 had voted 238 to 95 against abolishing the death penalty to one which in 1965 voted in favour, by 204 votes to 104, was surely due as much to the disenchantment with the Homicide Act 1957 expressed by Lord Goddard's successor, Lord Parker, and endorsed by his fellow Law Lords as with the supposedly liberalizing influx of post-1958 life peers.

But the role of judges in debates on this subject was called into question by a Scottish Law Lord, Lord Keith of Avonholm, in his maiden speech delivered during the 1956 debates. 'I am not entirely satisfied in my own mind', he said, 'that judges have any more reason, or are more qualified, to decide upon this question than any other member of your Lordships' House. The question is primarily a social question.'[15]

This brings us back to the common confusion between criminal law and penology. Parliament is well equipped with experts in the former field, but its access to expertise in the latter is more restricted. Some Members of Parliament, both lawyers and non-lawyers, undoubtedly do take an interest and acquire expertise of a high order in penal matters *per se*, but there is a tendency, particularly in the legal profession, to think that experience in watching criminals in court and handing out sentences is *by itself* enough to give an insight into social and moral issues of punishment and the treatment of offenders. It would be nice to have confidence that all sentencers do have such insight, but, despite recent improvements in training (sentencing conferences, visits to penal institutions, and so on) this is by no means always the case.

As will be shown in the next section our hypothesis about the limited involvement of Parliament in penal matters, particularly at the level of policy-making, is largely confirmed by the facts. That parliamentarians lack expertise in this field is as much a consequence of the fact of unremitting executive domination over penal policy-making as it is a cause of that domination—though these things tend to happen in vicious circles. Parliament's problem today is that, with the ever-growing extent and complexity of governmental activity, it is hard for it to become really expert at *anything*.

PARLIAMENT AND THE PENAL SYSTEM: THE SESSION 1971-2

There is no such creature as a 'typical' parliamentary session; 1971-2 has been chosen for this case study because of its proximity

[15] H.L. Deb., vol. 198, cols. 641 ff.

to the present rather than as a paradigm of anything in particular. Indeed, in several respects it was an unusual session. There was intense inter- and infra-party controversy over the European Communities Bill, which loomed over the whole session, and the Government's programme also included such contentious items as the two Bills on housing finance, the introduction of V.A.T. and the reorganization of local government. The entire session was set against the bloody backcloth of a deteriorating situation in Northern Ireland.

Penal matters had, therefore, to fight an unequal battle for even a small place in a heavily crowded timetable. But, on the other hand, the Government chose this session to bring in the fourth post-war Criminal Justice Bill containing, *inter alia*, such innovating features as community service orders, criminal bankruptcy—and drastically modifying the previous Labour Government's legislation requiring courts mandatorily to suspend certain sentences of imprisonment.

Parliament is rarely given an opportunity to pronounce upon broad issues of penal policy in the context of major legislation. Criminal Justice Bills have been spread thinly over the post-war years—1948, 1961, 1967, and now 1972. To these must be added such measures as the Criminal Justice Administration Acts of 1956 and 1962; the Prison Act 1952; and the Children and Young Persons Acts 1963 and 1969. There have been Bills with a narrower penological content, such as the various legislative excursions into the realms of capital punishment and such measures as the First Offenders Act 1958.[16] Numerous Bills dealing with substantive criminal law—such as the Theft Act 1968, the Firearms Act 1968, the Misuse of Drugs Act 1971, and the Criminal Damage Act 1971—have contained significant penal ingredients.

The Criminal Justice Bill was introduced in the Commons in November 1971 and received the royal assent in October 1972; it was one of fifty-nine Government Bills introduced during the session. On the floor of the Commons it occupied about twenty-five hours of debate out of the sessional total of nearly 2,000 hours; it took some sixty hours spread over twenty-five sittings of a standing committee at which the average attendance was 16·4 members. Proceedings in the Lords took some forty hours, about 5 per cent of the sessional total. Altogether, therefore, this important Bill was given about 125

[16] This is a rare instance of a private Member's Bill in this field; a more recent example is Lord Gardiner's Rehabilitation of Offenders Bill, first introduced during the session 1972–3. It became law on 1 Aug. 1974.

hours of parliamentary time, by no means an insignificant total given the competing pressures on the timetable.

The debates, particularly those in the Commons, involved a considerable contribution by lawyers.[17] Out of about 1,000 column-inches of debate at Commons second reading[18] (including opening and closing speeches) 600 were by speakers with professional legal backgrounds. There were twenty-one speeches in addition to those of the four front-bench spokesmen who opened and wound up the second reading debate. Nine second-reading participants sat on the standing committee of twenty-three members, ten of whom were lawyers.

In the second reading debate in the House of Lords more than half the time was taken up by lawyers, including one Lord of Appeal, Lord Morris of Borth-y-Gest, though this total includes about one-third of the column-inches which are taken up by opening and closing speeches made by the minister, Viscount Colville of Culross, who is a barrister. But there were substantial contributions too from two lay magistrates, from Lady Wootton (criminologist and sometime member of the Royal Commission on the Penal System in England and Wales), from Lord Wells-Pestell (founder of the Marriage Guidance Council and a former senior probation officer), from the Bishop of Rochester, and from Lord Donaldson of Kingsbridge (then chairman of NACRO).

There is a tendency for non-lawyers in debates on penal matters to adopt an almost apologetic tone for their temerity in trespassing on the territory of those supposedly more expert than themselves. Thus, after the Bishop of Rochester had claimed to be 'the first lay voice to be heard in this debate', Lord Donaldson retorted that '... no right reverend Prelate has ever been a layman. He has admitted that his wife is a lay magistrate. I claim to be speaking as the first layman tonight. My wife is not a lay magistrate and nor am I. I am not a lawyer, nor is she; I am not even a learned judge . . .'[19] This is a humorous but significant disclaimer from the chairman of an important organization in the field of penal reform.

Statistics reveal only the bare bones of the story. The provisional model of penal policy-making sketched earlier was based in part

[17] In the analysis that follows no distinction is made between front-bench and back-bench lawyers or between practising lawyers and non-practising: these distinctions may well be significant.

[18] H.C. Deb., vol. 836, col. 965 ff.

[19] H.L. Deb., vol. 332, col. 633.

upon the assumption that, when faced with departmental legislation, Parliament can seldom do more than endorse a *fait accompli*. There is much truth in this, but it is an over simplification. Although the Criminal Justice Bill emerged from Parliament looking very much the same (in principle at least) as when it went in, several concessions were won. In particular, the Government allowed a bi-partisan coalition to persuade it of the desirability of inserting a clause abolishing the property qualification for jurors and then let itself be defeated on the minimum age for jury service. It also accepted an Opposition amendment to increase penalties for unlawful harassment by landlords.

One cannot fairly gauge the efficacy of Parliament just by counting the number of amendments made[20]; it is equally important that significant issues get publicly ventilated. On the issue of abolishing mandatory suspended sentences, for example, the arguments on both sides were persuasive; in the end the Government triumphed by weight of numbers, but the underlying issues were fully and intelligently canvassed at all stages.[21] Penal policy evolves slowly; ideas that make little headway now may emerge triumphant in later years, all the firmer and clearer for their previous airing in Parliament. It is essential that issues are talked about in public, and Parliament remains good at doing just that.

The capacity and the willingness of parliamentarians to concern themselves with penal issues is reflected to some extent in the distribution of parliamentary questions to ministers. The breakdown by subject of penal questions in the 1971–2 session is shown in table 1.

It must be confessed that the choice of subject categories has presented serious problems, symptomatic of the blurred boundaries between this subject and others, like criminal justice and social policy. A question may, for example, be asked about the incidence of a particular type of crime; the questioner may be interested in this information for its own sake or he may be trying to underline the

[20] The subject of amendments is usefully discussed by V. Herman, 'Backbench and Opposition Amendments to Government Legislation', in D. Leonard and V. Herman (eds.), *The Backbencher and Parliament* (Macmillan, 1972), pp. 141 ff., though it is unfortunate that his analysis is confined to proceedings on the floor of the Commons.

[21] *H.C. Committee Hansard*, Standing Committee G, 7th sitting (18 Jan. 1972); 8th sitting (20 Jan. 1972). Report stage: H.C. Deb., vol. 838, cols. 1939 ff. Committee stage (Lords); H.L. Deb., vol. 333, cols, 531 ff. Report stage (Lords); H.L. Deb., vol. 335, cols. 1299 ff.

TABLE 1

Parliamentary questions on penal matters 1971–72

Subjects	COMMONS								LORDS			
	Home Office				Other Departments				All Departments			
	Oral		Written		Oral		Written		Oral		Written	
	No. answered	Col. inches	No. answered	Col. inches	No. answered	Col. inches	No. answered	Col. inches	No. answered	Col. inches	No. answered	Col. inches
Sentencing policy and practice	1	6·5	12	58·8	2	22·8	6	8·0	—	—	1	10·5
Capital punishment	—	—	5	9·3	—	—	3	6·0	—	—	—	—
Life sentences	1	1·0	2	6·8	—	—	—	—	—	—	—	—
Suspended sentences	1	4·5	5	30·5	—	—	—	—	—	—	—	—
Unpaid fines	—	—	3	10·3	—	—	—	—	—	—	—	—
Penalties for particular offences	2	12·0	18	57·6	2	7·9	2	2·4	—	—	—	—
Remands in custody	2	23·3	22	111·8	1	4·8	—	—	—	—	—	—
Conditions in named prisons/remand centres	1	6·0	27	72·8	—	—	—	—	2	10·3	—	—
Prison conditions (general)	2	11·3	17	45·7	—	—	2	6·0	—	—	—	—
Cases concerning named prisoners	—	—	7	16·7	—	—	1	3·5	3	91·9	1	4·3
Borstals, detention centres, attendance centres	1	3·2	10	23·2	—	—	1	2·3	—	—	1	4·8
Women prisoners/Holloway	—	—	—	—	—	—	—	—	—	—	—	—
Prison	5	32·0	26	65·7	—	—	—	—	—	—	—	—

Prison staff (and their accommodation) .	2	10·3	8	20·0	—	—	—	—	—	—	—	—
Prison buildings (other than above) .	2	41·7	—	—	—	—	—	—	—	—	—	—
Prison costs (other than above) .	—	—	3	7·3	—	—	—	—	—	—	—	—
Training, work, and education in prisons .	1	21·0	5	11·1	1	4·7	1	3·2	—	—	—	—
Pre-release, after-care and employment of ex-prisoners	1	6·4	6	10·7	—	—	10	13·7	1	13·5	1	—
Parole .	1	1·0	5	8·7	—	—	—	—	—	—	—	—
Prison statistics (other than above) .	—	—	8	16·2	1	14·6	1	2·0	—	—	—	—
Broadmoor and Rampton Hospitals . .	—	—	3	5·0	—	—	2	5·1	—	—	—	—
Probation Service . .	3	19·9	7	18·3	—	—	1	3·5	2	44·5	1	5·8
Miscellany . .	2	6·3	6	22·8	—	—	1	3·0	—	—	1	3·0
TOTAL	28	206·4	205	629·3	7	54·8	31	58·7	9	165·0	4	23·6

The number of column inches shown for oral questions includes supplementaries, though the latter are not added to the total number of questions.

No distinction is drawn between questions set down for written reply and oral questions answered in writing.

The other departments are as follows: Scottish Office (4 oral questions, 9 written questions); Attorney-General (4 WQ); Lord Advocate (2 WQ); Environment (2 OQ, 2 WQ); D.H.S.S. (8 WQ); Prime Minister (1 OQ, 1 WQ); and one WQ to each of the following (all asking the number of ex-prisoners employed in the department)—Defence, D.E.S., Posts, D.T.I., and Employment.

need for stiffer penalties. Such an oblique interest in penal matters is not reflected in the table. Similarly, readers may be forgiven for puzzling over the exclusion of matters like bail, prosecution policy, the detention of illegal immigrants, and criminal-injuries compensation, while matters like remands in custody and the pay of probation officers are included. Questions about, for example, the Hanratty and Bentley cases are also excluded on the grounds that, although they have penological connotations, they are primarily to do with the efficacy of the criminal-trial process. Finally, penal questions relating exclusively to Northern Ireland, where special circumstances apply, are not covered by Table 1. The author can only plead that any classification is arbitrary and submit that the categories chosen suffice for present purposes.

The figures can largely be left to speak for themselves. In 1971–2 a total of 4,547 questions were answered orally in the Commons; 217 of these were answered by Home Office ministers; only thirty-five (twenty-eight Home Office) dealt with penal matters as specified in the table. The corresponding figures for written questions were: a grand total of 24,047 of which 1,636 were answered by the Home Office and 236 of them (205 Home Office) dealt with penal matters. Prison disturbances (viz. the Brixton incidents) loomed large; so did Broadmoor (after the Graham Young case); the imprisonment of Pauline Jones—and the plight of women offenders generally—also featured prominently. There was a sequence of questions about the London weighting of probation officers' salaries, and Mr. Greville Janner Q.C., wanted to know which departments were employing ex-prisoners; none of them knew. The largest category concerned conditions in penal institutions of one kind or another—particularly Ashford Remand Centre, and Holloway and Brixton Prisons.

In the House of Lords questions are much fewer and the number on penal topics very small. But there is a tendency in that House to turn the question period into a small-scale debate; thus a question about Myra Hindley's celebrated 'walk' in the company of the Governor of Holloway was discussed for some fifteen minutes.[22]

In addition to questions, penal issues were raised in other parliamentary contexts. These were as shown in Table 2 (in chronological order). Adding up how much of the 1971–2 session was spent on penal matters (though this involves the arithmetical solecism of adding together essentially different things) we discover that the

22 H.L. Deb., vol. 335, cols. 476 ff.

TABLE 2

House of Commons	Column inches
Address in reply to the Queen's Speech—four speeches on penal issues (in wider context of 'law and order')	128
Christmas dissolution debate on a Home Office Report on prisons	136
Short mention of the *Pauline Jones* case at business questions .	5
Adjournment debate about Midlands Women's Remand Centre	90
Debate on Expenditure Committee on Probation and After-Care	268
Private Notice Question about overcrowding in Brixton Prison .	26
Easter dissolution debate on remanded persons . . .	165
Adjournment debate on variation of sentences among the Great Train Robbers	83
Government statement following the *Graham Young* case .	93
TOTAL	994

House of Lords	
Address in reply to the Queen's Speech—seven speeches on penal issues (in wider context of 'law and order')	234
Government statement following the *Graham Young* case .	74
TOTAL	308

Commons spent some 35 hours out of (nearly) 2,000 (1·75 per cent), plus 60 hours on the committee stage of the Criminal Justice Bill. The Lords spent about 43 hours out of 800, just over 5 per cent, the larger percentage being due almost entirely to the committal of the Criminal Justice Bill to the whole House and not to standing committee.

While one cannot say with much confidence how much time Parliament *should* be spending on one important subject at the expense of another, one can at least say that, given the diversity of parliamentary business, these look like respectable rations; but they dwindle almost to vanishing point if, as happens in more sessions than not, there is no Criminal Justice Bill or a measure of equivalent penological importance. Qualitatively speaking, moreover, it is clear that Parliament's role in the penal policy sphere is, to put it kindly, limited. Most questions and debates are either on matters of more or less transitory importance (particular events like the Graham Young débâcle or the Brixton disturbances) or are of fairly narrow interest (e.g. the pay of probation officers, the speaking of Welsh in English prisons) or their purport is unclear (e.g. questions on the crime rate). And, although it is comforting to feel that elected representatives will take up the cudgels on behalf of the oppressed and niggle away at the Government over an increase in recorded crime, the comfort turns out on closer inspection to be somewhat illusory. Ministers have all kinds of techniques for evading embarrassing questions; Question Time itself is all too brief, the Home Office comes up on the rota all too rarely—and when it does, questions range over the entire spectrum of its responsibilities, of which the penal system is only a part.

One cannot assume, moreover, that all the questioners and participants in debate have the expertise to frame meaningful questions, still less that they will be able to do anything useful with the answers when they have got them. In the last analysis ministers have an effective monopoly both of information and of initiative in policy making. This problem clearly relates to the perennial controversy about whether Parliament is ceasing to be a generalist institution and is becoming fragmented into specialist groups. The present writer's view is that this trend, provided it is not carried to absurd extremes, is inevitable and probably desirable—though it is not possible to argue the case fully here.

So the model outlined earlier is largely vindicated—or at least not refuted—by the facts, though research of a more wide-ranging kind would be needed before firm conclusions could be drawn. All policy-making is under the thumb of a Government backed by bureaucratic expertise, and Parliament's role is technically crucial (in that its consent is needed for primary legislation and for the spending of public money) but practically peripheral; penal policy is developed in the interstices of on-going administrative practice. Even debates on Criminal Justice Bill, although they are important as ventilators of public issues and for tidying up loose ends, do not involve Parliament in significant policy innovation.

CONCLUSION

The conclusion to be drawn from this brief excursion through parliamentary activity accords with one's initial impression that penal change takes place, if not in the teeth of public opposition, at least without explicit or tacit consent of the public in any real sense. Parliament, in ever-shifting alliance with the mass media, plays its part in the dissemination of information, but it cannot realistically be said to reflect or to transmit public opinion or social *mores*. As past and present debate on capital punishment shows, however, politicians are quite capable of probing away at latent public concern and then of invoking a rather synthetic spectre of national frenzy to underpin a personal crusade. But capital punishment is *sui generis*: most penal policy making is an administrative function which barely impinges upon Parliament and which involves the man on the Clapham omnibus hardly at all. Thus the principal constraints upon policy-making in this field are largely administrative in character; social *mores* play a part only in so far as they accord with the value systems of politicians and administrators, though the largely rhetorical phrase 'public opinion' crops up not infrequently in debates on crime and punishment.

The setting up in 1964 of a Royal Commission on the Penal System in England and Wales (unprecedentedly dissolved and replaced in 1966 by the Advisory Council on the Penal System) is symptomatic of a tendency of successive Home Secretaries to drop politically hot potatoes of radical penal reform into the laps of others—though this happens in other spheres of government also. The same tendency was displayed in the contortions of successive ministers in hiding behind the skirts of the private Members when confronted by the issue of capital punishment. Even if parliamentarians were properly equipped to see inside the minds of Home Office ministers they would be seeing only a part of the policy-making process; the deliberations of advisory bodies, the activities of pressure groups, and the thought-processes and techniques of those administering penal institutions are only sporadically and imperfectly revealed. But, to end on a slightly more sanguine note, it must be said that Parliament does at least ventilate issues of punishment which might otherwise die for want of a public airing. Given the complexity of modern government and the amorphous character of public *mores*, it may be that healthy ventilation of penal affairs is the most that we can reasonably expect from a parliamentary democracy.

4. Policy and Administration in Penal Establishments

J. E. THOMAS

WHEN people in the community contemplate the activities of the Prison Service they tend, naturally, to focus their interest on the relationship between the prison officer and the prisoner, against the background of a particular institution. But this vital relationship does not exist in isolation. It is subject to the decisions made at the centre of this most centralized of our public services. These decisions cannot be categorized as the result of policy-making, or of administrative decree, but are a compound of both. I wish to discuss the three most crucial of these grand decisions: those that have been made; those that are being made; and those that have yet to be made. It is these decisions, translated into action, that provide the context within which things happen, or do not happen, in penal institutions.

Before discussing current and future decisions I shall describe, briefly, decision-making in the past, and how the administration of the Prison Service in this country has evolved. An awareness of important events in penal history does more than simply make the present system intelligible. It demonstrates that many of the debates that we regard as peculiar to our age are, in fact, timeless and universal. Above all, a review of prison history will emphasize the radical, basic nature of policy decisions that are being made at the moment.

The history of the English prison system may be divided into a number of fairly well-demarcated periods.[1] At the end of each of these periods, there occurred a new and radical change of direction. The reasons for these changes are complex, but they have usually been precipitated by crises of some kind. At the present time our prison system is at the end of such a period. Provoked by critical events, decisions have been made, and continue to be made, which are changing the prison system.

The end of the first, longest, and remarkably unchanging period in prison history was brought about by the Prisons Act of 1877. Under

[1] For a discussion of the problem as to whether each period was an 'improvement' on its predecessors see Chapter 1, esp. pp. 1–15.

this Act, for the first time, central government took over the administration of all our prisons. Hitherto local prisons were the responsibility of the local Justices of the Peace. The whole of the New Prison Service was to be administered by a Prison Commission, which had five members. This conferred an administrative distinction upon the Prison Service which has continued. Unlike the hospital service, education authorities, or the police forces, local people have no statutory administrative function in respect of penal establishments in their vicinity. The sole local connection, the Board of Visitors, is not concerned with finance, staffing, or policy.

Writers on the period after 1877 tend to portray it as a kind of Prison Dark Age, with Sir Edmund du Cane, the chairman of the Commissioners, in the role of arch villain. The facts are not nearly so depressing. It was a time when deterrence was believed to be a sensible policy, effective in its aim of persuading criminals to abandon their anti-social activities. Prison was to consist, in the classic phrase, of 'hard labour, hard fare, and hard bed'. But the new administration brought considerable benefits to prisoners, not the least of which was an end to the capricious behaviour of local prison staff, and the establishment of a staff structure, which was carefully supervised, and ruthlessly disciplined if prisoners were ill treated. There was, however, one especially serious disadvantage. Before 1877, government Inspectors of Prisons were often very critical of local prisons. They were rigorously inquisitive, and the abuses they discovered in Birmingham prison in 1852 are only remarkable because a Royal Commission was set up to investigate. After centralization, the Inspectors became part of the Prison Commission, and the only criticisms that they made from then on were trivial. This raises basic, perennial, and hitherto unsolved questions about prison inspection, and these will be discussed.

This period, which saw the establishment of the Prison Service in the form in which, in all important respects, it remains today, ended in 1895. In that year the Gladstone Committee published its report. The committee reviewed much of the system, and made radical proposals. The most important was for a change in policy: 'We start from the principle that prison treatment should have as its primary and concurrent objects deterrence, and reformation.'[2]

---

[2] *Report from the Departmental Committee on Prison*, 1895 (H.M.S.O., Cmnd. 7702).

This famous statement has generally been regarded as the *imprimatur* for the ending of a discredited, exclusively deterrent policy, and for the ushering in of an Age of Enlightenment. In reality, apart from the establishment of the Borstal system, in a very rudimentary form, little happened for twenty-five years. Nevertheless, by its introduction of a reformative goal, the Gladstone Committee did bring one period to an end, and initiated another.

The grandness of its statement concealed the fact that the seeds of a major conflict had been sown, since the exhortation to achieve the 'twin tasks' set in motion a series of events which contributed, substantially, to the crisis in 1966. This conflict culminated in the Mountbatten Inquiry into security, following the escape of George Blake (sentenced to 42 years' imprisonment for spying[3]) from Wormwood Scrubs. There can only be, by definition, *one* primary task; the two proposed tasks of deterrence and reformation are manifestly incompatible. In addition, the committee took no account of the relationship of the supreme task—security—to the other two. The result was a confusion which served only to make staff despair.

The Gladstone initiative, in respect of reform, bore fruit in 1922 when Alexander Paterson was appointed as a commissioner. It was Paterson who was the driving force behind the many reforms which, in the inter-war years, made the English Prison Service famous throughout the world. All of these reforms cannot be catalogued here. They included improved educational facilities, more 'association' between prisoners in their free time, the abolition of the convict 'crop', and an expansion of the practice of prison visiting. Had it not been for the outbreak of war, he might well have succeeded in abolishing closed prisons for women altogether. Perhaps above all, Paterson is assured of a place of honour in penal history because of the introduction of the 'open' institution. In 1936, for the first time in England, prisoners from Wakefield slept in open conditions. Throughout the 1930s the first open Borstals were established. Some of these became penal legends—Lowdham Grange, North Sea Camp, and Hollesley Bay Colony—the last-named having the doubtful honour of numbering among its former inmates Neville Heath and Brendan Behan.

Paterson was the architect of the Borstal system as it stands today. It was a reflection, in many ways, of his personality, his experience,

3 [1962] 2 Q.B. 377.

and his faith. He believed that, given the right environment, *all* boys would improve. The key to success was the quality of the relationship between staff and inmates. Structurally, Borstal was modelled on the public school, with a housemaster, house staff, and much emphasis on sport, work, and the cultivation of qualities such as loyalty.[4]

In recent years the Borstal system has been under stress. The complaint has been made, often by the staff, that the assumptions about society, religion, and adolescent culture which underpinned the classical system are no longer valid. Or, that the inmates are more difficult than they used to be. Mounting criticism of this kind has encouraged pressure to alter the system. The proposals differ in degree, but have a number of common themes. It is not appropriate to discuss the question of the treatment of the Borstal age group here, nor is this necessary, since the Advisory Council on the Penal System has just carried out a major review. (Its report came out while this book of essays was in the course of publication.) There are two themes, however, that deserve comment, because in essence, they occur in many contemporary debates about the penal system.

The first is the growing tendency to make a sentence more flexible, by curbing the power of the courts to specify exactly how long a sentence should be. A rudimentary example is remission, and more sophisticated manifestations are the Borstal sentence, and parole. A very significant step has been taken recently by awarding social service departments of local authorities discretion over the treatment of children and young persons, which include decisions as to whether being sent away is appropriate. There are many advantages in this flexibility; decisions are not binding, and changes can be made as circumstances alter. Before this flexibility is too easily accepted as an incontrovertible advantage, it is well to exercise some caution when penal decision-making is moved from a court to an executive office, where evidence, and decisions about a course of action based on that evidence, are not openly debated or easily challengeable. However 'expert' a group may be, it should not be allowed to control too many parts of the machinery of criminal justice. This is the source of objections to the several proposals in recent years that social workers

---

[4] Paterson's creed was set out in a privately printed publication, *The Principles of the Borstal System* (1932). Paterson's work has been viewed with mixed feelings in recent years. See Gordon Hawkins, *The Ideology of Imprisonment*, especially his discussion of the views of Rupert Cross, pp. 105–108, *infra*.

should be involved in sentencing *and* treating young people. And they are sound objections.[5]

The next theme centres around a belief that *all* facilities for treating certain groups should be managed by one authority. For some time, for example, it has been suggested that Borstals should be taken out of the prison system, and should be made part of a comprehensive organization for the training and treatment of the 17–21-year-old group.

There is a tendency in many organizational situations to seek such a one-dimensional style of operation. It is more efficient to have one over-all authority. But rather than develop one style of institutional training which could not cope with diverse needs, it is surely better to maintain a set of alternative methods in the treatment of offenders which can only be a *real* alternative if administered by several authorities. The need for variety of treatment, incidentally, also justifies the retention of the detention centre. Borstals could usefully be kept as such and re-examined so that the best in its traditions and experience could be harnessed to new ideas. Many possibilities for development have been tentatively explored within the service—the 'Huntercombe Scheme'[6] having been one of the most promising. This plea for a variety of ways of dealing with young offenders includes at least an examination of the value of retaining detention centres.

There is one other reason, albeit negative, and perhaps unacceptable, for the retention of Borstals by the prison service. It is the beneficial effect on *prisons* of the presence in the system of institutions that are unequivocally for 'training'. The Borstal tradition, some of which is passed on to prisons through the transfer of staff, has been a stimulant in prisons.

The Second World War, and its aftermath, created a new situation. The war had brought new crises, especially of overcrowding and understaffing, which were coped with remarkably well. The reformative zeal was still present. There was an increase in the numbers of open institutions, home leave was introduced, and one of the most constructive experiments of all was begun—the hostel scheme. Initiated in 1953, it enabled selected prisoners to work outside the prison, in normal occupations, during the day. The new Prison Rules of 1949, made under the 1948 Criminal Justice Act, contained a

[5] Some of the issues involved in modifying the inflexibility of sentences are examined by Louis Blom-Cooper in *The Constitutional Framework of the English Penal System*, esp. pp. 25–31.

[6] For accounts by the Governor, and an officer, see *Prison Officer's Magazine* (May 1965), 120; (December 1966), 319.

historic statement of intent: 'The purpose of training and treatment of convicted prisoners shall be to establish in them the will to lead a good and useful life on discharge, and to fit them to do so.'[7] Thus was deterrence finally rejected as an aim of the prison system, however much it persists in the sentencing process.

But that serious crisis was developing, which had been immanent in the confused recommendations of the Gladstone Report. In the inter-war years the crisis, or rather the potential crisis, had been kept in check. There were many reasons for this, the most important being Paterson's status, influence, and adroitness, and an evident public sympathy for prison reform. These proved stronger than either the persistent warnings and complaints of the uniformed staff, or the drama of an event which remains unique in English prison history, the Dartmoor mutiny in 1932, during which the major part of the prison was taken over by the prisoners.[8]

Now, after the war, the crisis accelerated. Several situations arose which were to lead into the crisis that the Mountbatten Report tried to examine. There had been something of a change of attitude in the community. Punishment was in the air again. The 1948 Act for example, provided for the building of detention centres, those curiously atavistic establishments, committed to deterrence—the Gilbertian 'short, sharp, shock'—which continue to exist uneasily in a reformative milieu. Then the prison population soared. The system of men living three in a cell was introduced; in 1948 2,000 men, about 10 per cent of the population were so accommodated. In 1971 'more than a third' of the 38,000 men in prisons were sleeping two or three to a cell.[9] This practice remains the most deplorable single fact of prison experience in England. Nevertheless, in spite of these pressures, reforms were introduced, many of which were humane, some of which were expedient, some of which had training value. All meant that the prisoners had more freedom.

Prison officers now found themselves in an almost intolerable situation.[10] Their public statements reiterate, constantly, their anxiety

[7] Prison Rule No. 6, 1949. This was reiterated, in a slightly different form, in the 1964 Prison Rules, as Rule 1.

[8] The Government asked Mr. (later Mr. Justice) Herbert du Parcq to conduct an inquiry. This was published as *Report on the Circumstances connected with the Recent Disorder at Dartmoor Convict Prison*, 1932 (H.M.S.O., Cmnd. 4010).

[9] *Prison Department Annual Report*, 1971.

[10] For a detailed discussion of the place of the prison officer in the English prison system, see J. E. Thomas, *The English Prison Officer since 1850* (London, 1972).

at the burden being put upon them. Recruitment was poor, and those who stayed soon observed that as conditions improved for prisoners, they worsened for officers. The chances of being assaulted were greater than ever, and each reform, each increase in the freedom of mobility of prisoners, increased the risk. Officers were especially disgusted at the way in which it became fashionable to 'lionize' well-known prisoners. The sympathetic way in which the latter's complaints were received, contrasted strongly with the coldness with which officers were received when they asked for improvement in their conditions. It took thirty years of constant effort, for example, to secure the right to a staff Association. The officers felt alienated from the organization, and frequently said so. Many of their objections to changes were rational, and reasonable. But characteristic methods of coping with them were to ignore them, or to claim that they were exaggerating, or, most insidious at all, to imply that they were guilty of some collective personality defect which accounted for their being 'punitive'. But a solemn lesson has to be learned from this period. It is that no prison service can implement any kind of policy whatever, least of all a reformative kind, unless the uniformed officers are consulted, involved, and convinced that some attention will be paid to their problems. Officers know this; prisoners know this; policy-makers too must understand this.

At the end of the 1950s there was a greater need than ever before for competent administration at the centre of the service, for an appreciation of the very real difficulties being faced by the staff, and, in a service which was becoming more and more complex, especially through the introduction of specialists such as psychologists, teachers, and social workers, a desperate need to be able to recognize and contact the people who were making decisions. Instead, there took place one of the most disastrous administrative changes in recent years—the dissolution of the Prison Commission.

The Prison Commission, for most of its existence, was dominated by professional *prison* administrators. In 1946, for the first time, administrative-class civil servants were appointed to key positions, and pressure arose for its abolition, and restructuring as a department of the Home Office. The disadvantages of a small administrative body with a powerful chairman are obvious enough: for example, he might be a tyrant. But this is less traumatic than a situation where the 'head' of the service is also the head of other departments, or where, as happened, the centre becomes so confused that there is no administrative structure that is intelligible to staff or inmates.

But as well as noting the disastrous nature of this change, one must observe another important and highly relevant lesson. The only people who supported dissolution when it was first proposed in 1961, were the Government front bench. Everyone else who made a public statement including newspapers, Members of Parliament, penal reformers, and retired prison staff, were against abolition. There then emerged a new and distinctive style of coping with opposition which senior prison administrators have employed on several occasions since. Because of the opposition, the matter was dropped. Two years later, in 1963, an Order in Council quietly ended the life of the Commission. This technique of giving in to pressure, and then, later, gently introducing the change without provoking public debate has been employed in other highly important matters. In 1963, for example, the Advisory Council on the Treatment of Offenders brought out a report[11] in which it recommended that welfare work in prisons should be expanded, but that this should not be the responsibility of the probation service. In spite of this, and with no public explanation or discussion, the probation service *did* become responsible. This change effectively altered the essential nature of the probation officer's job, and made it impossible to explore properly the prison officers' request that *they* should be involved in welfare work. In the same way, a proposal in 1969, that direct entry to the governor grades should be stopped, was effectively opposed. In December 1972 an announcement was made in Parliament that entrants to the governor grades under the age of twenty-four must have served as uniformed officers. Such a condition radically alters the whole pattern of recruitment to key posts in the Prison Service, and will ultimately exclude the kinds of people who have made such significant contributions in the past. In the end, all such changes affect the lives of prisoners. Later in this discussion, there are more examples of this rather alarming practice.

This atmosphere of administrative confusion and of staff frustration was bound to lead to a major crisis, a fact of which governors and officers were well aware. Three events in the 1960s provided the catalyst. The first was the abolition of capital punishment. Most murderers conform and collude with their imprisonment because of their hope of release. But after abolition, some murderers were

[11] *The Organization of After-Care* (H.M.S.O., 1963), esp. p. 23.

imprisoned for offences of such gravity that it is highly unlikely that they will be released for a very long time, if at all. Unless present policies change, their numbers in prison will continue to rise. The second factor was the commission of crimes of such novelty, and on such a scale that the perpetrators were awarded very long sentences. Included among these were the 'great train robbers', and certain spies. The third event was the escape of some of these prisoners from institutions where attention to matters of security had become lax. These escapes drew the attention of the community to the fact that the escape rate was very high, and that, confronted by prisoners who saw no advantage in collaborating with the staff, no prison was secure. And so, in 1965, the Mountbatten Inquiry took place.

It is not possible to discuss the report[12] in full. Broadly, it addressed itself to two major problems: the question of effectively controlling the new categories of prisoners which have been described, and the relationship between the prison department and the institutions. These are, and will continue to be, the central matters affecting the whole direction of prison administration for many years ahead.

Mountbatten recommended that a special security prison should be built to house what he defined as Category 'A' prisoners. These are prisoners who because of violence or 'security considerations' must in no circumstances be allowed to get out. This recommendation was accepted. But two years later, the Advisory Council on the Penal System reviewed the problem of long-term prisoners, and recommended that, instead of 'concentrating' high-risk prisoners in one institution, they should be 'dispersed' to a number of prisons which would have special security arrangements including dogs, floodlights, and closed-circuit television.[13] This is now prison-department policy.

The dispersal of Category 'A' prisoners has a certain amount to commend it. Some reformers believe it to be undesirable to concentrate such prisoners because they would be labelled as outcasts, and marked as beyond redemption. While they are part of a fairly normal prison group, they will avoid such a stigma. It is argued too that the tensions generated by the concentration of this group in an institution would be immense, not only on inmates, but on staff. Dispersal, however, has even worse effects.

[12] *Report of the Inquiry into Prison Escapes and Security*, 1966 (H.M.S.O., Cmnd. 3175).
[13] *The Regime for Long-term Prisoners in Conditions of Maximum Security* (H.M.S.O., 1968).

The problem of the 'A' prisoners should be important, but relatively minor. The dispersal policy makes it a problem that affects the entire prison system, and justifies its inclusion in this discussion of major issues. One lesson that prison staff learned from the events of the 1960s is that, above all, an 'A' prisoner must not be allowed to escape. Naturally, in the dispersal prisons there is elaborate 'perimeter security'. It is claimed that, if this security is sound, then there can be freedom inside. In the traditional prison this cannot be so, since the design of the Victorian prison, within which most of these prisoners are located, militates against such an assertion. At the time when these prisons were built, security was based on a system of separation in individual cells. Prisoners cannot be allowed that great freedom which is envisaged.

There is an even more unpleasant effect of dispersal. It is that prisoners who are not 'A' men are being subjected to unnecessary constraint, since it is impossible to compartmentalize the treatment of different groups within the same prison. This fact, which necessitates a variety of institutions with specialized functions, is the basis of any classificatory system. The effect is manifestly unjust. According to the 1971 Annual Report of the Prison Department, there are six dispersal prisons with a total population of 3,393, of whom some 10 per cent are category 'A'. This means that some 90 per cent of the inmates of these prisons are under unnecessarily oppressive security conditions.

The effect is actually even more widespread than that. If a specially designed prison were brought into service, then the problem of containing this group would be defined as a limited, highly specialized matter. Instead, dispersal not only affects six prisons, but also tends to generate a sense of crisis throughout the entire prison system. There is an emphasis on security which, in respect of most prisoners, is excessive. There are new roles for staff, dog handling which some regard as a particularly offensive technique, and security work. These have strengthened the emphasis on security.

The unpleasantness of the fact that there are now men who will spend most of their lives in prison cannot be avoided by suggesting that they are the same as ordinary prisoners. They are quite extraordinary; their sentences are extraordinary, their needs are extraordinary, and their treatment should be extraordinary. Failure to accept this will provoke more of those crises in prisons, which have already begun. The building of a special prison would go some way to allowing the Prison Service to develop methods of training and treatment both for 'A' prisoners and for the rest—that is the bulk of the penal population.

The second problem that was discussed in the Mountbatten Report concerned the relationship of the Prison Department and those working in the institutions. Mountbatten was very critical of the isolation of the department, and its apparent inability to communicate with the institutions. To remedy this, he recommended the creation of a new role, that of an Inspector-General, who could be identified by staff and inmates as a decision-maker. That he was to be powerful was indicated by the intention that he would have close contact with—even direct access to—the Home Secretary. In other words, there was to be some degree of restoration of the old office of Chairman of the Prison Commission. Uniformed staff were especially pleased about this proposal, and greeted the newly appointed Inspector-General with great enthusiasm. But such a role is not consonant with the traditions of the civil service which more and more eschew charisma and embrace anonymity. After only three years, in 1969, the Inspector-General was 'separated from executive functions' as the result of a 'Management Review',[14] which was never published, or publicly discussed. It would appear that this change was made because a new Inspectorate was to be established.

There are, naturally, problems in allocating great power to one man in a Prison Service. But in a firmly structured hierarchy it is essential that the head of the organization is recognizable to staff. There is a real danger of a resurrection of that feeling that 'Head Office' has no people in it, which the staff expressed so persistently in the years before Mountbatten. The problem of combining strong leadership and direction with civil-service traditions is one that, above all in the Prison Service, urgently needs to be faced.

The Inspector-General had another component in his role; to inspect. This issue of inspection leads to a third question which the report did not discuss; the relationship of the community with its prison system. Although this is a perennial problem, it is one that has not been satisfactorily resolved in England, and in the years ahead it is likely to be more important than ever before. The root of the problem lies in the fact, universal, well documented, and entirely natural, that prison administrators will try to dissuade the community from taking too close an interest in what goes on in penal

[14] *Prison Department Annual Report* 1971, p. 57.

institutions. All sorts of objections are marshalled; that prisoners will lie and manipulate, that their privacy should not be invaded, or that visitors are subversive in a variety of ways. All such objections are partially or occasionally true. The immediate justification is that the presence in a prison of 'A' prisoners necessitates a curb on community interest in the form of lectures, voluntary work, and similar activities. The history of prisons shows that informed and intelligent interest on the part of the community prevents policy and administration from being based entirely on exigency, or on a precedence which is no longer relevant. In future years, claims about security should not be allowed to restrict public interest in prisons.

There are three points at which the community touches penal establishments. These are all due for reappraisal. The first is the official Inspectorate. This has never been a success since 1877, for the reason that the Inspectors are too close to the administrators, a situation which Mountbatten tried, unsuccessfully, to rectify. The problem derives from the administrative uniqueness of the Prison Service, already discussed. There is an entirely different situation in the police service, probation service, or education, where Inspectors, as used to happen in the Prison Service, are reviewing the work of people with whom they have little or no organizational connection. At the moment it is proposed that a specialized Inspectorate should be set up, and this body would carry out detailed inspections of the institutions. Two major criticisms may be made of this proposal. Firstly, that the Inspecting team will be members of the Prison Service, which means that, once again, they will be inspecting their own work, and that of their erstwhile colleagues. Secondly, the validity of such inspections cannot be assessed because they are not published, and the community has to be content with generalizations which appear in the annual reports.

The second point of contact between community and institution is through the Board of Visitors, that vestigial reminder of local control. This body has three main functions: to inspect, to adjudicate on serious offences, and to hear certain kinds of requests. Their powers, on paper, are impressive; for example they approve Borstal discharges, and they can suspend a member of staff. An energetic board member who exercises his power to remedy defects gets more support from many staff, not to say prisoners, than he ever appreciates. As a supervisory body, they are generally ineffective for many reasons. One is that they tend to be composed of professional committee men who really cannot give up the necessary time. Another is that they are naturally apprehensive about challenging apparently confident and competent prison staff. Again, they are aware of the dangers of creating a fuss, and will tend to behave in predictable ways. It is always difficult to make supervisory bodies more critical, but there is a need to encourage boards to be much more inquisitive and intrusive. It might be possible to do so by encouraging a new kind of membership of the boards, although this is mere speculation.

The direction of prison affairs can be influenced by the work of an impartial Inspectorate, and by the effective involvement of Boards of Visitors. Policy-makers and administrators can also be influenced by outsiders, and there are two groups especially which, in the history of prisons in England, have caused differences to be made— Members of Parliament and organized pressure groups. Some members of these groups have been effective because they have never lost sight of the truth that the making of much prison policy is not a complicated matter, although people who are responsible will allege that it is. The inherent conservatism of prison services has often been challenged by such people. Unfortunately these influences on prisons are in some danger.

In the past, the influence of Members of Parliament in shaping prison policy has been considerable. Persistent, well-informed discussion in Parliament has challenged, effectively, convenient assumptions about prison. This tradition has been dying in recent years. This is partly because many of the most outrageous features of prison life—flogging, for example—have been abolished. Also, reforming M.P.s, like other groups, are in something of a quandary about the best way of coping with the new groups of prisoners. This trend away from interest in prisons is not likely to be arrested by the encouragement given to M.P.s to interest themselves in much grander matters, such as European affairs. For these reasons it is necessary to stress that their interest is vital.[15]

Prison matters do not attract many pressure groups, largely because the treatment of criminals cuts across the usual political divisions, and defies alignment with any particular party. Such groups, most especially the Howard League for Penal Reform, have been quite effective in suggesting or encouraging change. In the past,

15 The complexities of the relationships between Parliament and administrators in respect of penal policy are dealt with in detail by Gavin Drewry in Chapter 3.

officials have been susceptible to pressure, and reformers have been reasonable enough to take into account the difficulties of the service. But now, as elsewhere in public administration, officials are becoming rather less susceptible to pressure. Their definitions of what is 'realistic' or 'possible' are becoming increasingly difficult to challenge. This places the organized reform bodies in a very difficult situation which can be resolved in three ways. One is to argue that reform is impossible without the goodwill of the people who run the prison system, and therefore one must simply continue to press gently. But the price of maintaining this goodwill, especially at the post-Mountbatten crossroads, may be too high. Another way out of the difficulty is to concentrate on non-prison matters—new forms of non-custodial sentences, for example. The third way is to become more radical. A more aggressive pressure for reform would echo the current new radicalism in other groups seeking change in a wide variety of matters. As administrators become less and less willing to be influenced, pressure groups become more and more impatient. It is the reluctance of the traditional penal pressure groups to become more radical, together with a greater degree of education and sophistication on the part of prisoners that has led to a new phenomenon, a pressure group of prisoners and ex-prisoners, which calls itself Preservation of the Rights of Prisoners.

Over the course of the next thirty years, the significance of the Mountbatten Report, and the events surrounding it, will become clear. These were not just isolated phenomena, provoked by an abnormal situation, and easily resolved by a relatively minor decision. The Report set new policies in motion. Already decisions have been made which are altering the foundations of the system, the most notable being implementation of the 'dispersal' policy. But I have also stressed that these decisions are not irrevocable. In spite of a developing gap between government departments and the community which is by no means confined to prison affairs, it is to be hoped that society, to whom prisons belong, and in whose name the prisoners are dealt with, can still make an impact. The community, especially through its committed pressure groups, has a vital part to play in the moulding of the Prison Service of the future. Here, more than in most areas of public administration, is it necessary for an informed public to influence the decisions of the professional administrators.

5. The Evaluation of Penal Systems

PETER NOKES

THERE are two ways of approaching the task of evaluation. On the one hand we may inquire what results an organization is intended to achieve, and then ascertain by objective criteria whether, or to what extent, it achieves them. This is to refer the issue of evaluation to that of *effectiveness* or *efficiency*. On the other hand we may, without inquiring too closely into what is intended, yet inquire what is achieved, whether intentionally or otherwise, and then ask whether these effects are desirable. We may, if we wish, go on to ask whether, being desirable, their desirability is sufficient justification for their cost, the most familiar example of this kind of approach being that of cost-benefit analysis.

There is no doubt, however, that in respect of penal systems the first is the more familiar approach. Virtually all systematic evaluative studies of penal systems, or of particular forms of penal treatment (for example Kassebaum, Ward, and Wilner's recent study of the effectiveness of group-counselling regimes[1]), have up to the present been conducted in terms of the idea that evaluation means the assessment of efficiency. Nevertheless it is not entirely clear that this is the most useful approach, for a number of reasons.

Ultimately the issue of efficiency must always refer to the issue of objectives. Thus in the study mentioned the conclusion that group counselling is ineffective is meaningful in the light of the premise that group counselling is intended to reduce recidivism rates. (Or was intended at the time they were conducting their research: it is necessary to say this in view of the tendency of enthusiasts for group counselling, in the face of negative findings, to argue that their objectives were other than those on which the findings were based.)

Clearly we cannot say how effective a technique is unless we have some idea of what ends the technique is intended to achieve; nor by implication can we say how well an organization is doing until we

[1] G. Kassebaum, D. A. Ward, and D. M. Wilner, *Prison Treatment and Parole Survival: an Empirical Assessment* (John Wiley, 1971).

have some idea of what it is intended to do. The same applies to a watch, a car, or any mechanism, and ultimately this approach refers to the idea of the organization as a mechanism, as a means to an end. The idea is familiar enough and is entirely understandable. Contemplation of any organization, especially perhaps an organization we are not very familiar with, generally provokes the reflection that all this must be *for* something, that this complex of buildings, people, and routines was not assembled for the sheer pleasure of doing so. It may seem that this is the only possible way of thinking about an organization. Yet it is not the only way, and not necessarily the most helpful way of thinking about prisons.

For to raise the issue of objectives in connection with prisons is immediately to establish us in an area that is as unsatisfactory as it is familiar. What are the purposes of imprisonment? The unsatisfactoriness and the depressing familiarity are both due to a complex of problems surrounding the very idea of organizational objectives, to assumptions we tend to make about the status of objectives generally, and so to associated problems of knowing what we are talking about when we talk about efficiency.

MULTIPLE OBJECTIVES AND 'PRIMARY TASKS'

It is not an easy matter to sort out. Nevertheless a first and obvious difficulty relates to the presence in penal institutions (and in many other kinds of organization, including hospitals and schools) of multiple and contradictory objectives. The familiar debating subject referred to above (what are the purposes of imprisonment?) generally provokes the reflection at an early stage that there are indeed respects in which the aims of security and rehabilitation, for example, conflict. We might therefore conclude that since both these aims, at least, must be pursued, neither of them can ever be maximized, certainly not rehabilitation and perhaps not even security. It would then follow that the efficiency of penal institutions in terms of any single objective can never be more than limited. This would be a sensible and realistic conclusion, and the debate could be wound up.

And yet, of course, the debate is never wound up. The question we must ask is, why not? For one thing to take this view of matters would deprive us of the right to charge the prison system with inefficiency. This may appear an outrageous suggestion, but any serious assessment of the place of the penal system in contemporary British society must take account of the fringe benefits that it

affords, which is a point I shall return to later. Certainly the traditional polarizations in terms of which we feel justified in speaking of
'Us' and 'Them', and in saying such things as 'Society must make up
its mind' must break down under any serious scrutiny. We are all
members of that society. Thus to the question 'Does our penal system
make sense?' (the theme of a recent Howard League conference) it
is perfectly reasonable to answer, 'Yes, it does.' It depends on what
we mean by sense, but in the perspective of the organization
theorist, viewing the penal system as itself existing within an external
system of conflicting pressures, it certainly makes sense, and in this
perspective we might fairly conclude that prisons are probably about
as efficient as it is possible for them to be.

Yet this is not a perspective most of us want to adopt. However
sensible and inescapable the conclusion, we feel that it is unsatisfactory. Things may be so, but in our heart of hearts we feel that they
ought not to be so, and from the feeling that they ought not to be so
it is but a short step to the conclusion that they need not be so, and
are in fact not. And certainly there is another way of regarding systems.
We can acknowledge the truth of the matter, and yet regard ourselves
not as detached from systems, viewing events in a state of remote
contemplation, but as part of them, and therefore entitled to put
pressure on them. Objectives, after all, are intentions, which is to say
that they exist only in people's minds. But there is some reluctance
to acknowledge this. Hence, perhaps, the common dislike of functionalism and systems theory, both of which force on our attention our
essentially political status.

For political status is difficult to acknowledge when we feel ourselves
to be at the mercy of events. Hence, perhaps, what one can only
describe as a game, commonly played on management courses, of
Hunt the Objective, as though objectives were somehow *immanent*
in the organization itself, that they had got mislaid, and that once
rediscovered all would be well. There is an equivalent game, commonly played by assistant governors under training, of Hunt the
Role. Here the implicit assumption is that roles exist if only we could
find them, or if only the trainers would come clean. The assumption
behind both games is that the process of establishing objectives is
one of inspection, not of intent. The advantages of viewing matters
in this way are obvious. The notion of an immanent objective, as
opposed to one located in the intentions of individuals, simultaneously discharges us from the responsibility of deciding what is to be

done, and avoids the awkward problems that might arise if we were each to decide to do something different.

Moreover, the issue of decision is avoided in a situation where prison officials feel themselves not to be in a position to take decisions anyway. It thus reflects the divorce in this country between penal policy and penal practice. But who does make the decisions? The curious thing is that the higher echelons of the prison department engage in analogous activities. During the 1960s the British Prison Service engaged in a series of attempts to find an extra-political basis for penal practice. All these attempts, ranging from flirtations with psychiatry and the Human Relations movement in the early part of the decade to management theory later on, seem to have had in common a belief that the necessary unifying ideology, when found, would be in some sense *scientific*. Needless to say they were confirmed in this belief, especially in respect of the presumed 'sickness' of convicted criminals and their associated need for 'treatment', by the unsophisticated criminology of the day. Criminologists seem to be changing their minds about this, but it would be a mistake to suppose that the Prison Service is yet out of this scientific thicket. The belief still survives that all problems are managerial problems, and that one day with the help, if not of the Manchester Business School then of somebody else, the Prison Service will be able to sort itself out.

The belief that objectives are immanent in an organization acquires some apparent justification if we view organizations as natural organisms, which in turn provides some justification for ideas of 'scientific management'. Management theorists seem to be less certain of the scientific status of their activities than they once were, and it is just as well, since in deference to these ideas some extra-ordinary things have been said and done. One of them is the introduction of the belief that there is always present within an organization the genuine possibility of organizational death, and that the issue of organizational survival can supply one source of paramount and therefore self-evident objectives. It is a comforting belief for those in conflicted situations since it reassures us that in any organization there is always some one thing (in the 'game' the plural is dropped) that has to be done, in terms of which efficiency is properly to be measured, and that what has to be done is so necessary and inevitable as to render all other considerations secondary. This is the issue of 'primary tasks', which always relates, directly or indirectly, to the issue of survival.

It is not entirely clear why it should be so important to establish the existence of single paramount or overall objectives, but that it is so felt is beyond dispute. For example the present writer has a vivid recollection of an occasion, at the Glacier Institute of Management, when a party of hospital administrators (who also have these problems) were informed that it was impossible to have more than one objective, and that if one thought on the contrary that one did, then only one was an objective: the rest were 'constraints'. It is difficult to comment on this view, since it is difficult, as it was at the time, to know exactly what is being said. At any one time an organization may be on with one thing rather than with another, just as an individual may be; the trouble is that to neglect over a period of time all the other things that need to be done leads to a situation where they all become pressing. The result is a state of oscillation. In just this way the British Prison Service oscillated, in the 1960s, between the objective of rehabilitation after the Report in 1963[2] of the Advisory Council on the Treatment of Offenders (the predecessor of the Advisory Council on the Penal System), to the objective of custody after the Mountbatten Report of 1966,[3] and will no doubt oscillate back again in due course.

Perhaps more common is a variety of the single-task theory which acknowledges the existence of multiple objectives, but sees them properly arranged in a hierarchy. This is made explicit in the principle of 'Management by Objectives', which is a second school of management thinking that was briefly entertained at one point. In the context of an industrial organization the doctrine does seem to make an immediate and obvious kind of sense. Thus according to one exponent of the principle, an essential feature of improving management performance is 'clarifying with a manager the key results he will achieve in line with company objectives and gaining his contribution to and understanding and acceptance of them'.[4] The essential preliminary is the identification of organizational objectives; the next step to see that individual activities are 'in line': 'To go no further than clarifying divisional or sectional goals encourages a partisan and selfish attitude: "As long as I get my results I'm in the clear, whatever the overall situation." When managers can see their

---

[2] *The Organization of After-Care* (H.M.S.O., 1963).
[3] *Prison Escapes and Security*, 1966, Cmnd. 3175.
[4] J. W. Humble, *Improving Management Performance* (British Institute of Management, 1965).

unit's contribution integrated with the total organizational goals cooperation is encouraged.'

The trouble is that in organizations like prisons, sectional goals are not always arranged in a hierarchy in just this way. There can be unity of this kind at a sectional level, but it cannot be supposed that this will be consistent with the all-out pursuit of different goals in another section. This is not so much because all-out efficiency in one department involves making exceptional claims on scarce resources, although this is obviously important, but because the objectives of different groups of staff may be opposed, often by their terms of contract.

This is particularly likely to be the case in organizations with a long history. The late Dr. K. Rice, of the Tavistock Institute of Human Relations, defined the 'Primary Task' of an organization as 'the task which it is created to perform'.[5] But this neglects the extent to which original purposes may be rendered irrelevant by time. Organizations last, surviving even major policy changes. Faced with a change in social need or in the climate of opinion we do not scrap existing organizations but adapt them to new purposes. Prisons are indeed veritable archaeological deposits of policy—each represented by a separate grade of staff—accumulated over the last hundred years or so. Hence a situation where custodial staff, treatment staff, educational staff, and others may each see the central purposes of the organization to be pre-eminently their own concern. What is therefore individualized treatment from one point of view is favouritism or a security risk from another, and legitimately seen as a problem. This is not to say that the problem is beyond solution. The task of managing prisons might well be seen as the reconciliation of conflicting interests. It is a position often reached by penal administrators. The point is that it is not the conception of management implied in the passage quoted. Nor is it a conception likely to find much favour with those who see the future of the Prison Service to lie in the adoption of modern management techniques from the worlds of industry and commerce.

Rice defines the 'Primary Task' alternatively as 'the task that an organization must perform to survive'.[6] This formulation has the advantage of directing attention to those respects in which

[5] A. K. Rice, *Productivity and Social Organization: the Ahmedabad Experiment* (Tavistock, 1958).
[6] A. K. Rice, *The Enterprise and its Environment* (Tavistock, 1963).

management thinking in the social services is dominated by the model of the industrial or commercial organization existing in a state of competition, and by the assumption that there must always exist the possibility of going out of business. For Rice the issue of objectives, and so of efficiency rests ultimately on the question of what circumstances would inevitably lead to organizational death. But even in respect of industrial and commercial organizations there are difficulties with that idea: 'Those companies which do not plan to create and capitalise on growth opportunities are unlikely to profitably survive the pressures of competition in the long term—though it must be admitted that some companies appear to have a remarkable inbuilt capacity to survive in spite of persistent bad management.'[7] But this means that they must survive for other reasons, and this is certainly true of social service organizations.

PURPOSE AND FUNCTION

These reasons are to be found less in the realm of formal objectives, and the effective implementation of these objectives, than in the 'latent' functions that such organizations serve. The distinction between 'manifest' and 'latent' functions is R. K. Merton's.[8] Merton's use of the word 'function' in both connections does have the disadvantage, however, of failing to attach sufficient importance to the special status of publicly made statements. In this paper a distinction will therefore be drawn between *objectives*, which belong to the realm of public statement, and *functions* which belong to the realm of empirically observed relationships.[9]

Even casual observation of the industrial scene suggests that notwithstanding anything management theorists have to say to the contrary, the provision of employment is an important function of all organizations, and in certain circumstances a sufficient guarantee of their continued existence. Additionally many organizations become involved in interdependent relationships with the industrial scene in ways that have little to do with official statements of intent, but which none the less make their efficiency in terms of these statements irrelevant to survival. This is conspicuously true of many kinds of school. An important function of schools, using the term strictly in the sense defined above, is simply that of looking after children

[7] Humble, op. cit.

[8] R. K. Merton, *Social Theory and Social Structure* (Free Press, 1957).

[9] P. L. Nokes, 'Purpose and Efficiency in Humane Social Institutions', *Human Relations*, 13, 2 (1960).

while one or other parent goes out to work. Schools do not *have* to be efficient, however much we would like to think otherwise.

As for prisons, apart from the function of containment (which may obviously be an objective too) and getting deviant individuals out of the way of the rest of society, they have an important expressive function in testifying to the things that a significant section of society feels ought to happen to people who break the law.

In this respect 'going to prison' is the relevant issue, entirely separate from 'being in prison' and undergoing any specific kind of regime for any determinate period of time, and raises the interesting question of whether all we need preserve of our older prisons is the façade, to permit the sight of the delinquent going through the gates. The act is expressive or symbolic, as well as being instrumental. It is an important distinction, and one that draws our attention to those respects in which symbolic functions of this kind are self-perpetuating unless continually tested: people continue to be sent to prison at least partly because prisons are seen to be the obvious places for them to be sent. Notwithstanding public and judicial enthusiasm for prisons, there is a fair degree of indifference about what goes on inside them, and although it might appear that there is nevertheless an interest in how long it goes on for, recent Dutch experience suggests that even this interest may evaporate—except in special cases— once the possibility is visibly withdrawn.

Now this line of thinking does seem to offer a possible solution to the problem of efficiency, since functions can obviously be turned into objectives. If efficiency is a measure of the relationship between what we intend and what we achieve, then efficiency can be increased either by bringing achievements in line with intentions, or by adopting as intentions what can and perhaps must be achieved. The point is not in the least frivolous, since the perceived efficiency of an organization has an important bearing on both public credibility and on staff morale. Social service organizations invariably tend to adopt aims that are well in advance of practical possibility. This is desirable in so far as they thus perform an important expressive function in testifying to the aspirations of society at large. Nevertheless there are associated problems. For example, the adoption of an objective of treatment in the nineteenth- and early-twentieth-century mental hospitals led, in the absence of any known technique of treatment, to a situation where these hospitals suffered in respect of both public esteem and staff morale.

This is a point which it is difficult to apply to prisons with sufficient delicacy. Nevertheless it is at least possible that the public image of the prison might improve if it stopped claiming to do what it conspicuously is not doing, and concentrated instead on what it can do reasonably well. It is not a question of adopting an objective of mere containment, although obviously this would be acceptable to a significant section of the public. But it does raise the question of what significance we can continue to attach to certain kinds of objective, and in particular the precise interpretation that is to be given to the vexed issues of rehabilitation and of 'treatment'. The issue of evaluation has therefore an unexpected bearing on policy.

THE PRISON AS A TREATMENT AGENCY

The idea of the prison as an agency of 'treatment' seems to derive from a number of sources. One source of the model is no doubt the belief, common in the 1960s but less heard of these days, that 'crime' is a form of 'illness'. The penal administrator, on this line of thinking, is properly to be conceived of as a therapist. From another point of view the idea is obviously a development of the idea of rehabilitation, with this addition—that the idea of treatment, with its medical or quasi-medical overtones, appears to legitimize more explicitly the idea of the prison as a 'people-changing' agency.

A currently fashionable view of organizations is that they can always be seen as 'conversion processes', by which one thing is turned into another, and, in particular, undesirable things or states are converted into desirable things or states. Thus in a factory raw materials are 'imported' into the organization, processed, and 'exported' as finished products. Ultimately the image is that of an oven, dough being put in, cooked, and so transformed into bread. It is certainly possible to see organizations in these terms. Whether it is more than temporarily illuminating is a different matter. Acute general hospitals are, in a sense, mechanisms for turning sick people into well people (or presumably dead people). Universities can be seen, and alas increasingly are seen, as mechanisms for turning non-graduates into graduates. It is by no means clear, however, that schools can be seen in the same way, as mechanisms for turning the uneducated into the educated, if only because children leave school not when they are educated but when they are sixteen. The time boundaries of the process are set by considerations other than the successful completion of the task. It is a consideration that applies equally to prisons.

One obvious question raised by the idea of the prison as an agency of treatment is, simply, what forms of treatment are available? It is noteworthy how, after all the claims made by enthusiasts for the principle, the only methods that have seriously been tried are those, like group counselling and social casework, whose outcomes are only very problematical and that consume time. It could hardly be otherwise. In a hospital, more specifically an acute general hospital, the successful completion of a course of treatment is followed in the normal course of events by discharge. But a method of penal treatment that did guarantee basic behavioural or personality change in the direction of reducing a disposition to criminality would pose awkward problems about release. Hence a situation where the treatment idea is retained only by redefining the term 'treatment' in such a way as to empty it of all meaning. Inmates are rarely deceived in these matters, and this only adds to the air of chicanery that surrounds the Prison Service.

The idea of the organization as a mechanism is associated with the principle of essentially temporary involvements. Patients stay in a hospital until their treatment is completed and no longer; workers go home from the factory at 6 o'clock or thereabouts. In both cases involvement in the organization goes no further than is necessary to secure the achievement of a manifest task, since it is supposed in both cases that 'real life' lies elsewhere. The fact that the supposition is incorrect, as Elton Mayo showed in his classic studies of factory organization, and the fact that it is certainly not true of long-stay hospitals does not alter the principle. Notwithstanding all we know of the unofficial satisfactions that spring from even temporary involvements, the practice of referring to factory workers as 'hands' and patients as 'cases' still persists as a technique of depersonalization, testifying to the idea that while on the premises life is in a sense supposed to be suspended. But in residential establishments like prisons people do not go home very soon at all; their lives are lived where they are.

It is time, in fact, that transforms a mechanism into a social system, and this subtly affects the nature of the task. Organizational efficiency is inevitably reduced by the presence of people. Some accommodation has to be reached between official purposes and the needs of individuals on the premises. This applies even when the people concerned are all staff, and at least formally committed to the organizational objectives, and when they all go home at night. It is doubly the case when the majority of the people concerned are permanent and reluctant members. No organization can be merely a machine, certainly not a long-stay organization, and perhaps least of all a prison.

It is perhaps the most difficult thing to come to terms with about long-stay organizations. It is precisely this difference between the formal and the informal, the official and the unofficial, between what is supposed to go on and what does go on that management theorists find most difficult to handle. From the standpoint of rationality these appear merely irritating limitations on the running of an efficient organization. Perhaps even dangerous limitations. Thus one important aspect of the distinction is that between the formal authority structure of an organization and its informal power structure. But to use this language in connection with prisons is to refer to what has been called 'the corruption of authority', since it is clear that important aspects of the power structure may be controlled by prisoners themselves.

And yet this melodramatic phrase indicates the presence of very problematical assumptions about what an organization can do or be. Even a prison: it is a commonplace among experienced prison officers that their control rests ultimately on a tacit agreement between themselves and their charges. Prison disturbances are due not to the acquisition by prisoners of new sources of power, but to a decision to use those sources of power that are always present. Certainly there are problems, yet it is difficult to see the force of a position that would deny what is quite inescapable. In fact these characteristics of long-stay organizations may be seen not as handicaps but as opportunities. It depends on how we view organizations, or what assumptions we make about the nature of organizational life.

TWO PERSPECTIVES ON ORGANIZATIONS

The issue turns on the difference between the organization viewed as a means of getting some external task done, and the organization viewed as a place of residence and a way of life, between the ideas of 'association' on the one hand and of 'community' on the other.[10]

The ramifications of the idea of community have been very fully

[10] R. MacIver, *Society* (Macmillan, 1937).

worked out by Professor R. A. Nisbet in a long and careful analysis of the 'unit ideas' of the sociological tradition.[11] Although his theme is the history of ideas about the nature of society as a whole, his remarks are directly applicable to the management of residential organizations, since they indicate how we habitually view such organizations in two quite different and indeed contradictory ways.

Thus the idea of community, as it developed in the nineteenth and twentieth centuries, is to be contrasted with that of 'mass society'. Nisbet shows how the theme is characteristically associated with a distaste for the impersonalities of modern industrial and political society, with a desire for emotional as well as contractual relations between men, and with regrets for the supposed intimacies of earlier forms of society. The idea is manifested most explicitly in the establishment of small-scale residential communities, utopian in inspiration, where people gather together with the aim of living a satisfying and enriching life. Communities, from this point of view, are ends in themselves, while associations, also small social groupings, are nevertheless essentially means towards the achievement of an externally defined goal. Villages are perhaps the best examples of pure communities, whereas factories are generally cited as examples of associations. The distinction is not absolute, since associations where people spend any considerable amount of time together invariably acquire community characteristics. This is a complicating factor in the analysis and indeed in the management of places like long-stay hospitals, prisons, and even factories. All owe their existence to the presence of externally defined objectives, and are therefore in principle associations, but because of their community aspects can never be entirely efficient as mere utilitarian structures. Obviously this varies from case to case, but the tendency for an association to acquire the characteristics of community certainly increases in proportion to the length of time its members spend in contact with one another, and this is therefore a matter of practical importance in the running of residential institutions, including prisons.

There can be little doubt that this has been long understood by many of those concerned in the running of penal institutions. Much traditional practice reflects an intuitive appreciation that a prison is not after all a kind of factory, but something quite different. Nevertheless it cannot be supposed that the value of the community

[11] R. A. Nisbet, *The Sociological Tradition* (Heineman, 1967).

idea has ever been adequately exploited, mainly because the necessary vocabulary has never been developed. The appreciation remains after all intuitive, and therefore without political force. It has not been exploited even in 'therapeutic community' experiments, because the habit of thinking of all organizations as means to an externally defined end, and therefore as temporary, survives even there.

The essential difference between the two approaches is manifested in the significance that is attached to activities within the organization. In an association all activity is, in principle, supposed to be directed towards the achievement of the organizational task. This is made entirely explicit in the doctrine of Management by Objectives. All activity is seen as instrumental, a means to an end. But it is impossible in any experience that extends over a period of time to sustain this degree of purposiveness, since other questions then become obtrusive, questions to do with the quality of life. These considerations are fully acknowledged in the idea of community, since the absence of any conception of an end that has to be achieved is associated with the notion of activities as expressive, as ends in themselves. It would, for example, be foolish to think of school orchestras as ingeniously calculated means towards the achievement of some precisely envisaged educational goal. This is not why we have them. We have them because school organization in Britain has been from the first very much influenced by the idea of community, since pupils are necessarily present for a number of years. Since they are, and since communities are therefore not merely means to an end, but ways of testifying to the existence of shared values, effort is given to the material expression of these values.

This may appear a fanciful way of thinking about prisons; nevertheless it should be only too apparent how in prisons the idea of the experience as temporary conflicts with the need to make something of the *now*. (It is the point that W. R. Stirling makes with some force in Chapter 10 below.) A total fixation on life beyond the sentence leads only to a neglect and impoverishment of the present, and is therefore only a cruel denial of realities. It is indeed a question of the quality of life that is generated within a community of prisoners, and especially long-term prisoners. If the idea of community implies, as one of its components, the idea of commitment, of readiness on the part of an inmate to settle down and indeed to live, then the question arises of what is the quality of the experience to which he is being invited to commit himself. To condemn this process of settling down as one of 'institutionalization' is appropriate only when the experience is impoverished.

It is also a question of idealism, and at this point it may very well be felt that this is to go too far. Prisons, it may be felt, ought not to be made pleasant since they are places where people ought not to be at all, and the sooner they are out the better. But this is irresponsible. It is not denied that an associative model has a place, perhaps even a treatment model. It depends on our readiness to distinguish between those prisoners we have a realistic hope of doing something with, those who should never have been there in the first place, and whom we are going to get rid of, and those whom we are simply going to lock away for a very long time. The problem now is that of the long-term prisoner, and our preoccupation with 'treatment' has left us without any ideas of what we are going to do with him. Even for the short- and medium-term prisoner enthusiasm for the idea of treatment needs to be tempered with caution. It is worth remembering that a declared objective of treatment in the mental hospitals came to be associated with abysmal standards of general patient care. There is a pathology even in idealism.

Needless to say this requires some adjustment in the way we habitually think about organizations. It requires us to acknowledge the necessity of compromise: the fact that multiplicity of objectives means that efficiency in terms of any one objective can never be more than partial. Of course we acknowledge this in practice; the point is that it is too easily taken to indicate failure. Yet the sense of failure may stem from the inappropriateness of the models we employ. The need, in fact, is for a subtler perspective, for a systems perspective.

In the face of this it may be argued that the point is already fully acknowledged. But that is not so. If acknowledged the point is acknowledged only formally; it has not in the least affected the way we habitually think about prisons. It is denied, for example, by the management approaches already referred to. It is equally denied by the continued attempt to evaluate in terms of simplistic notions of efficiency, and here one can see a possible reason for the persistence of naïve and inappropriate models. One suspects in fact that in such evaluative studies more is going on than appears at first sight, notably an exercise in catching the penal administrator out. The fact that discussion of penal objectives can take place at all indicates that penal objectives are problematical, but in that case we must ask where people who conduct evaluative studies of this kind get their statements of objective from in the first place. In fact they are generally assumed, or else taken from official policy statements. But the status of such statements is itself problematical, as we all know very well. Hence to do this is really to distort the reality of the situation, to commit the essential fraud of concentrating on what is said rather than what is done (which may be done very well) and then catching the victim out. It is to play the game of, 'Now I've got you, you bastard'. The activity is informed from the outset by hostility to prisons as such. With the rights and wrongs of this I am not concerned here. I am merely concerned to point out that this contaminates the quality of discussion.

I think we have to recognize that academics have not always been as dispassionate in these matters as might appear. It cannot be taken entirely for granted that there is a general desire to see penal systems improve. The literature of residential institutions is, as Professor Kathleen Jones has suggested, part of the literature of protest, and careers are made this way. The quality of penological comment is not high, and is so partly because to take prisons seriously would deprive many people of the opportunity to engage in very gratifying forms of behaviour. There is a considerable amount of pathology in a situation where criticism of penal administrations on the grounds of failure to contain comes from the same quarters as criticism on the grounds of their previous failure to rehabilitate or to treat. Of course functionalism and systems theory do take the steam out of radicalism, yet it is doubtful whether it is any longer enough to be merely a penal reformer in the traditional sense. It is certainly not a sufficient definition of criminology.

Prisons are probably about as 'efficient' as it is possible for them to be. This does not mean that they cannot be evaluated on other grounds, that change is not needed, or that it is impossible to change them. Change is needed, and change is possible, but only if we have a serious alternative in mind. It depends on what we want, not what we don't want, and establishing what we want is hard work.

6. Aspects of European Penal Systems

NORMAN BISHOP

INTRODUCTION

IT is not my intention to present, even in summary form, a general survey of European penal systems since I doubt the usefulness of doing so in a book which is primarily concerned with development, improvement, and growing-points. When Dr. McLachlan, elsewhere in the present book, says (of penal reform and penal history) 'the more extraordinary fact to me is still how little the penal system has changed' he might well have included much of Europe too. Alper and Boren[1] in their study of international action and concern about crime prevention and the treatment of offenders list some eighty major international conferences which took place between 1846 and 1970. At these, rules on the treatment of prisoners, parole, indeterminate sentences, probation and other alternatives to imprisonment, work programmes, prison wages, open institutions, and aftercare were repetitively discussed. The authors comment:

It could be expecting too much therefore in reviewing the impact of the history of international action and concern in the field of crime, to be able to derive . . . an unbroken series of successful breakthroughs in the search for the precise causes of crime, the effective prevention of delinquency, or successful methods of re-adjusting the acknowledged criminal to a law abiding life in society . . . Despite the ideas so hopefully advanced from time to time during the 150 years under review, the history of penology by no means represents a constantly rising level of humane treatment. What little progress has been made, as set down in these pages, has been over a long, slow, and tortuous route. The pendulum may perhaps be a more accurate measure of penal progress than any other as it swings alternatively between rival philosophies and treatment methods within the ambit of a narrow number of modes, understandably limited by the human condition of those who are kept and those who keep.[2]

[1] Benedict S. Alper and Jerry F. Boren, *Crime: International Agenda* (Lexington Books, 1972).
[2] Alper and Boren, op. cit., pp. 155–6.

That the route in penal progress is indeed long, slow, and tortuous may be seen by a brief look at the European status of probation, in itself, one would have thought, a well-tried alternative to imprisonment over decades in many countries. In fact France introduced legislation on probation in 1958, Belgium did so as late as 1964, Luxembourg laid a Bill before the Chamber of Deputies in October 1971 on probation for certain first offenders, while Italy and Turkey have no provision for probation for adults at all.

But it can scarcely be helpful to dwell excessively on what has not improved, and I shall present instead some account of ideas, legislation and practice to be found in Europe which reflect current dissatisfaction with imprisonment because of its high monetary cost and low rehabilitative efficiency. English practice is reflected in this book, and so I have excluded it. But I have tried to report approaches and practice that would seem to have some relevance for English developments. Much of my material comes from Germany, Holland, and the Nordic countries. Partly this is a question of the potential relevance of their experience; partly it is because they are all countries in which challenging changes are occurring; and partly it is because information about them is easier to get than in some other European countries. I have tried to organize this report around three main headings—legislative approaches to restricting the use of imprisonment, new practice in the enforcement of prison sentences, and the status of treatment ideology.

RESTRICTIONS ON, AND ALTERNATIVE PENALTIES TO, IMPRISONMENT

Undoubtedly the most effective way of limiting the use of imprisonment is through legislative control of the courts' power to impose it. Alternative penalties may be provided instead. An example is to be found in the Criminal Law Reform Acts (1969) in the Federal Republic of Germany which provide that short prison sentences, i.e. ones not exceeding six months, may only be imposed quite exceptionally.[3] In the ordinary way these sentences will be replaced

[3] For a short account in English of this legislation, see the Council of Europe's bulletin *Exchange of Information between the Member States on their Legislative Activity and Regulations*, N.S. 4 (Strasbourg, 1971). I have also drawn on a memorandum on alternative penal measures to imprisonment in the Federal Republic of Germany submitted to a sub-committee of the European Committee on Crime Problems by Dr. H. Horstkotte of the Federal Ministry of Justice at Bonn (Council of Europe document DPC/CEPC/XXVII (72) 5).

by fines. Only where there are special reasons—and the term is to be narrowly interpreted—may short-term imprisonment be used. General deterrence, especially if deemed necessary 'for the protection of public peace', may be such a reason but the court is obliged to suspend the sentence where there are favourable indications for future law-abiding behaviour by the offender. Nor can considerations of general deterrence be taken into consideration when deciding on suspension. On the contrary, where a short prison sentence is used *solely* on grounds of general deterrence, it *must* be suspended.

The Criminal Law Reform Acts also provide that prison sentences of between six months and one year must also be suspended where the prospects for future law-abiding behaviour are good and where no exceptional necessity arises for enforcing a sentence of imprisonment on grounds of general deterrence. When a court suspends the sentence it may impose special duties on the offender or issue special directives. Examples of the former can include reparation for damage done, making a financial contribution to the State Treasury or certain non-profit-making institutions, or performing community service. Directives relate to work, leisure, contact with undesirable persons, etc. Table 1, on the use of these measures, relates to adults prosecuted under the Penal Code and does not include young persons dealt with under Juvenile Court Law. (The latter includes those up to eighteen and, under certain circumstances, can include those between eighteen and twenty-one.) Administrative fines, used, for example, for certain traffic offences, are not included in the table's data.

TABLE 1

*Persons sentenced under general criminal law for major and minor offences**

Sanction			1968	1969	1970
Unsuspended prison sentence	.	.	23·8%	16·1%	6·5%
Suspended prison sentence†	.	.	13·2%	13·9%	9·5%
Fine	.	.	63·0%	70·0%	84·0%
			100%	100%	100%
Absolute numbers .	.	.	572,629	530,947	553,692

* From the Federal German Ministry of Justice memorandum cited in footnote 3, p. 84.

† Includes probation orders, since they commonly occur on suspension of a prison sentence exceeding nine months.

Norman Bishop

The general effect of the Criminal Reform Acts seems clear. There has been a decisive shift away from both unsuspended and suspended prison sentences in favour of fines.

Austria is tending to a similar approach, that is, through new legislation to restrict the use of imprisonment. A relatively high proportion of sentences passed have involved deprivation of liberty. In 1967, 41 per cent of all convicted adults were so sentenced, while 51 per cent were fined. It should, however, be noted that 55 per cent of the prison sentences passed were in fact suspended. During 1971 a Government Bill was presented on the over-all reform of the substantive criminal law.[4] Under section 36 of the Bill provision is made for the use of fines as a general rule rather than short prison sentences of up to six months. The Bill also provides for the use of a 'day fine' system similar to the one that has long been in use in Sweden. (Under this system the severity of the penalty that it is desired to impose is measured by the number of day units specified. More days means a severer penalty, fewer days a less severe penalty. The actual sum of money to be paid for each day unit imposed is then related to the offender's financial circumstances.)[5] The maximum number of day units proposed in the Austrian Bill is 360. The minimum monetary value has been put at 10 Austrian schillings and the maximum at 5,000 schillings. Should the fine not be paid, imprisonment can follow, with each two days not paid resulting in one day in prison. At the time of writing, the Bill is still under consideration.

Although, so far as I am aware, there is nothing dramatically new in the legislative field it is certainly interesting to look at Holland since it is a European country which has, over a long period, taken very seriously the damaging and costly effects of imprisonment, and has tried to find alternative methods. It is noteworthy that in a country with somewhat more than 13,000,000 inhabitants the prison population is today less than 3,000. Even Sweden, which is often thought to have a low prison population, cannot equal this, for there

[4] See *Bulletin on Legislative Activities*, 1.5 (Council of Europe, Strasbourg, 1971), for a short account in English of this Bill, 'Regierungsvorlage eines Bundesgesetzes über die mit gerichtlicher Strafe bedrohten Handlungen—Strafgesetzbuch'. A further account is given in the Council of Europe *Newsletter on Legislative Activities*, 3 (April 1972).

[5] The 'day fine' system is briefly described in the report of the English Advisory Council on the Penal System on Non-Custodial and Semi-Custodial Penalties and Disabilities.

the daily average prison population is about 4,700 for a country with slightly more than 8,000,000 inhabitants. The relative proportions of the daily average prison population per 100,000 of the national population are thus 22 and 61 respectively. For England and Wales the proportion is 72 per 100,000 inhabitants.[6]

Under Dutch law the main penalties are imprisonment (which means fairly long to very long sentences), light imprisonment (that is, short prison sentences), and fines. There is also a sanction for those offenders deemed to have no responsibility or diminished responsibility for their actions which entails placing them 'at the disposal of the Government' in a mental institution. The prison sentences can be unconditional and therefore served in their entirety or, if they are for one year or less, conditional. A conditional sentence means that the court suspends enforcement providing certain conditions are fulfilled for a probationary period of at most three years. Common conditions imposed are probation under the supervision of a rehabilitation officer, psychiatric treatment, attendance at a clinic for drug or alcohol misusers, making good the damage done, bans on visiting certain persons, as well as certain deprivations in connection with traffic offences. But community service of the kind provided for in the laws of England and Germany is not possible under existing Dutch law.

In Holland important powers are given to the public prosecutors to waive prosecution, with or without conditions, and to restrict the scope of prosecution 'in the general interest'. In practice waiving of prosecution has become relatively frequent. Thus in 1968 about 45 per cent of the 30,000 cases taken up by the public prosecutors in Holland's nineteen District Courts were dealt with by waiving prosecution. Of these about 27,500 were waived without conditions being imposed. The most frequently used conditions were probation, supervision under a rehabilitation officer, and payments of compensation.

By far the most important alternative to imprisonment is a fine. Extensive provision is made for the use of this alternative. To a considerable extent this reflects the changing values that come with increased economic opportunity and a rising standard of living and, on the other side, the high cost of imprisonment. It is only where an offence is punishable by imprisonment for six years or more that

[6] First Report from the Expenditure Committee, Session 1971–2, 'Probation and After-Care', (H.M.S.O., London, 1971), p. xxv.

fines may not be used as an alternative. They can also be used in combination with unconditional and conditional prison sentences. As well as fines, 'settlements' are possible for offences of no great seriousness. This means that, without the intervention of a court, an arrangement can be made with the public prosecutor to pay an appropriate sum in settlement to his department. Statistics on the use of fines and settlements show that between two-thirds and three-quarters of the offences against property are dealt with in this way and slightly more than half of offences against morality or traffic laws. For the years 1955–64 the number of fines and settlements unconditionally imposed for serious and minor offences has been fairly constant at approximately 1,000,000 per annum and rather more than this for the period 1965–70. The average value of the fines imposed has risen from 10 guilders in 1955 to 42 guilders in 1970. For this latter year the State's revenue from the 1,000,000 or so fines imposed was about 45,000,000 guilders. (At about 3,000 guilders per month to keep a man in prison it would *cost* the State that to keep a mere 1,250 offenders in prison for a year!) Finally it may be noted that the Ministry of Justice did a follow-up study on the payments of fines imposed during the month of May 1970 and found that imprisonment for non-payment of fines was 0·8 per cent of the number imposed for District Courts and 0·5 per cent for Cantonal Courts.[7]

In Denmark in February 1972 a Working Party set up by the Minister of Justice to study a number of questions concerned with reducing the volume of imprisonment, published its report.[8] From the report it appears that for the period 1960–9 the number of unsuspended prison sentences imposed rose from 2,900 to about 4,500, i.e. from about 25 per cent of the total sanctions imposed to about 34 per cent. Conditional prison sentences rose from 2,000 to 2,800, i.e. from 16 per cent of all sanctions to 21 per cent. In January 1971 Denmark had a daily average of nearly 70 persons in prison per 100,000 of the national population—a figure which comes close to that for England at 72 per 100,000, and is more than three times higher than that for Holland. The report has a number of recom-

[7] Information and figures taken from a memorandum on alternatives to the legal sanction of deprivation of liberty submitted by the Dutch Ministry of Justice to Sub-committee No. XXVII of the European Committee on Crime Problems in the Council of Europe.

[8] 'Betaenkning vedrørende nogle af—og nedkriminaliserings-spørgsmål', Betaenkning Nr. 650, Statens Trykningskontor, Copenhagen, 1972.

mendations for diminishing the size of the prison population. The main principle behind the recommendation is a simple one, namely, that a general but moderate lowering in the level of punishment would produce sizeable total reductions. Thus, for example, under Danish law the courts were *obliged* to take account of the offender's previous record when passing sentence and the Working Party considered that this had led the courts to use unnecessarily long sentences for recidivists. A new and more flexible provision was proposed by the Working Party which, with some of the other proposals, now finds expression in a Government Bill.[9] The Working Party also held, after investigating the criminal records of a sample of offenders, that conditional sentences of imprisonment could be used to a far greater extent than at present. In this connection work carried out by the Swedish researcher Bengt Börjeson[10] was quoted. (Börjeson's study showed that after controlling for background factors associated with the risk of recidivism, recidivism after deprivation of liberty was more likely than after the use of sanctions not involving deprivation of liberty. Despite the care with which the research was carried out it has not been immune from criticism on statistical grounds. On the other hand no findings to show *better* results after deprivation of liberty have yet been demonstrated in the Nordic countries.) The Working Party's proposals on a moderate lowering of the level of sanctions can be summarized as follows. Half of the very short detentions used could be changed to fines and the remainder should not be longer than fourteen days on average. Similarly, half of the prison sentences up to six months could be made conditional and the remainder could be unconditional but for, on average, three months only. Sentences of between six and nine months' imprisonment could be reduced to six months only. The nine-month to one-year sentences could be reduced to nine-month ones and so on. The effect of such a lowering for the year 1971 would have been to reduce total imprisonment time by about 550 years, a reduction in prison time of about 25–30 per cent.[11]

In the foregoing paragraphs I have given examples of the ways in

[9] 'Forslag til Lov om aendring af borgerlig straffelov', Justitsmin, j. nr. L.A. 1972–20002–163, Ministry of Justice, Copenhagen, 1972.

[10] Bengt Börjeson, *Om påföljders verkningar*, with English summary (Almquist & Wiksell, Stockholm, 1966). See also N. Bishop, 'Prison Research in Sweden', report presented to the American Academy for the Advancement of Science, December 1972, available from Box 12 150, 104 24 Stockholm.

[11] Betaenkning Nr. 650, Chapter 10.

which European countries are seeking to reduce the crippling burdens imposed by imprisonment. I do not wish to give the impression, however, that all efforts are going in this direction. On the contrary, many, perhaps most, of the European States are sharpening laws and practice that relate to dangerous and organized crime and especially the organized, commercial transporting and selling of drugs. For example, in Sweden the maximum penalty for this latter offence has gone up from six to ten years' imprisonment.[12] Denmark has increased the maximum penalty for hijacking aircraft from nine to twelve years' imprisonment.[13] During the latter part of 1971 the Danish Director of Public Prosecutions carried out a study and presented proposals for more efficient action against organizers and instigators of crime on a large scale.[14] I have, however, presented no information on these aspects because usually there is no lack of support for such measures and also because it is very difficult to discuss their effectiveness without considering the work of the police. But the problem of *unnecessary* imprisonment still commands too little support and interest as well as too little realistic investment in alternative measures. I have preferred therefore to address myself more to this latter question.

PRACTICE

In the previous section I have set out a number of legislative approaches to a reduction in the use of imprisonment. In this section I shall consider a number of ways in which the actual enforcement of imprisonment is carried out primarily from the point of view of reducing its negative effects and trying to get some positive experience into its content. I take for granted that the major evils associated with imprisonment are those of loss of personal autonomy, deprivation in matters of personal and especially heterosexual relationships, deprivation of goods and services, and being cut off from normal society in a highly artificial environment where relations between staff and inmates can too easily be organized only along a power dimension.

The well-known problems of prison have, over the last few years,

12 See *Newsletter on Legislative Activities*, 3 (April 1972) and 4 (June 1972), Council of Europe, Strasbourg.

13 See *Newsletter on Legislative Activities*, 4 (June 1972), Council of Europe, Strasbourg.

14 See *Newsletter on Legislative Activities*, 1 (Jan. 1972), Council of Europe, Strasbourg.

produced a crop of riots and revolts. In America they have reached dramatic and tragic levels of intensity. In Europe, even if they are less dramatic, they are not less tragic and widespread. They have been noted, to name a few examples, in the Regina Coeli prison of Rome, in a number of Swedish and English prisons and, towards the end of 1971 in Toul prison in France. Often they are accompanied by inmates' demands for improved conditions which will lessen the pains of imprisonment. What are the current actions of prison administrators to try to redefine the prison situation?

Following the events at Toul, a committee of inquiry was set up by the Ministry of Justice which itself in January 1972, on the basis of the inquiry's results, proposed some reforms which seem essentially modest.[15] Despite the fact that French prison sentences are supposed to be enforced under the watchful eye of a judge responsible for humane and correct enforcement, the system has not worked well and has since been reinforced by the setting up of a commission to ensure proper consultation between the supervising judge, the prison governor, and his staff, especially in matters of disciplinary punishment. Solitary confinement as a disciplinary punishment may no longer be imposed for up to ninety days—only up to forty-five days. Home leaves will be given to prisoners who have served half of their sentence and whose discharge will take place within three years. In addition it was proposed to improve prison work and payment schemes, staff training, 'work-out' schemes and after-care. These matters have already been settled by administrative regulation. In a Bill on procedure and enforcement of prison sentences it is proposed to give supervising judges competence to decide on requests for conditional release where the sentence is of less than two years. A system of remission, under the control of the supervising judge, is to be provided as a reward for good behaviour. The remission will be three months per year of sentence, and remission gained can be taken away for misbehaviour.

A number of countries have ways of making the serving of short sentences of imprisonment less likely to inflict harm on the offender's family and social and professional life with, possibly, some reduction in the likelihood of the offender being stigmatized by his prison sentence. Thus in Belgium very short-term prison sentences can be served at the weekends. Under Article 50 of the Belgian Penal Code

[15] See *Newsletter on Legislative Activities* 1 (Jan. 1972), 2 (Feb.–Mar. 1972); 3 (Apr. 1972); and 5 (Sept.–Oct. 1972), Council of Europe, Strasbourg.

sentences not exceeding one month can be served in up to fifteen weekends counting these from 2 p.m. on Saturdays to 6 a.m. on Mondays. Each night inside is the basis for reckoning one day's imprisonment. A similar possibility formerly existed in Germany but has been superseded by the new legislation abolishing short-term imprisonment. In Sweden, providing the offender is not remanded in custody at the time of sentence, the correctional administration has formal responsibility to decide in which region imprisonment must be served and the regional director decides on the prison. This information is transmitted to the offender by police in the offender's home locality. The offender then has the right to begin his sentence at once if he wishes. He makes his own way to the prison in which the sentence is to be served. However, the county council authorities can grant a delay in enforcement for up to six months if there are valid reasons. Circumstances connected with work, studies, family matters, and, in the case of women, pregnancy, are examples of reasons which can be cited. Where it is a question of sentence of one or two months the authorities customarily grant delays in enforcement. One practical consequence of such decisions is that February, with only twenty-eight days in it to serve a sentence, is regularly the month of highest use in Swedish prisons! Pardon and clemency measures are also used relatively frequently to permit some delay in the serving of sentences on personal and compassionate grounds.

Short prison sentences are often, though not invariably, served in open prisons. The regimes in such prisons can be arranged so that there is a lowered level of personal deprivation. Renbaek prison on Jutland, Denmark, for example, has no physical barriers; the staff are in civilian clothing; coin-operated telephones can be used freely by inmates; inmates have keys to their own rooms; television and other leisure-time activities are not subject to restrictions on hours; prisoners have their own money and wear their own clothes (Renbaek provides overalls for work); work or educational activity is not obligatory, though the prison provides no pay without participation in work or education; inmates attend school and church freely in the nearby town; and there are no posted lists of rules. The avowed intention of the regime is to de-dramatize imprisonment by getting rid of its more punitive features. Leave is granted for eight hours every other week or two days per month providing the inmate can get back in time to spend the intervening night in the prison. Three-hour visits are permitted every Sunday. No special arrangements are made for sexual activity during visits, but the visiting rooms provide for privacy and comfort. Contraceptives are on sale from machines in the main toilets. Renbaek is the most liberal of the Danish open prisons, and certainly the closed prisons have far more restrictive regimes.[16]

The closed prisons of Sweden are probably somewhat more liberal than their Danish counterparts, with the exception of the largest closed security prison, Kumla. The recent history of reform is as follows. At the end of 1970 a wave of strikes occurred in Swedish prisons, notably in Östråker (a main security prison) over disagreements between the inmates and the administration, chiefly concerning visits, leaves, and other means of contact with the outside world. Early in 1971 the National Correctional Administration agreed to meet representatives of the prisoners for discussions of these matters.[17] (Long before the strikes it had been decided that prisoners were not deprived of the right of association simply by the fact of imprisonment and inmate councils exist in all but the smallest prisons.) The discussions resulted in a number of agreed improvements. Among them was a reduction in the qualifying time for leave in closed prisons from ten months to seven months. Leaves are granted thereafter every two months providing they are not abused. In the open prisons the qualifying time is four months. Other points were improved visiting facilities (couches in the visiting rooms and privacy), reduction of letter censorship and experimentation with coin-operated telephones in certain prisons. Prisoners, however, who have more than two-year sentences to serve must have their leave rights decided by the National Correctional Administration and, where long sentences have been passed for drug offences (and especially where there is a question of deportation on conclusion of sentence), far more restrictive rules are applied. But only 10 per cent of the 11,000 admissions each year serve more than one year; 24 per cent serve between six and twelve months and 66 per cent serve less than six months. During 1972 about 18,000 leaves were granted of

[16] General information on the Danish prison system can be found in 'Beretning om Faengselvaesenet i Danmark, 1965–66', Statsfaengslets Trykeri, Nyborg, 1969 and 'The Penal System of Denmark', Prison Department, Ministry of Justice, Copenhagen, 1968.

[17] See the account written by Director-General Bo Martinsson of the National Correctional Administration, 'Prison Democracy in Sweden', Swedish Information Service, New York, 16 Apr. 1971. A more critical account is given by the Norwegian sociologist, Thomas Mathiesen, "The Politics of Abolition", *Scandinavian Studies in Criminology*, Vol. 4, Universitets-forlaget, 1974, pp. 129–172.

which 9 per cent were misused by late return or failure to return and 3 per cent in some other way, e.g., drunkenness, drugs.

Arising from the report of a major governmental committee on the treatment of offenders, new legislation and practice is being prepared which will more closely integrate prisons and outside society.[18] No further large institutions will be built (Kumla, the largest, has 435 places; other prisons fewer). Instead, the existing large prisons, somewhat reduced in number, will take difficult offenders for whom a high level of security must be provided, as well as those serving extremely short sentences chiefly for purposes of general deterrence, e.g. certain drunken drivers. The remainder of the institutions will be small (sixty to eighty inmates) and locally based so as to facilitate frequent and flexible contact with the prisoner's own home area. The present regional system of management will be superseded by smaller administrative areas corresponding closely to counties. After-care preparation will be in the hands of the probation officers. The new arrangements will come into force over a five-year period beginning in 1974. At the time of writing the proposals have received general and parliamentary approval. New legislation is being prepared. The proposals constitute major guide-lines for Swedish corrections for many years to come.

For long since many European countries have had excellent prison-work programmes. This has been especially true of Germany and Sweden. Both countries may be criticized for not yet providing adequately for work-release. On the other hand, rapid fluctuations in the national economy's stability, with bursts of unemployment, has not greatly encouraged prison authorities to diminish their internal arrangements for constructive work. Nevertheless the Gustav Radbruch-Haus at Frankfurt is a step in the right direction.[19] It takes forty-six prisoners, some of them with fairly long sentences, for the last third of their time and sends them to outside employers to work for full market wages. Prisoners pay for their board and lodging, and must save against the day of release. Tillberga open prison in Sweden also pays prisoners the equivalent of full market wages (about £100 per month) but here it is for production work performed inside the prison. As in Germany the aim is the betterment of the

[18] 'Kriminalvård' (SOU 1972:64). The report is in Swedish. A short stencilled summary in English is available from the Information Service of the Royal Ministry for Foreign Affairs, Stockholm under the title 'Proposals for Reform of Swedish Criminal Care' (Sept. 1972).

[19] Reported in *Dagens Nyheter*, Stockholm, 18 Mar. 1973.

prisoner's financial and social situation. Prisoners who apply to come to Tillberga from other prisons should preferably have at least six months to serve. They must agree to prepare a budget plan in collaboration with the prison's social assistants. The increased wage may be used to pay off debts and damages, to provide family allowances, and for savings against release. Leaves are granted fortnightly after a two-month qualifying period (one month if the inmate was on regular leave schedules before coming to Tillberga). The scheme has been in operation only since November 1972 but the initial signs are that prisoners regard it favourably and wish to take advantage of the opportunities offered.[20] A similar experiment is planned for a closed prison.

Another development in prison work has been the emergence of what, literally translated from Swedish, are called 'self-steering groups'. The use of these forms of industrial democracy has been known since before the beginning of the century.[21] More recently industrial enterprises in Norway and Sweden have been attracted to the idea of organizing work so that small groups of workers have considerable freedom in the way that they will organize their work tasks. Usually group wages are paid rather than individual ones. A well-known recent example is the Saab car firm which has, at its Södertälje factory, abandoned the conveyor-belt principle in favour of these small self-determining groups. Volvo also is working on these lines. The same principle has been in use at Nortälje prison since the beginning of 1971.[22] It will be extended to certain other prisons gradually. No one claims that in prison the method is foolproof. There is always the risk that prisoners with physical or psychological difficulties in performing work will be rejected by these small groups because they constitute a handicap to group-earning potential. But under good staff guidance the method can bring a more creative atmosphere to the workshop and provide a situation in which men who have experienced little satisfaction in their work lives begin to do so.

Two other experiments may be briefly described. At Gruvberget in the northern part of Sweden the National Correctional Administration has bought a small village which formerly belonged to a lumber

[20] Carl-Henrik Ericsson, 'Labor-market Wages for Prisoners', stencilled account in English available from the Information Service of the Royal Ministry for Foreign Affairs, Stockholm, December 1972.

[21] Hyacinthe Dubreuil, *A Chance for Everybody* (Chatto & Windus, London, 1939). [22] Carl-Henrik Ericsson, op. cit.

company. A number of small houses are grouped round a local church, school, and stores. The countryside around is wild and beautiful, and provides good opportunities for walking, skiing, etc. A small staff is permanently in residence. Groups of prisoners and staff come from different establishments to spend one or two weeks in Gruvberget. In addition the prisoners are joined by wives and children and live together in the village's houses on their own. Some of the time in Gruvberget is given over to study courses, usually dealing with citizen rights and responsibilities outside prison, and, of course, activities are arranged in keeping with the time of year.

The other experiment is with a modified therapeutic community in a closed prison, Gävle. The prison is very small with places for at most forty prisoners. The aim has not been to set up a psychotherapeutically oriented prison regime but rather to try to give prisoners and staff maximum autonomy to work out meaningful ways of running the prison. In order to do this community meetings are held three times a week and a number of other small groups have been set up. There is little doubt that change has occurred in the amount of communication taking place between prisoners and staff. The number of contacts with the world outside prison has also been substantially increased without serious difficulties arising from diminished security. Changes in the rules for the running of the prison are discussed, negotiated, and then implemented on a basis of contractual agreement. Such forms of change involve the prison's organizational environment too, and new forms for improved communication with regional and national management systems have been found necessary. The most serious difficulty to date has been the problem of shift systems for basic-grade staff which have prevented their involvement to the degree that they, the prisoners, and the National Correctional Administration, wish for. A research study is being carried out on the development of this experiment.[23]

THE STATUS OF TREATMENT IDEOLOGY

In many of the countries of Europe penal practice is based on the belief that a substantial proportion of offenders are in need of

[23] Gruvberget is described in the report entitled, 'Kriminalvården 1972 (SOS)', Kriminalvårdsverket, Stockholm, 1973 (English summary included). For a report on Gävle, see: Landerholm-Ek, A-C, *Försöksverksamhet vid Gävle Fångvårdsanstalt med modifierat terapeutiskt samhälle*, Utvecklingsenheten, Kriminalvårdsstyrelsen, Stockholm, 1972 (English summary provided).

'treatment'. The underlying assumptions derive basically from the fields of biology, medicine, and psychiatry. The offender is seen as in some way sick or defectively socialized. Individualized treatment provided through various kinds of psychological and medical expertise offers, it is believed, opportunity to cure or resocialize the offender. In practice this philosophy can and does lead to extensive diagnostic services. (A good example of such a diagnostic centre is the Rome–Rebibia Institute in Italy which undertakes extensive clinical examinations of offenders.) In order to carry out treatment, appeal is often made to specialized institutions—especially for psychopathic offenders or multi-recidivists—and to indeterminate sentences. Considerable power is given also to the administration responsible for the treatment, notably in the matter of release from the treatment system. This approach is especially marked in Latin Europe, but is by no means limited to it. A distinguished account which urges the importance of individual treatment needs as the main criterion in deciding what measures society should use with offenders, is given by Ancel.[24] It is this complex of ideas and practice that is called the 'treatment ideology' in the Nordic countries and, after a long period of acceptance, has come increasingly to be questioned and attacked. The issue is an important one for it profoundly affects the kind of criminal policy and penal system one wishes to have.

The principal criticisms directed against the treatment ideology are as follows. First, it is pointed out that most of the treatment given to offenders is coercive in character. In this way it is different from the treatment usually given by a doctor to a patient. Moreover, in the latter case there is usually no conflict of interest between the doctor and his patient. This is not true of the offender in a treatment situation. Here conflict of interest is built in; the offender is in a weak bargaining position and in fact much treatment has been conducted without due regard for adequate legal safeguards for the rights of the offender. This all might—just—be acceptable if treatment actually produced results, but the evidence for successful penal treatment is both meagre and unreliable. And indeed, say the critics, it is not hard to see why, for treatment ideology starts from an assumption of *abnormality*, while in fact the opposite is true. Criminality is so widespread that it is difficult to maintain that it

---

[24] Ancel, Marc, *La Défense sociale nouvelle: un mouvement de politique criminelle humaniste* (Editions Cujas, Paris, 1966). See also *L'Individualisation des mesures prises à l'égard du délinquant* (Éditions Cujas, Paris, 1956).

is essentially abnormal. Given the problem of coercive treatment and the conflict of interest between treater and treated, the absence of treatment results and the disparity between the gravity of crimes and the time served under indeterminate sentences, many Nordic lawyers and social scientists are seeking to redefine the basis for society's measures against offenders. I summarize two practical results arising from this thinking.

At the moment of writing, March 1973, the Danish Government has put forward a Bill which will have the effect of greatly reducing the scope of the indeterminate sentence.[25] Youth imprisonment, which may be compared with Borstal training, is to be abolished completely. The courts will pass sentences, if the Bill is approved, of determinate length on young offenders. It will be, however, for the administration to determine in which sort of establishment these sentences are to be served and the appropriate programmes to be organized. Hitherto internment sentences on serious, allegedly dangerous, recidivists have been of the indeterminate type. These, under the Bill's proposals, will now be sharply diminished. Only those crimes that clearly imply danger to the community will be susceptible of indeterminate internment.[26] Serious recidivism in connection with property offences, for example, will result in determinate sentences passed by the court.

In Finland a government committee presented a report at the end of 1972 on various kinds of suspended sentences and on conditional release from prison.[27] The report has attracted much attention since it represents a new approach within the Nordic countries. Where sanctions are carried out under conditions of freedom the Committee has recommended that a clear distinction be made between control measures, which can be coercive, and treatment or social-service help, which must be offered and voluntarily accepted. To emphasize this point the committee has proposed that the correctional agencies should only be responsible for the control measures. Treatment and social-service help should be carried out by the community's normal agencies. The committee, in an attempt to

25 *Forslag til Lov om aendring af borgerlig straffelov, af lov om ikrafttraeden af borgerlig straffelov m.m. og lov om rettens pleje*, Justitsmin. j. nr. L. A. 1972–20002–181, Ministry of Justice, Copenhagen, 1972.
26 See also Dr. Prewer's essay, 'The Contribution of Prison Medicine', Chapter 8, below.
27 A Swedish summary, translated from the Finnish, is available in *Tidskrift för Kriminalvård*, No. 2, 1972, Box 418, 801 05 Gävle, Sweden.

diminish the need for using imprisonment in cases where considerations of general deterrence would appear to demand it has proposed a new sanction, 'punitive supervision'. The aim of this sanction is to provide a punitive alternative in free society to sentences of, at most, six months' imprisonment or a reinforcement of an ordinary suspended sentence where considerations of general deterrence call for it. Punitive supervision means reporting to the police two or three times a week. It is intended to be a short-term firm warning, the duration of which would be from three to nine months (three months only if used in conjunction with a suspended sentence). So far as conditional release from prison is concerned the committee has recommended that release should take place after half of the sentence has been served (minimum time actually served must be three months). The parole period would be the portion of the sentence not actually served. But the real innovation here is the recommendation that parole *supervision* should be completely abolished since, in the committee's view, it amounts, with its confusion between control and help, to no more than an extra punishment with no real significance for individual support or the prevention of future criminality. New crime would be the only ground for revoking parole, though not if the offence is normally punishable by a fine. None of the foregoing is to diminish human contact and helping work. On the contrary the committee proposes that intensive contact work be developed during the prison period which can continue afterwards if the offender wants it. This can also be a bridge to helping services in the community. The essential point is that these forms of treatment are to be offered for voluntary acceptance and in principle be independent of correctional agencies. In practice the committee recognizes that it will not be possible to give immediate effect to this latter proposal and so has put forward suggestions for a special organization to provide social services to clients in the correctional system.

As I have said, the debate on criminal policy in the Nordic countries has focussed strongly on the issues of inmate rights and the status of the treatment ideology. Let me end with a quotation from a perceptive Swedish journalist, Svante Nycander.

The debate has reflected above all the contradiction between the demand for justice, i.e. fixed, unambiguous rules applied identically to all persons, and the need for individualisation from the standpoint of both care and security. The prisoners and their representatives tend to assign priority to justice rather than treatment, the authorities to treatment rather than justice.[28]

At the moment, I believe, the trend is towards justice.

[28] Svante Nycander, in *The Swedish Dialogue: Criminal Welfare—Voices from Newspapers, Magazines and Books*, published in English by the Swedish Institute, Stockholm, 1973.

7. The Ideology of Imprisonment

GORDON HAWKINS

THE REFORMIST IDEOLOGY

By the ideology of imprisonment is meant what Sir Lionel Fox called 'the principles of imprisonment as a legal punishment'.[1] In other words, it refers to the justification for, or rationale of, the use of imprisonment as a form of punishment.

There is no point in reviewing the history of this matter. That has already been admirably done by Fox himself in the first four chapters of his classic text, under the general heading 'What Is Prison For?'[2] It will be sufficient here to summarize briefly his account of the twentieth century's answer to that question.

Fox's statement of 'the principles underlying the contemporary system of prison treatment'[3] is expressed principally in terms of what he refers to as 'these two well-worn coins of penological currency',[4] deterrence and reform. He suggests that in the twentieth century 'a viable synthesis' of these classic principles has been achieved by the introduction of a third notion which he calls 'the conception of training'.[5]

As to deterrence Fox quotes Sir Alexander Paterson's celebrated dictum that 'Men come to prison as a punishment not *for* punishment'.[6] The implication is that so far as deterrence is held to be a function of imprisonment it is fulfilled by the deprivation of liberty for a prescribed period and that in view of the suffering 'inevitably inherent' in that experience no deliberately punitive treatment of the offender in prison is necessary.[7]

The concept of reform is defined as 'the substitution of the will to do right for a will to do wrong'. This is said 'to come from something inside the man' which 'can be reached by the right personal influences'. It is, says Fox, a 'delicate and very personal growth'.[8]

[1] L. W. Fox, *The English Prison and Borstal Systems* (1952), Chapter III.
[2] Id., pp. 3–74.   [3] Id., p. 73.   [4] Id., p. 71.
[5] Id., pp. 18 and 66–73.
[6] Id., p. 72; see also S. K. Ruck (ed.), *Paterson on Prisons* (1961), p. 23.
[7] Id., pp. 71–2.   [8] Id., p. 72.

Consequently he is sceptical about its attainment 'by specific features of treatment labelled "reformative"'.

'The conception of "training"', we are told, 'seeks to provide a background of conditions favourable to reform . . . by personal influences . . . it concentrates on the social rehabilitation of the prisoner.'[9] At another point Fox quotes an official account of policy and practice in the administration of prisons in England and Wales where it was said that 'for all suitable prisoners with sentences of suitable length, the prison regime should be one of constructive training, moral, mental and vocational'.[10]

Fox goes on to say that this approach was 'recognized and established by Parliament in the Criminal Justice Act 1948 which provides that rules shall be made for "the training of prisoners"'. Moreover it 'sets in the forefront of those rules the statement that "the purpose of training and treatment of convicted prisoners shall be to establish in them the will to lead a good and useful life on discharge, and fit them to do so"'.[11]

This rule, which was then Rule 6 of the Prison Rules 1949, has since become Rule 1 of the presently effective Prison Rules 1964. It expresses the ostensible official policy of the British prison system today. In so far as that policy rests on a theoretical basis, the theory in question is that stated in Fox's book and outlined above.

It is quite clearly a reformatory theory of punishment which owes a great deal to those Fox refers to as 'the heretic Americans'.[12] Indeed he explicitly acknowledges the debt, writing of George Canning's bringing the New World in 'to redress the balance of the old' as a 'beneficent process' the effects of which 'were nowhere more marked than in our prison system'.[13]

It is true that Fox's formulation may seem more sophisticated than those of the Pennsylvania Quakers. But in so far as he differs from them, the difference is largely, to use his own phrase, 'one of means rather than ends'.[14]

It is notable that the dominance of this ideology has not been confined to English and American prisons. There has been what Fox calls 'international diffusion' on an extensive scale. In fact he includes in his book an appendix designed to illustrate this phenomenon. There he sets out a selection of extracts from published reports and studies reflecting contemporary international opinion

[9] Id. p. 72.   [10] Id., p. 128.   [11] Id., p. 73.   [12] Id., p. 63.
[13] Id., p. 32.   [14] Id., p. 56.

regarding the theory and practice of punishment. The selection does, as he says, 'show a striking correspondence of thought, whether as to the principles of penal punishment or its application, across the five continents of the world'.[15]

THE NEW CRITICS

It is also true to say that until very recently there has been little tendency to question the assumptions underlying this dominant theoretical orientation. This is not to say that the general public or the popular press have not been critical; but rather that among academic penologists, correctional administrators, and workers in the field, writing in what Fox called 'responsible publications on penal matters',[16] although differences about matters of method and interpretation have been continual, there has been relatively little dispute about principles and ends.

In the last few years, however, the situation has changed. The assertion, in the McKay Commission Report, that 'Attica is every prison; and every prison is Attica'[17] may be a rhetorical exaggeration. But both in the United States and the United Kingdom there have been serious disturbances in many prisons. And criticism which in the past has been aimed largely at failures to implement declared policy is now being directed at policy itself.

For the purpose of this discussion two recent publications in which criticism is levelled at the basic assumptions of 'progressive' penology will be considered. The publications in question are first, Professor Sir Rupert Cross's *Punishment, Prison and the Public* (1971) and second, the Report on Crime and Punishment in America prepared by an expert Working Party for the American Friends Service Committee and published under the title *Struggle for Justice* (1971).

REFORMATION AND DEFORMATION

The essence of Cross's critique is succinctly and conveniently stated by the author in his Introduction. 'Doubt is cast', he says, 'on the possibility of there being a real reformation in any save the most exceptional cases, and it is even suggested that the belief that prison could be reformative has had a baneful influence.'[18]

[15] Id., pp. 140, 444, 451.   [16] Id., p. 130.
[17] *Attica: The Official Report of the New York State Special Commission on Attica* (1972), Preface XII.
[18] R. Cross, *Punishment, Prison and the Public* (1971), Intro. XV.

On the question as to the extent to which prisons are reformatory
Cross confesses to 'profound scepticism'.[19] 'The chances of deterioration in prison', he says, 'are at least as great as those of reform'; and
'if analogies have to be drawn, prisons are more like cold storage
depots than either therapeutic communities or training institutions.'[20]

He rejects the idea of the conversion of prisons into therapeutic
communities as based on the wholly inappropriate model of the
mental hospital.

We are asked to imagine such a hospital in which people are detained
against their will although they fall right outside the Mental Health Act,
in which the detention may have to continue long after a cure has been
effected, and in which the vast majority of the patients are not, and never
have been, either mentally ill or subject to any form of nameable or treat-
able personality disorder.[21]

As to work, education, and vocational training he is dubious about
the extent to which rehabilitation is achieved by these means. 'It is
common knowledge that a prisoner who works well inside is often
not prepared to work at all outside. Education in prison may amount
to little more than filling in time, and comparatively few prisoners
are fit for vocational training.'[22]

While Cross is highly sceptical about the reformative potentialities
of imprisonment he says that 'no one would be disposed to doubt
the existence of deformative risks'.[23] 'There is a real danger that
someone who is already a bad man when he goes into prison will
come out worse; hence the crucial importance of what can best be
described as "anti-deformative action" in our prisons.'[24] In fact he
concludes that 'the main aim of prison reform should be the prevention of prisoners' deterioration'.[25]

It follows also that 'the period of imprisonment should be as
short as it possibly can be compatibly with the aims of the sentence
whether they be denunciation, deterrence, the protection of the
public or all three'.[26] In practice however 'the baneful influence of
the myth that prison is reformative'[27] ('or could be reformative if
only the authorities were given time enough'[28]) has resulted in a
substantial increase in the average length of prison sentences in
Britain since the 1930s,[29] and a good deal of 'unnecessary suffering'.[30]

[19] Id., p. 84.   [20] Id., p. 85.   [21] Id., p. 80.   [22] Id., p. 84.
[23] Id., pp. 73–4.   [24] Id., p. 86.   [25] Id., p. 85.   [26] Id., p. 86.
[27] Id., p. 101.   [28] Id., p. 102.   [29] Id., pp. 101–2.
[30] Id., p. 165.

A RADICAL CRITIQUE

The Report on Crime and Punishment in America compiled by the American Friends Service Committee's Working Party (which incidentally included Caleb Foote, Professor of Law and Criminology at the University of California at Berkeley and John Irwin, Associate Professor of Sociology at San Francisco State College, both of whom have served terms of imprisonment) is considerably more polemical in style and substance than Professor Cross's book. Thus the American criminal justice system is condemned as 'an instrument of white Anglo-domination and a barrier to the development of full power within communities of oppressed peoples'.[31]

The report is said to be inspired by 'the desire to transfer power from the police/courts/prisons to the people'.[32] The reader is told a number of times that 'the construction of a just system of criminal justice in an unjust society is a contradiction in terms'[33] and warned of the 'impossibility of achieving more than a superficial reformation of our criminal justice system without a radical change in our values and a drastic restructuring of our social and economic institutions'.[34]

Another respect in which the Friends Working Party's critique differs from that of Professor Cross relates to the type of criticism that they direct at the protagonists of reformatory penology. For whereas Cross confines himself to attacking the actions and statements of the reformists, the Working Party almost invariably also impugns their motivation.

To give an example, Cross is extremely critical of Sir Alexander Paterson who is generally regarded as one of the most influential, inventive, and energetic penal reformers of this century. He speaks of Paterson's writings as containing 'a plethora of aphorisms and clichés, call them what you will'.[35] He refers to the memorandum that Paterson submitted to the 1932 Committee on Persistent Offenders as 'rather glib'[36] and as revealing 'the pulp which underlay so much of Paterson's penology'.[37] He accuses him of using arguments which are sophistical[38] and remarks of one of his statements, 'it makes me feel sick'.[39] And he is equally damning about some of the practical consequences of Paterson's influence on penal policy.[40]

---

[31] *Struggle for Justice: A Report on Crime and Punishment in America.* Prepared for the American Friends Service Committee (1971), p. 112.
[32] Id., p. 171.   [33] Id., p. 16; see also e.g. pp. 13 and 99.
[34] Id., pp. 12–13.   [35] R. Cross, op. cit., p. 131.   [36] Id., p. 163.
[37] Id., p. 164.   [38] Id., p. 166.   [39] Id., p. 131.   [40] Id., pp. 165–6.

Nevertheless Cross nowhere questions Paterson's sincerity or integrity. His account of his career, personality, and work as a Prison Commissioner is a fair one and he acknowledges the beneficent influence of 'the spirit of Paterson' on staff/prisoner relationships, as well as 'a vast and continuous amelioration of prison conditions' for which he is credited with the principal responsibility.[41] Moreover he is equally objective in his treatment of the other three Prison Commissioners whose achievements he discusses in some detail.[42]

The Friends Working Party found nothing to praise in the activities of those they label the functionaries of the criminal justice system. 'By and large', they say, 'the functionaries of a criminal justice system are either members of the politically and economically dominant classes of society or totally subservient to these classes.'[43] In so far as those functionaries support the 'treatment-oriented prison reform movement'[44] their attitude is seen as hypocritical and their motives as discreditable.

Thus what is called 'the individualized treatment model' is said to have 'never commanded more than lip service from most of its more powerful adherents'.[45] 'Prison administrators' who 'embraced the rehabilitative ideal' are said to have done so because it increased their power over inmates. 'It wasn't treatment that excited them. It was the prospect of having greater control over their prisons.'[46] Prison personnel are described as 'unthinking, unfeeling functionaries within institutions'.[47]

A major factor in the reform movement is said to have been 'the mixture of hatred, fear and revulsion that white, middle-class Protestant reformers felt toward lower-class persons ... These difficult feelings were disguised as humanitarian concern for the "health" of threatening subculture members. Imprisonment dressed up as treatment was a particularly suitable response for reformers' complicated and inconsistent feelings.'[48]

Inevitably this is reflected in prison regimes, so we find that 'as part of treatment and rehabilitation, cultural assimilation is forced upon' offenders. In other words attempts are made by 'officials [who] exaggerate their own importance' and 'the uptight caseworker' to impose 'a middle-class life-style' and 'the increasingly outmoded

---

[41] Id., pp. 31–2.   [42] Id., pp. 7–41.
[43] American Friends Service Committee Report, p. 134.
[44] Id., p. 29.   [45] Id., p. 39.   [46] Id., pp. 85–6.   [47] Id., p. 120.
[48] Id., p. 85.

Protestant work ethic' on them. 'Accepted correctional practice is dominated by indoctrination in white Anglo-Saxon middle-class values.'[49]

In this connection it is interesting to note that Professor Cross is equally critical of Sir Alexander Paterson's belief in 'the merits of inculcating middle-class values, derived from the public school, in the minds of Borstal boys'. He sees it as a 'pernicious manifestation of the disease of "PLU" (people like us)'. Moreover he thinks that the English penal system 'has been bedevilled' by this notion 'that the world would be a better place if only it were inhabited by people like us'.[50] It is notable, however, that he does not accuse those responsible of being motivated by 'hatred, fear and revulsion . . . toward lower class persons'.[51]

Perhaps the essential difference between the two approaches is that whereas for the most part Professor Cross adopts an empiricist approach to penological questions the Friends Working Party is more inclined to refer to principles which seem to be regarded as self-evident. Thus to give an example: on the question of the death penalty Professor Cross states that he is 'an abolitionist on the capital punishment issue', but that he would 'certainly wish to reconsider my position if confronted with convincing evidence that a substantial number of criminals would abandon the use of guns if capital punishment for murder were restored'.[52] The Friends Working Party on the other hand merely states flatly, 'Out of respect for the innate worth of every human being, we are deeply opposed to the death penalty and fervently hope the Supreme Court will have abolished it as cruel and unusual punishment by the time this report appears.'[53]

The truth is that the authors of the Working Party Report, as they state candidly in their first chapter, "approach criminal justice from a Quaker perspective',[54] although it cannot be said that this leads them to take a particularly indulgent view of the role played by earlier Quakers in the development of penal reform. In fact they

[49] Id., pp. 43 and 119–20.   [50] R. Cross, op. cit., pp. 131–2.
[51] American Friends Service Committee Report, p. 151.
[52] R. Cross, op. cit., pp. 170–1.
[53] American Friends Service Committee Report, p. 151. On 29 June 1972 in *Furman* v. *Georgia*, the Supreme Court stopped short of holding the death penalty *per se* 'cruel and unusual punishment' (although at least two Associate Justices were prepared to do so). The majority held that the death penalty as at present administered was applied unevenly and was discriminatory.
[54] American Friends Service Committee Report, p. 16.

come very close to categorical repudiation in the preface to the report where they say:

It would be naïve not to acknowledge the blunders that an uncritical faith can produce. The horror that is the American prison system grew out of an eighteenth-century reform by Pennsylvania Quakers and others against the cruelty and futility of capital and corporal punishment. This two-hundred-year-old experiment has failed.[55]

THREE LESSONS

Yet despite the fact that Professor Cross and the Friends Working Party see the history of penal reform in a different perspective they reach some very similar conclusions. This can be seen clearly if we look at the 'three salutary lessons' which Cross says are provided by 'the sad history of twentieth-century English attempts to cope with recidivism'.[56]

The first lesson, according to Cross, is 'the extreme importance of avoiding calling the same thing by different names'. He refers in this connection to Paterson's proposal to the 1932 Committee on Persistent Offenders 'to abolish all prisons' and replace them with 'training centres' and 'places of detention'; a proposal which was later reflected in the provisions of the Criminal Justice Act 1948. He condemns 'this kind of gerrymandering with words' as not only dishonest and misleading but also productive of unnecessary suffering in that offenders are sentenced to longer periods than they might otherwise receive because of the illusion that they are not being sent to ordinary prisons.[57] A very similar point is made by the Friends Working Party when they say that

Many proposals that seem to urge the abolition of prisons are really exercises in label switching. Call them 'community treatment centres' or what you will, if human beings are involuntarily confined in them they are prisons . . . it confuses analysis and obscures the moral nature of our act to pretend that we are not employing punishment . . . proposals that we should 'abolish prisons' or 'end the crime of imprisonment' are destructive of thought and analysis when all that is contemplated is a reshuffling of our labels or institutional arrangements for coercive restraint.[58]

The second lesson that Cross enunciates relates to the futility of incarcerating offenders for more protracted periods in order that they may be trained.

[55] Id., Preface V.   [56] R. Cross, op. cit., p. 163.
[57] Id., pp. 163–5.
[58] American Friends Service Committee Report, p. 23.

We must now face the fact [he says] that if what is wanted is training, it had better take place out of prison. We can no longer delude ourselves into thinking that we are getting the best of both worlds by deterring the offender and others by depriving him of his liberty and, at the same time, training him to lead a useful life.[59]

As the Friends Working Party Report puts it: 'After more than a century of persistent failure, this reformist prescription is bankrupt.'[60] The report emphasizes at some length 'the difficulties inherent in implementing treatment in prison'[61] and makes the point also made by Cross[62] that the 'adoption of the rehabilitative ideal' has resulted (in this case, in California) in a steady increase in the length of sentences.[63]

Cross's third lesson to be learned from twentieth-century attempts to deal with the recidivist is 'that we have made no progress whatsoever'. In fact he says: 'Judged by the standard of the number of habitual criminals in and out of our prisons, our system is no better than it was in the days of the Gladstone Report.'[64] The Friends Working Party Report, referring to the California correctional system 'which has pushed further toward full implementation of the rehabilitative ideal than any other correctional system in the United States'[65] reaches a similar conclusion.

There is evidence that people are not being helped any more by a median stay of three years in a rehabilitatively oriented prison than they were by approximately two years in a basically punitively oriented prison. One indicator of this lack of change is the consistent recidivist rates. Through the years approximately 40 per cent of the persons released on parole in California have been returned to confinement two or three years after release.[66]

THE CRUCIAL DIFFERENCE

The foregoing collation of passages from Professor Cross and the Friends Working Party Report gives a somewhat misleading impression of an identity of approach. In fact there are many significant differences other than those already mentioned above. But the essential point in this context is simply that they both regard the

[59] R. Cross, op. cit., pp. 165–6.
[60] American Friends Service Committee Report, p. 8.
[61] Id., pp. 97–8.   [62] Cross, op. cit., pp. 101–2.
[63] American Friends Service Committee Report, pp. 91–2.
[64] Cross, op. cit., p. 166.
[65] American Friends Service Committee Report, p. 83.   [66] Id., pp. 91–2.

reformist justification for imprisonment as untenable. Moreover they agree that in practice the reformist ideology 'lengthens sentences and increases suffering'[67] without producing any countervailing social benefit. Both parties take the view that by causing 'prisoners' deterioration'[68] imprisonment, however treatment-oriented, will do more harm than good.

The Friends Working Party Report goes further and says that 'Imprisonment with treatment is identical with traditional imprisonment in most significant aspects.'[69] It argues that although 'progressive penology' inspires internal institutional reforms the changes involved are trivial when measured against 'the basic evils of imprisonment'. Those evils are defined as follows:

It denies autonomy, degrades dignity, impairs or destroys self-reliance, inculcates authoritarian values, minimizes the likelihood of beneficial interaction with one's peers, fractures family ties, destroys the family's economic stability, and prejudices the prisoners' future prospects for any improvement in his economic and social status.[70]

It is true of course that many of these criticisms of imprisonment as a penal method are not particularly novel. Thus when the Friends Working Party complain that 'much that passes for reform is a façade', that 'penal programs are inhibited by bureaucratic and custodial restraints', that 'most institutional employment and training programs are not relevant to the future employment possibilities of the prisoners', and that 'only a minority of those who receive vocational training for some occupation while in prison work at that trade when released',[71] even the slightest familiarity with the literature of penal reform over the past half century will serve to inoculate the reader against any sense of astonishment.

The crucial difference between the kind of critique we are discussing and that of previous critics lies not so much in the nature of the specific faults found as in the nature of the practical implications which are seen to follow from the unfavourable assessment. Thus penal reformers have in the past for the most part taken the line that while most prison correctional or rehabilitative programmes have proved unsatisfactory this is due not to any defect in the underlying theory but to failure adequately or properly to implement that theory. The implication is analogous to G. K. Chesterton's celebrated

[67] Id., p. 97.		[68] Cross, op. cit., p. 85.
[69] American Friends Service Committee Report, p. 25.
[70] Id., p. 33.		[71] Id. p. 33.

aphorism about 'the Christian ideal': 'It has not been tried and found wanting; it has been found difficult and left untried.'[72]

The Friends Working Party Report explicitly rejects this line of thought. It notes that 'the experts—even the most enlightened and progressive—line up solidly in support of the system, asking only for more of the same. Most established penologists and criminologists support the treatment and individualized treatment principles . . . We venture to hope that this report will inspire reconsideration by such experts'.[73] The report is decisive about demands for such things as more money for corrections, 'more and better trained personnel at higher salaries', 'careful classification of inmates', 'more "experts" for the courts', 'improved educational and therapeutic programmes in penal institutions', and 'small "cottage" institutions'; all of which are dismissed as 'all this paraphernalia of the "new" criminology'.[74]

'The premise of such an approach', says the report, 'is that the programs are on the right track but have never been given a fair trial, that the blame for past failure is public and legislative inaction.'[75] The report goes on to say that in fact even if all the proposals mentioned were implemented this would not either 'serve legitimate public interests or alleviate the major abuses of our present programs'. This is because there is 'compelling evidence that the individualized-treatment model, the ideal towards which reformers have been urging us for at least a century, is theoretically faulty, systematically discriminatory in administration, and inconsistent with some of our most basic concepts of justice'.[76]

TWO COMMENTS

What conclusions can be drawn from such a brief survey of this development in penological theory? Obviously at this stage no final judgements are possible. Nevertheless 'comment', as C. P. Scott observed, 'is free'. He also said that 'facts are sacred',[77] although in this field it would be more accurate to say that verified facts are scarce. This in part explains what a fellow contributor to this volume has called in another publication 'the tradition of unsupported assertion which is general in literature on prisons'.[78] However, at

[72] G. K. Chesterton, 'The Unfinished Temple' in *What's Wrong with the World* (1910).   [73] American Friends Service Committee Report, p. 156.
[74] Id., p. 8.   [75] Id., p. 11.   [76] Id., p. 12.
[77] C. P. Scott, in the *Manchester Guardian*, 6 May 1926.
[78] J. E. Thomas, *The English Prison Officer since 1850* (1972), Intro. XIV.

the risk of appearing to support that tradition two observations are offered.

The first thing to be said is that the debate we have been considering represents a significant advance if only because it goes beyond the usual sleight of hand with, what Fox called, the 'well-worn coins of penal currency'.[79] At the same time it is a welcome relief to encounter discussion of penal reform which is conducted in terms of something other than pious aspiration. Both Cross and the Friends Working Party are sceptical about the familiar reformist rhetoric, although in the case of the Friends this is counterbalanced to some extent by the provision of some of their own brand. Nevertheless both parties are familiar with and responsive to the evidence which leads Cross to say that 'we have moved into an era of penological pessimism'.[80]

There is in fact abundant evidence which might well give rise not merely to pessimism but to total cynicism. George Orwell writing, in his celebrated essay 'Inside the Whale', about the work of American novelist Henry Miller talked of Miller as one who abandoned 'the Geneva language of the ordinary novel' and dealt with the Realpolitik of everyday life.[81] In the field of penology one can find a similar contrast between the writings of senior penal administrators and those of prison officers and ex-prisoners. To give only one example, the account of corrective training in 'the Geneva language' of Sir Lionel Fox in *The English Prison and Borstal Systems*[82] and the account given by former corrective trainee Frank Norman in *Bang to Rights*[83] scarcely seem to belong to the same universe. Moreover, although there are no mis-statements of fact in Sir Lionel's account, anyone with any first-hand experience of corrective training will affirm that for a veridical account of the realities of the system it is to Mr. Norman's book that one must refer.

But it is not only in the works of ex-prisoners that one finds today a concern with the Realpolitik of the prison system. As Noel McLachlan points out in his contribution to this volume, 'criminologists today are a good deal more sophisticated—or cynical—about their "expectations".'[84]

Certainly, in relation to imprisonment, serious research workers

[79] L. W. Fox, op. cit., p. 71.   [80] Cross, op. cit., p. 100.
[81] G. Orwell, *Collected Essays, Journalism and Letters*, i (1968), p. 544.
[82] L. W. Fox, op. cit.   [83] F. Norman, *Bang to Rights* (1958).
[84] N. McLachlan, 'Penal Reform and Penal History', Chapter 1 above, p. 1.

have, in recent years, come to speak in a fashion much closer to that of ex-prisoners than to the bland pronouncements of official and unofficial prison reformers. Thus we find Richard Sparks in *Local Prisons: The Crisis in the English Penal System* saying that 'the majority of those men, who inhabit the local prisons, have (at least in recent years) had nothing even approximating to reformative treatment'.[85] J. E. Thomas in *The English Prison Officer since 1850* says that 'the possibilities of training and treatment in a prison are few and limited because of the very nature of imprisonment'[86] and speaks of 'a reformative prison system' as something which 'will exist only in official literature'[87] unless radical organizational changes are made. F. E. Emery in *Freedom and Justice within Walls* goes even further and argues that 'if we feel that we have to have the security afforded by the medium- and maximum-security prisons, then we should accept that these will be custodial institutions not reformative institutions . . .'[88]

But if the increased realism to be found not only in the English studies but also in American correctional research is to be welcomed, the question remains whether the appropriate response is the kind of categorical rejection of the reformist ideology found in Professor Cross's book and in *Struggle for Justice*. This brings me to my second and final point which relates specifically to the ideology of imprisonment.

In this connection one of the most striking features of the debate about the use or uses of imprisonment is the way in which the concept of 'The primary purpose' dominates discussion. Not only do we frequently find ourselves rehearsing all over again the familiar championship battles between such popular contestants as retribution, deterrence, and reform but we are commonly expected to accept the notion that there can only be one winner, or that at the most there may be a draw, as in the case of Sir Lionel Fox's 'system of treatment in which reform would hold a primary and concurrent place with deterrence'.[89]

It is true that sometimes when the debate is confined specifically to imprisonment other contestants such as custody, control, security, treatment, and training enter the ring. But here too we encounter

[85] R. F. Sparks, *Local Prisons: the Crisis in the English Penal System* (1971), p. 94.   [86] J. E. Thomas, op. cit., p. 221.   [87] Op cit., Intro. XIV.
[88] F. E. Emery, *Freedom and Justice within Walls* (1970), p. 97.
[89] L. W. Fox, op. cit., p. 63.

the same pursuit of primacy. Thus we find even so sophisticated an observer as J. E. Thomas writing of 'the overall primary task of the system, which is control'[90] and of 'this primary task of control'.[91]

Professor Cross supports a different candidate. 'The prevention of deterioration', he says, 'is just as important as the promotion of reform . . .' In fact he goes further and says 'the main aim of prison reform should be the prevention of prisoners' deterioration'.[92] Reform is dismissed as 'incidental to, not the object of, imprisonment'.[93]

Yet it is surely a mistake to talk about the 'primary task of the system' or 'the object of imprisonment' in this way. Indeed earlier and in a different context Professor Cross quotes as 'the most telling remark of the century on the philosophy of punishment'[94] a passage from Professor H. L. A. Hart's *Punishment and Responsibility* which points both to the crux of the problem and also to its resolution.

In the passage to which Cross refers, Hart writes of the complexity of punishment and of the multiplicity of aims which in the case of punishment, as in that of many other social institutions, may be pursued.[95] Yet if we acknowledge, as we must, this multiplicity of purposes in relation to the institution of punishment, we must also recognize that precisely the same may apply to some of the particular methods of punishment such as imprisonment. So that rather than seeking for the primary purpose or the principal aim of imprisonment in general we should realize that confinement in penal institutions may be used, in relation to different categories of prisoner, for quite different purposes.

Of course this point is unlikely to strike anyone with the force of a revelation. After all Sir Lionel Fox himself said plainly enough: 'Clearly, then, whatever prison is for it is not for one clear and single purpose.'[96] But this did not prevent him from seeking to devise some 'viable synthesis'[97] of the principles under which we should regulate the treatment of prisoners. He saw that there was something ridiculous about all that 'anxious balancing of how much, without undue derogation from deterrence can safely be conceded to reform'.[98] But he continued to play the game, even if he played it with more finesse than his predecessors.

In the end his gloss on the reformist theory in terms of 'the

[90] J. E. Thomas, op. cit., p. 217.   [91] Id., p. 218.
[92] Cross, op. cit., p. 85.   [93] Id., p. 86.   [94] Id., p. 54.
[95] H. L. A. Hart, *Punishment and Responsibility* (1968), p. 3.
[96] L. W. Fox, op. cit., p. 15.   [97] Id., p. 18.   [98] Id., p. 71.

conception of training'[99] proved no more satisfactory than the recipes it replaced, as is evident from the critiques we have been considering. But it does not necessarily follow from those critiques that we are wrong to regard the reformation or rehabilitation of the prisoner as a legitimate objective. The truth is rather that we are mistaken in regarding it, or any other single purpose, as the over-all primary task and only justification of the prison system.

Thus there may be prisoners coming within the top security category under the present English regulations[100] in respect of whom the primary task of the system could only be defined in terms of control and containment. Although both humanity and prudence would dictate that we should also pay attention to the prevention of prisoners' deterioration. At the other extreme there is unquestionably a substantial number of offenders whose imprisonment serves no purpose that could not be better achieved outside prison. In between there will be many different categories of prisoner for whom a variety of different objectives, educational, vocational, disciplinary, remedial, or therapeutic might feasibly be selected as primary.

Could it be that the persistence of the all-purpose penitentiary in which the majority of prisoners serve their sentences is in part due to the belief that there must be some single dominant purpose to be fulfilled by such establishments? This of course is precisely what the Pennsylvania Quakers believed, and the reformist ideology was their answer to the question of what that purpose should be.

The principal lesson to be learned from their critics, however, is not that the Quakers' answer was wrong. It is that the question was mis-conceived and that the search for some universal formula is delusive. If that is understood then there is some hope that in rejecting the reformist ideology we shall also, at long last, abandon the total institutions intended to embody it. For all the evidence points to the conclusion that the penitentiary system was, quite literally as it happens, a monumental mistake.

The most obvious practical corollaries of that conclusion are firstly a substantial diminution in the use of imprisonment and the further expansion of alternatives to institutionalization; and secondly the development of much smaller, specialized custodial establish-ments designed to meet the diversity of our penal needs and purposes.

[99] Id., p. 18.
[100] Earl Mountbatten, *Report of the Enquiry into Prison Escapes and Security*. Cmnd. 3175 (1966), 212–17.

8. The Contribution of Prison Medicine[1]

R. R. PREWER

THE Duke of Wellington is reported to have said that the whole business of life is to endeavour to find out what you don't know from what you do; he then went on to make his famous remark about guessing what was on the other side of the hill. In trying to prognosticate what part the medical services are likely to play in the penal system during the remainder of this century, it will be useful not only to review the present situation but to look back at the way in which it has developed.

The doctor came late upon the prison scene. We now accept it as a basic principle that Society owes a duty to those in captivity, to provide them with good hygienic conditions and to care for them when they are sick. Yet, so far as I am aware, no regular medical attention was provided in any English prison before 1692, when one of the surgeons from Bart's was appointed to visit the inmates of Newgate, only a short walk from the hospital.[2] Another eighty-two years were to pass before Parliament, newly awakened to the problems of the gaols by John Howard, passed 'An Act for Preserving the Health of Prisoners in Gaol', which required that a reputable surgeon or apothecary should be appointed to every prison. These gaol surgeons were often men of skill and integrity, as a reference to the old medical records will show; but they were badly paid, and often had to provide medicines from their slender stipend. It was not until Millbank penitentiary was completed in 1821 that a resident surgeon and a visiting physician were appointed to care for the 1,100 prisoners it contained. It is interesting to observe that even in those days an occasional prisoner was released to one of the great London hospitals for surgical treatment, not only from Millbank but also from the Hulks at Woolwich. As each of the big new prisons was

---

[1] This essay is published by permission of the Home Office, but does not necessarily represent official views.

[2] Anthony Babington, *The English Bastille* (1971), p. 64.

opened by the Government—Parkhurst, Pentonville, Portland, Dartmoor—one or more whole-time medical officers were appointed as a matter of course; infirmaries were provided, and very soon 'infirmary warders' also. Indeed, Pentonville was under the control of eleven commissioners, of whom two were medical men of great eminence, one a physician and the other a surgeon.

The inmates of prisons today are on the whole fairly healthy people. If one looks at the photographs of prisoners taken a century ago, an undue proportion appear to have squints or curious conformations of their heads, or strange shapes of face; not a few look abnormally old for their years. Many of these men would be in hospitals for the subnormal today. But very few prisoners now look anything like the popular idea of what criminals should do. If a comparison should be made between a group of recidivists and another group of the same age and background, taken from the population as a whole, it is doubtful whether any physical characteristics would be found to differentiate one group from the other. Repeated examinations at various prisons lead to the detection of many minor abnormalities, and an attempt is made to remedy them wherever possible; squints are improved, many scars and tattoos removed, and orthopaedic deformities corrected. Bearing in mind how little care some inmates seem to have taken of their health when at liberty, it is extraordinary that they live as long as they do. Probably prison itself has been the preservative.

Today there is comparatively little serious illness in the average prison community, and few of the operations performed in the four surgical centres are of an urgent nature. Psychosomatic symptoms, on the other hand, are very common, especially during the earlier part of a sentence. Far more men report sick in prison than would do if they were at liberty, but this is no indication of physical ill health. Inmates frequently worry unnecessarily about their physical condition, and fear that they will not survive to enjoy their release. Others report sick because of boredom, a desire to avoid work or other compulsory activity, to seek attention regarding non-medical matters, to air a grievance, to extract concessions from the doctor, or merely to meet men from some other part of the prison. Whatever the cause, all these cases have to be sorted out and investigated. The daily standard of medical care is equivalent to that of good general practice outside; the prison medical officer has instruments, equipment, text-books, nursing assistance, and a consulting-room which are as good, or better than, those in the average general practice. If he wishes to obtain the opinion of a consultant, he can send his patient to an outside clinic in the great majority of cases, or (if he wishes) can call a consultant into the prison. In the larger establishments there may be some hundreds of consultations in the course of a year. It is usually easy to obtain X-rays, pathological reports, and physiotherapy; and in the larger hospitals there are technicians and equipment for recording the electrical activity of both the brain and the heart. Many of the hospital buildings are antiquated and inconvenient by modern standards, but this is no reflection on the work carried out in them; it is not walls that make the city.

So much for physical medicine. To turn to mental illness, the Victorians were much embarrassed by the presence of insane prisoners in their model establishments, because they tended to disrupt the smooth running and strict discipline of which they were so proud. The treatment of psychotics in those days was still primitive, and control before the days of tranquillizers was a major problem; great care had to be exercised in preventing disturbed patients from attacking each other or from injuring themselves. For many years Bethlem Royal Hospital took many of the worst cases, and housed them in a special wing. It was not until 1863 that Broadmoor was opened, and rapidly filled up with 'criminal lunatics'. Before many years had passed Broadmoor became over-full and various expedients were adopted to accommodate the excess of psychotic prisoners. In the early years of this century Parkhurst asylum was opened in what had previously been a separate wing for small boys, close to the main prison; it closed in 1913, when Rampton asylum was completed. Since the end of the last war, the rising tide of recorded crime and the greatly inflated prison population has again led to difficulty in finding hospital accommodation for some mentally ill patients, and delays of weeks or even months are not unknown. The position has been aggravated by the 'open door' policy of ordinary psychiatric hospitals, by which many chronic schizophrenics (among others) have been allowed to discharge themselves from hospital, to wander about, and get involved in crime. It is only fair to point out that even today psychotic patients are relatively uncommon in a prison setting; but the problems that they cause are out of all proportion to their numbers.

Psychopaths, on the other hand, are all too common; indeed, a large number of recidivists are psychopaths, perhaps 50 per cent of the population of some prisons. There is nothing new about this, except the label. A century ago many prisoners were classed as 'weak-minded', and a little research into the old records shows that many of these men were not mentally subnormal persons. There were violent epileptics, depressives, early cases of dementia, both due to senile changes and to alcohol; but there were also eccentric individuals, given to unpredictable outbursts, and a perpetual menace to both staff and other prisoners. Some of these may have been schizophrenics, but others were clearly psychopaths. In the middle of the nineteenth century the weak-minded convicts were concentrated at Dartmoor, and a little later at Millbank and Woking; finally, when Parkhurst had become an adult convict prison, they were sent to that establishment. The weak-minded were segregated in C Hall at Parkhurst, and subjected to close medical supervision; they were employed on work specially suited to their capacity, and minor breaches of discipline were dealt with in a lenient manner. So useful did this regime become that special rules were approved for C Wing by the Home Secretary; by 1897 every convict in the country who evinced any marked mental abnormality was sent to Parkhurst for observation. Although the 'weak-minded class' seems to have died a natural death between the wars, the tradition of tolerance and understanding of the mentally unstable was not lost.

Fifty years ago the prison medical officer was concerned with the health of the prisoners, with the hygiene of the establishment, and with the ascertainment of the mentally sick; nobody at that time had suggested that he had any part to play in curing his charges of their tendency to commit crimes. In Victorian days the chaplain was the official responsible for rescuing criminals from their evil ways; for the rest, it was left to the working of 'the System'. But in the early years of the new century Freud's theories were attracting attention, and interest grew in psychotherapy after its successful application to the treatment of war neuroses. Soon the first psychiatric clinics began to appear. In 1932 the Committee on Persistent Offenders suggested that psychological methods might be applied to the treatment of certain types of offender; two years later the first psychotherapist was appointed to Wormwood Scrubs.[3] Shortly before the Second World War, East and Hubert issued their conclusions on prison psychotherapy in a report entitled *The Psychological Treatment of*

[3] *Report of the Inter-Departmental Committee on Persistent Offenders*, 1932, Cmnd. 4090.

Crime.[4] Their chief recommendation was the establishment of a special prison, which was to serve as a treatment centre, a base for criminological research, and as a suitable environment for housing the more pronounced misfits from other parts of the Service. Owing to the war, no progress was made until 1962, when Grendon Psychiatric Prison came into existence. It is clear that what East and Hubert envisaged was not only a treatment unit, but also a centre for the more grossly psychopathic prisoners; perhaps they underestimated the difficulty of carrying on entirely separate regimes in the same institution. Moreover, the East–Hubert report was written when the general prison population was low; after the war it went up by such leaps and bounds that no one institution could possibly house all prison psychopaths, not even the worst ones.

Grendon eventually emerged as a therapeutic community, in which every activity and every inhabitant, staff as well as prisoners, work together to the same end. The aim is to give the inmate an understanding of himself and his difficulties, to renew his self-confidence, and to send him out better fitted to avoid further offences. Psychotics and those of sub-average intelligence are not accepted. The candidate for Grendon must be recommended by the medical officer of the prison or Borstal where he is serving his sentence, and his suitability or otherwise is then decided by the Grendon authorities. Those who eventually arrive find themselves in an environment unique within the prison system. There are substantial amenities in this establishment, and in return the inmate must give his co-operation. Those who fail to co-operate or who tend to retard the progress of others, are sent away. The average Grendon inmate is a young recidivist, who generally carries a poor prognosis; he usually stays in the prison for between eight and ten months.[5]

At the other end of the psychopathic spectrum are those who will not co-operate in any kind of treatment, will not control themselves, and readily indulge in violence or threats of violence. Indeed, violence is the greatest problem facing penology today, whether inside prison or in the community as a whole. Reference to the old records shows that there were some savage assaults on warders and on other convicts far back in the last century; but they were exceptional.

[4] W. N. East and W. H. de B. Hubert, *The Psychological Treatment of Crime*, (1939).
[5] J. Gunn, 'Psychiatry and Prisoners: a Retrospective Look at Grendon Prison', *Prison Service Journal* (October 1972), 13.

Assaults on staff were visited with severe floggings, and the violent were restrained by fetters of various kinds; those who attempted to escape were put in leg-irons. Round the perimeter of the convict prison were armed sentries; and at Dartmoor the Civil Guard marched into chapel with fixed bayonets, and stood facing the assembled prisoners. But one by one these forms of restraint were abandoned, until today there is little sanction left for the violent man, except to lock him up. Meanwhile the number of grossly unstable inmates has increased, and many of these men will resort to violence on little or no provocation; they have what is called a low threshold for frustration. When an undue proportion of men such as these find themselves in the same establishment, there is a risk that a small spark will ignite the barrel, and an explosion of destructiveness will result. It was to meet this situation that C Wing was again brought into use at Parkhurst in May 1970, in order to house a special unit for the more grossly psychopathic inmates of the prison. To dilute the pure culture of psychopath, so to speak, some men who had recovered from serious mental illnesses, as well as some unstable dullards and others, were added to the C Wing population. Apart from segregation from the rest of the prison, the regime rests principally on the division of the inmates into small groups, each of which is the responsibility of one member of the uniformed staff; he has to be thoroughly conversant with his charges and their histories, and generally to act as their adviser and friend. In this way the early signs of trouble are detected, and violence prevented or minimized. The staff is drawn from both the hospital and discipline sides of the service, with the latter preponderating. Case conferences are held, at which individuals are discussed. Whether in C wing or in the neighbouring hospital, these disturbed inmates are cared for by the same medical officer. If a man refuses work, he stays in his cell and loses his pay; if he works well, he is suitably rewarded. Minor breaches of discipline are regarded with a tolerant eye, but repeated misconduct will lead to transfer back to the mental-observation landing of the hospital. Those who improve in their behaviour may be tried out in the main prison, and if they succeed in adjusting to normal prison conditions they remain there. In this way C Wing is the safety-net beneath the main prison, and the hospital is the safety-net beneath C Wing.

It has been objected that C Wing offers nothing except the old carrot-and-stick approach; but this is to misunderstand the whole conception of what this unit is about. No claim is made that these men are being 'cured', for there is no cure for psychopathy; the only hope lies in that gradual maturation which comes with the years, and robs all but a very few of their fight and fire. Even so, we must be doing something in the present, and the aim of C Wing is to control its inmates on a day-to-day basis. If a violent psychopath goes through just one day without some untoward incident, it is a cause for satisfaction, and as much as we can expect in our present state of knowledge. Moreover, the main prison runs more smoothly without its disturbed inmates. A bonus lies in those officers who have served in the Wing, and who carry elsewhere their experience of handling violent and unpredictable men.[6]

We have traced briefly the development of Grendon and C Wing at Parkhurst, two of the growing-points in our treatment of the criminal today, and in both of which Medicine plays the major part. Three other developments are worthy of mention, as offering hope where none existed a few years ago. One is the treatment of sexual offenders at Wormwood Scrubs by means of hormone implants. The implant is a small pellet inserted under the skin, the contents of which are slowly absorbed into the body; after the first few days the patient experiences a sharp drop, and possibly a total loss, of sexual desire. He has to return after a few months for a replacement, or desire will reappear. It is not pretended that a hormone implant is a cure for sexual deviation—indeed, it throws out the sexual baby with the deviant bath-water; but it has proved a very effective way of keeping such offenders out of mischief. Unfortunately, many sex offenders will not accept this form of treatment, probably because it is so efficacious; others commence it and then fail to come back for replacements when once they have obtained their liberty. There is reason to believe that even more useful drugs will shortly become available for this purpose.

The second development lies in the treatment of alcoholism at Wakefield and other centres, and in the treatment of drug addiction. The methods used are not any different from those used in clinics elsewhere, so that no elaboration here appears to be necessary. But it must be emphasized that alcoholism in recidivists is frequently but one facet of a behaviour disorder, and the results of treatment are generally disappointing. Experiments are still proceeding on the

[6] B. D. Cooper and A. J. Pearson, 'C-Wing at Parkhurst', *Prison Service Journal* (October 1972), 3.

application of behaviour therapy to other forms of delinquency besides alcoholism and drug addiction.

Another gleam on what is otherwise a rather gloomy therapeutic horizon comes from one highly specialized technique of brain surgery. It has been discovered that the electrical coagulation of a small mass of cells known as the Amygdaloid Nucleus, deep in the brain, will reduce or abolish the aggressive element in the sexual drive. This method was pioneered in England at the Wessex Neurological Centre. Only two patients have been treated in this way, but results so far are promising. Suitable cases are not easy to find, yet this method gives hope when all else has failed. It is possible that cerebral surgery may have other surprises in store for us in the future.

Apart from these more specialized forms of treatment, there are still the older methods available. Medication, for example, is of great value in the control of psychopaths, and by judicious use of tranquillizers the incidence of violence in penal establishments is greatly reduced. The consent of the patient is essential, and in practice he is the one who usually raises the issue. Some men require prolonged medication, but in most cases it is possible to withdraw it gradually over a long period, once control of tension has been achieved. Many different substances have been used, but the ideal drug without side-effects, which will prevent violent outbursts and yet not interfere with normal thought-processes, eludes us still. Even when armed with a specific remedy, we shall still have the task of preventing its misuse.

Psychotherapy, on the other hand, has not proved the panacea in the treatment of crime that the last generation had hoped. Group therapy has proved useful with certain types of offender, but some are unable to withstand the pressures that a group engenders. The hardened recidivist will frequently refuse to play, or tends to exploit the group situation for some ulterior purpose. It must be faced that many criminals do not want to be any different, and are quite satisfied with their way of life, except that they do not want to get caught. It may be of value to be able to tell a court that one was under psychiatric treatment on a previous sentence, and some prison inmates appear anxious to take out such an insurance policy; others are convinced that a request for 'treatment' may accumulate merit when their cases come up before the Parole Board. But, like Scrooge when he was asked for a subscription to charity, the majority wish to be left alone. However, supportive therapy is of great value in

helping the inmate through the bad patches of his sentence, and it is
here that prison psychotherapists can be of considerable assistance.
All the most rewarding work done in a prison comes through
talking with individuals, sometimes when they are ill or in personal
difficulties, at others in the ordinary course of the day's work. Rap-
port between captives and those charged with their care not un-
commonly builds up over the years; sometimes old lags become our
old friends in a prison environment, and in most cases a curious
'live and let live' relationship emerges as one sentence succeeds
another. All such relationships constitute a form of psychotherapy
in its widest sense.

I would suggest, therefore, that at the present day the general
standard of medical care in English prisons is in no way inferior to
that provided by the National Health Service; we have the machinery
for treating, or sending elsewhere for treatment, those who are
mentally ill; and we have the outlines of a system for controlling (but
unfortunately, not curing) the psychopath and other types of grossly
unstable inmate. It is now time to try to predict what lies on the
other side of the hill, and where the next twenty-five years will take
us. And first I must express the hope that some reduction in the
number of prison inmates may be seen before long. For the past
quarter of a century the Prison Service has had to run faster to try to
stay where it is, and close personal attention can only be given to a
small minority of the horde of new inmates which has poured in
upon us. It is reasonable to suppose that the provisions of the
Criminal Justice Act 1972 will soon begin to take effect, and that a
decline in the prison population will ensue. Whether such a decline
would continue, or whether some of the new sanctions may prove to
have the boomerang-like effect of the suspended sentence, remains
to be seen. Toughness and consistency in working the Act will be
essential; any weakening in its application to individuals may
eventually increase the number sent to prison. For since the abolition
of capital punishment, prison remains the ultimate sanction for
crime, the long stop of the whole penal system. If we had only half
the number of men in prison which we have now, we could concentrate our resources and deal with individual cases, more in the way in
which Grendon and C Wing do at the present time. But one must
be realistic, and after an initial decline in numbers, the probability is
that a rise will again occur, although at a slower rate than we have
known during the last two decades. In an ideal society, a large

proportion of those in prison today should never be there; equally, a small minority should never be let out.

This leads on to the problem of violence. All the indications are that violent crime will continue to increase, and that the more serious cases will undoubtedly lead to more long prison sentences. It would be useful if we could predict those who were likely to return to violence after their release. Unfortunately there is no infallible test to which such persons can be subjected, though there are one or two useful pointers. One is the so-called M.M.P.I. test, which can generally be relied upon to pick out the psychopath, but not specifically the violent psychopath. Another is the observation that if a man has had two convictions for violent crime in a comparatively short period, a third can be predicted with some confidence; the probability rises steeply with each succeeding offence of this nature. It must not be thought that those who have been labelled as 'inadequate' are not dangerous; on the contrary, some of these individuals indulge in such offences as rape and arson, and some commit crimes involving extreme violence. Some murderers fall into the 'inadequate' group. Dangerous psychotics are not common, whether in the community or in prison, and in the majority of cases they can be detected fairly readily. The most dangerous group is made up of aggressive psychopaths and the more paranoid members of the criminal fraternity; a few epileptics are dangerous, and so are a small number of mentally subnormal (and borderline subnormal) patients. I venture to predict that further units based on C Wing at Parkhurst will soon be set up within the prison system to control such problem cases under sentence. A weak point in the present system is the difficulty in following up the dangerous man after his release; it is not sufficient to inform the Mental Health authority and the police of the district to which he is going, or even to write to his general practitioner—that is, if he has one. Criminals, more especially those who are mentally unstable, will not always conveniently settle down in the place to which they are released; they often disappear, and their new neighbours know nothing about them. Legal safeguards may be necessary to prevent some who are known to be dangerous from being discharged on to an unsuspecting public; indeed, some form of indefinite sentence of detention in a special hospital or prison may be indicated here.

To provide a high standard of psychiatric care for the most disturbed inmates, a number of large new prison hospitals will be required, each serving an area or group of other establishments. They will be built in accordance with the recent practice of the National Health Service, in which both physical and psychiatric patients are treated in the same hospital, although in separate departments. This would provide comprehensive medical care for all but a few inmates; the remainder would still require temporary release for highly specialized forms of surgery or medical treatment, and certain cases dealt with under section 72 of the Mental Health Act 1959 would still require transfer to the special hospitals. In these new central hospitals, prison nursing staff would receive good all-round experience in a custodial setting. The prison nurse is a versatile individual, and must be prepared to jump from surgical or medical work to handling dangerous psychopaths or psychotic patients at short notice; even in a surgical ward his patients may produce grossly psychopathic behaviour. I hope, and would go so far as to predict, that within a few years prison nurses will be given the same basic training as all other members of the nursing profession, with the addition of specialized instruction to fit them for their unique duties.

Prison nurses—with the exception of a few specialists—are males. Twenty years ago no woman worked inside a male prison, with the exception of the theatre sisters at Wormwood Scrubs and an occasional typist. All this has changed, and over the past decade we have had the appointment of women medical officers, psychotherapists, psychologists, pharmacists, radiographers, physiotherapists, and so on; and all four surgical units have sisters and nurses attached to them. The influence of women has been a good thing, and they are treated with respect and consideration by the inmates, except on the rarest occasions. This influence is likely to grow with the passage of time.

Both doctors and nurses who work in prison have the tradition of psychiatry behind them, and through long experience of psychopathic patients have much to offer to fellow prison officers in the way of training and example. Both Grendon and Parkhurst C Wing are teaching ordinary prison staffs to control and understand difficult inmates. The medical officer can provide advice and support to the Governor and his immediate subordinates in a variety of ways, and can join usefully in the general management of the prison by participating in committees and staff meetings. It is essential that both doctors and hospital staff should identify themselves with their colleagues in other branches of the service, and they can best do this by belonging to it themselves. Prison medicine is a speciality in its own right, just like military or aviation medicine. I sincerely hope that the Prison Medical Service will not be merged in the National Health Service; whether it will or not must await the recommendations of Lord Butler's Committee. But it would be wrong to assume that the prison doctor lives and works in isolation; by means of postgraduate courses, lectures, clinical meetings, contact with individual consultants, and occasional mutual assistance, he is well acquainted with his N.H.S. colleagues and keeps abreast of recent advances.

After-care is going to receive a lot more attention within the next few years. Perhaps some system can be evolved by which contact can be maintained with the psychopath during his periods of liberty. At the present time a number of different agencies and different persons may be concerned with him; they all need to be drawn together, so that whether the discharged prisoner is in a hostel, or hospital, or his own home, those who have assistance to offer will know all about him, and can pass information from one to another. It may be that hostels will be set up in connection with certain prisons, and even clinics where the ex-patient can see his old doctor or psychotherapist. At the present day far too many unstable men disappear into the blue, and are not heard of again until somebody at another prison calls for their old case papers, because they are back again inside.

It will be clear by now that I do not expect any dramatic changes in the contribution which Medicine has to make to the prison system during the next twenty-five years; there is no therapeutic Utopia on the other side of the hill, no psychiatric magic wand to wave over the habitual criminal. After long experience of recidivists, I have become (to use the words of Sir Thomas Browne) 'complexionally superannuated from the bold and courageous thoughts of youth and fervent years'. During the past decade medical facilities in prison probably have improved to a greater extent than they had done in the previous fifty years, and this process of improvement is going to continue. New hospitals will be built, still more equipment provided, larger and better staffs recruited. Our methods of recognizing the mentally unstable, and more especially, the potentially dangerous, will become increasingly efficient; we shall learn more about the psychopath, and will grow more adept in controlling him while he matures. It is always possible that some new form of medication may be discovered—if it will not eliminate violent conduct, it may yet prove to be more specific than anything we have at present. Hormones and related chemical substances may prove highly effective in reducing the number of persistent sexual offenders. It is possible that brain surgery may produce solutions to a few of our most intractable problems. But as one peruses the old records, and realizes that we have not come so very far since mid-Victorian times, it seems possible that half as long again may pass before any revolutionary changes occur in our methods of treatment. One thing is quite certain, and that is that Medicine in its wider sense is going to play a larger and larger part in both the treatment and control of those offenders who come into penal institutions, be they many or be they few; and in this context, it is suggested that treatment and control are merely two sides of the same coin.

9. The Role of Psychologists in the Penal System

GORDON TRASLER

THE first prison psychologist was appointed in 1946. He, and the handful of colleagues who joined him during the next three or four years, owed their jobs to the prevailing climate of optimism about penal matters—confidence that effective programmes of treatment were being developed in prisons and Borstals, and that the problems of retraining offenders were gradually yielding to the endeavours of penologists. Psychologists were regarded as diagnosticians, the users of tests (and occasionally of interview techniques) for the purposes of assessment. It was therefore envisaged that they would work mainly in the Borstal allocation centres and in the Corrective Training allocation wing, investigating trainees and assigning them to appropriate training institutions and work programmes; and also that they would assist prison doctors in identifying handicapped or sick individuals who needed special care.[1] The work of psychologists was wholly located within the institutions that employed them; they did not furnish advice to the courts (although prison medical officers sometimes incorporated their findings in reports on remanded offenders), and they had no contact with the non-custodial sector of the penal system.

The 1950s and 1960s brought a considerable increase in the numbers of psychologists and psychological testers (non-graduate aides), and some changes in their prescribed role. There was much more participation in treatment—in group and individual psychotherapy, and counselling—and psychologists began to take a hand in administrative matters. Less time was devoted to the assessment of individual offenders. Intensive investigation of Borstal trainees at the allocation centre was gradually abandoned (partly, it seems, because of the discovery that psychologists' assessments were contributing

---

[1] See R. L. Morrison, 'The Roles of Prison Psychologists', *Howard Journal*, 10, 2 (1959), 125–34; and A. Straker, B. A. Johnson, T. J. Ager, J. H. Fitch, and E. S. Darling, 'The Work of Prison Psychologists', *Occupational Psychology*, 37 (1963), 1–19.

little to allocation decisions),[2] and clinical testing for purposes of psychiatric diagnosis formed a smaller part of the work-load of most prison psychologists than it had done in the early days of the service.

In a quarter of a century of development, the Prison Psychological Service has continued to expand. Its present staff establishment of some seventy-five graduate psychologists, and perhaps a third as many non-graduate testers, must make it one of the largest psychological teams in western Europe. There are also, of course, many psychologists with specialist knowledge of delinquency and criminality employed in the classifying schools for young offenders and in the 'special hospitals' at Broadmoor and Rampton. It is clear that psychologists have a major role in the day-to-day functioning of the correctional[3] system in England and Wales, and it is surprising that this substantial body does not, so far as one can ascertain, have an influential voice in the shaping of penal policy. Nor, for that matter, has it contributed as strongly to research and public discussion on the treatment of offenders. The reasons for the neglect of this potential seem to be largely organizational—that is to say, they have to do with the way in which psychologists are deployed within the correctional system, and the kinds of work that they are called upon to do. The purpose of this essay is to consider how these defects may be put right, and—in particular—to attempt to forecast the roles that psychologists can, and should, play in the new patterns of penal provision that are emerging. We shall first look at the contemporary developments in the underlying philosophy of the correctional system.

If the Prison Psychological Service owed its existence to the post-war enthusiasm for training represented by the Borstal system and the new device of Corrective Training, it grew to maturity in a period of growing disillusionment with such measures. The change of heart was not a local phenomenon: penologists in the Scandinavian countries (and even in the United States of America, where a number of ingenious and costly experiments in the treatment of offenders were still in progress) had already begun to doubt whether it was realistic

[2] R. V. Sewell and M. Williams, 'A Study of Allocation Practice', unpubl. paper, Psychology Department, Wormwood Scrubs (undated).

[3] Unfortunately we do not have a suitable word to denote the whole system—custodial, semi-custodial and non-custodial—of provision for offenders; in its absence, we must resort to this American term, without intending to imply a particular view of the objects of the system.

to try to effect permanent changes in the behaviour of men and women through training carried out in the artificial conditions of a penal institution. There was also increasing concern about the risks to the traditional safeguards of the liberty of the individual which seemed to be inherent in the enthusiastic pursuit of the goal of effective treatment. Nor was the new scepticism confined to custodial measures; the validity (both practical and ethical) of the notion of the *treatment* of offenders was questioned as it had never been in the 1940s and 1950s. The results of evaluative studies were not encouraging; they showed, with depressing consistency, that none of the experimental custodial training regimes introduced in the post-war years had any measurable effect upon the reconviction rates of those subjected to them.[4] The effect of all this on the morale of the staffs of penal establishments—and not least upon the psychologists, despite the 'diversification' of their roles—was profound. If what happened in penal institutions had no effect upon subsequent recidivism, what was the point of elaborate and expensive attempts to match individuals to treatments?

This was also a period of increasing anxiety about the destructive effects of confinement in an institution. A series of essays—some sociological, others the reported comments and recollections of those who had experienced imprisonment—emphasized the social deprivation, the erosion of social skills, and the damage to vital roots of family and friendship, that were common (if not inevitable) concomitants of imprisonment. Studies[5] of prison cultures underlined the futility of attempts to harness the powerful coercive forces of the inmate social system for correctional purposes.[6]

Suspicions that the correctional system might be operating as a means of promoting rather than diminishing the propensity to commit criminal offences gave rise to another, less obvious, shift in correctional attitudes. The assumption that the central task is to diagnose, and then to eliminate, those lesions of personality that lie

[4] D. A. Ward, 'Evaluations of Correctional Treatment: Some Implications of Negative Findings', in L. Radzinowicz and M. E. Wolfgang, *Crime and Justice*, iii (Basic Books, 1971).

[5] For example, D. Clemmer, *The Prison Community* (Holt, Rinehart & Winston, 1966); G. M. Sykes, *The Society of Captives* (Princeton University Press, 1958). See also a brief discussion in G. B. Trasler, 'The Social Relations of Persistent Offenders', *Sociological Review Monograph*, No. 9 (Keele University Press, 1965), pp. 87–97.

[6] Cf. S. Cohen and L. Taylor, *Psychological Survival* (Pelican Books, 1972), pp. 201–7.

at the root of an individual's criminality has gradually been replaced by the more modest goal of identifying the causes of recidivism— some at least of which are probably to be found within the penal system itself. In a sense the British penal system has become less ambitious. The comprehensive objective, confidently expressed in the Prison Rules—'to encourage and assist [the offender] to lead a good and useful life'—which was the original inspiration for custodial training programmes and education, now seems to be unrealistic and perhaps impertinent, arrogating to the correctional system goals that properly belong to the individual himself. The notion that the correctional system ought to aim to 'straighten' the offender, to remedy all his weaknesses, to refurbish his values, his attainments, his social skills and his spiritual responsiveness, has been displaced by a more modest and practical goal: endeavouring to avoid further criminal convictions (or 'preventing reoffending', as current jargon inelegantly expresses it). The effect of this upon the strategy of corrections is to give new emphasis to the principle of minimum intervention: that is to say, the system may try to do what is nec- essary to diminish the likelihood that the offender will transgress again (with certain strict limitations on what methods it can employ to this end) but ought not to do more.

One of the results of these developments in penological thinking has been the beginning of a trend towards the integration of the custodial and non-custodial sectors of the correctional system. Custodial methods are increasingly regarded as a last resort, to be adopted only when there are overriding reasons for isolating the offender from the community, and (secondly) as part of a genuinely integrated programme of care; not as 'hospital' treatment followed by resettlement, but as a period of physical restraint within a longer process in which the offender is supported in his attempts to come to terms with his social environment and personal circumstances. The logical consequence of this approach to the care of offenders is a blurring of the distinction between custodial and non-custodial treatments, and perhaps some transfer of decisions as to when and for how long the offender must be isolated from the community.

In this new climate of opinion and policy, the roles that seemed appropriate for prison psychologists in the 1950s and 1960s are rapidly losing their relevance. Fundamental changes in the organiza- tion of psychologists in the correctional field, in their function and duties, and in their relations with colleagues will be needed. These may be identified conveniently by looking at each of the three sorts of activity to which prison psychologists devote their time: namely, work with individuals; research; and advising administrators.

Much of the work that prison psychologists have traditionally done with individual offenders has been based upon the conception of the custodial sentence as a programme of treatment that is to a large extent independent of whatever experiences the individual may have had in the past, and only marginally influenced by the kind of life he expects to lead in the future. The implicit object of the psychologist's activities, on this view, was the optimal distribution of resources within the custodial system—the best possible matching of training facilities to trainable material. But in abandoning the belief that the penal institution is the main agency of treatment, the psychologist must accept a new frame of reference: the offender in the whole correctional system. It is likely that an increasing proportion of his time and energies will in future be invested in the task of contributing to decisions about individual offenders. We have already noted the two trends in contemporary penological thinking which have this implication. One is the increasing integration of the custodial and non-custodial sectors of the correctional system. The other (developed by Louis Blom-Cooper in an essay in this volume) is the likelihood that the responsibility for decisions to release from custody to some other form of treatment will eventually pass to an executive authority—instead of being controlled by the courts, which is usually the practical position at present. The over-all effect of these two developments would be to make the whole range of custodial and non-custodial provisions available for any offender as and when they seemed appropriate. Such a state of affairs would call for new procedures; it would, for example, be necessary for a provisional plan to be drawn up for each offender when he was first committed, on the basis of what was known (and could be discovered) about him at that stage, and there would have to be a continuing review and revision of this plan in the light of his response. There would, of course, be much greater flexibility in ways of dealing with the offender and, since all of these consecutive decisions would be delegated to one executive, this body would be in a position to call upon whatever information and expertise the whole correctional system could provide.

In such circumstances the psychologist would have a key function, using his skills in the assessment of offenders and the measurement of behavioural change to provide part of the factual basis for decisions made by the authority. He would gain a valuable opportunity to develop his knowledge of the behaviour of the individual throughout both the custodial and non-custodial phases of his sentence—effectively to trace his career through to his return to an ordinary life—and in doing so to validate assessments and executive decisions against the true criterion of social adjustment. The essential condition for improving performance in judgement and decision-making—the ability to check the reasons for each decision and the basis for each judgement against the outcome—would be present.

In recent years (as we have already noted) psychologists in prisons and Borstals have devoted less and less of their time to work with individual offenders, and more to their other role as researchers and advisors on organizational and administrative problems. Why should this trend be reversed? Most of the work that psychologists have done with individuals has been directed to decisions about the assignment of offenders to particular training institutions or regimes, working in the allocation centres and providing advice for the courts (for example, on suitability for Borstal training). Increasing pessimism about the effectiveness of training regimes seemed to weaken the case for so substantial an investment of psychologists' time in these tasks; and the demonstration that the psychologist's contribution to allocation decisions seldom, in practice, modified recommendations that would have been arrived at on other grounds was adduced as a reason for transferring resources from the investigation of Borstal trainees to other, apparently more productive tasks. (This is not, of course, a necessary conclusion; however pessimistic one may be about the general effectiveness of treatment processes, it is likely that there are some individual differences in response to a given regime, even if they are in the negative direction—that is to say, that some individuals are more damaged than others by this experience.) But if the changes in the correctional system that have been outlined above are fully implemented, there will (of course) be a fundamental change in the nature of decisions relating to individual offenders. The psychologist's task will no longer be restricted to 'one-off' recommendations about offenders in the light of the information available at the time; he will be involved in a series of decisions about the same offender, concerning the transition from one form of correctional provision to another—from custodial care to hostel accommodation to supervision in the community, for example. It is surely arguable that contributing to serial decisions on the basis of gradually accumulating information about the offender's response to the correctional system will offer more scope for the skills of the psychologist—and more opportunity for the development of such skills and of systematic experience—than he has had before.

'The correctional worker stands on a shifting knowledge base', as Conrad has pointed out,[7] and for this reason continuing and vigorous research is essential to the maintenance of a correctional system that will retain the confidence of the public. Since they are the only group of trained behavioural scientists employed in the custodial sector of the penal system, prison psychologists have consistently argued (sometimes in the face of discouraging opposition) that research is, or ought to be, one of their major concerns. Some of the disagreements about the role and direction of correctional research stem from confusion as to what sort of activity the term denotes.

It is sometimes claimed that the collection of information about the characteristics of individuals entering a correctional programme or institution (called 'headcounting') may properly be regarded as research, since it is necessary to know with whom the system is dealing.[8] But although this notion is comforting to those whose desire to contribute to research is frustrated by heavy clinical commitments, it is seldom realistic. We already know a great deal about input populations, and we also know that the attributes which distinguish one such group from another, are usually artefacts of the criminal-justice process that are not difficult to identify by direct inquiry. On the other hand, an assessment routine designed to elicit information about individual offenders which can be used to make correctional decisions about them is unlikely to yield the sort of parametric information that the prison administrator needs, and will certainly produce a great deal of data that are irrelevant to that application. For example, it is probably important to know that a young criminal is semi-literate and aggressive, and comes from a broken family, if one is placing him in a Borstal. But if (which seems doubtful) knowledge of these characteristics of the Borstal population has policy implications, it could be obtained simply and quickly

[7] J. P. Conrad, 'Research and the Knowledge Base of Correction', *Crime and Delinquency*, 13/3 (1967), 444–54.

[8] See, for example, comments by a psychologist at Grendon prison, quoted in T. Parker, *The Frying Pan* (Hutchinson, 1970), pp. 161–2.

by appropriate sampling procedures—finding out things of this kind does not necessitate a continuous census. What the education officer wants to know, on the other hand, is how many of the boys currently *in his Borstal* need help with problems of semi-literacy and who they are: measures of the prevalence of reading difficulties in the Borstal population is of no use to him.

The experience of generations of social scientists has shown that the most promising style of research consists in systematic attempts to answer carefully specified questions—not in the accumulation of bits of information in case they might eventually turn out to be useful. There is no shortage of precise questions needing to be answered. The suspicion that existing custodial measures are not merely ineffective, but in certain respects positively dangerous, suggests that priority ought to be given to studies of correctional regimes and of the characteristics of the correctional system as a whole. As Conrad points out,[9] the inconclusiveness of most attempts to evaluate treatment programmes may be the result of adopting too simple an index of effectiveness—typically the rate of recidivism in the period immediately following release. It is naïve to expect regimes to be sufficiently different in their impact upon the offender to yield genuine and stable differences in recidivism rates, especially as input populations tend to be highly heterogeneous in apparently relevant respects. To the clients of the system, the common features of correctional regimes are usually much more significant than the intended rationale of a particular programme. Curbs upon freedom of movement and decision, submission to people in authority, the loss of social status implicit in being subject to a court order, and (in the case of custodial sentences) the characteristic and degrading features of institutional life, probably make more of an impression on an offender than does the presence or absence of group-counselling sessions or of graduated rewards for good conduct.

The fact is that we know little about what actually goes on in the correctional system. Such work as has been done—mainly by sociologists—points to the key role of unintended social effects, of which those who design correctional measures are often quite unaware.[10] Psychologists have paid little attention to the impact of prison

[9] J. P. Conrad, op. cit.
[10] To give examples of British work—T. P. and P. Morris, *Pentonville* (Routledge & Kegan Paul, 1963); S. Cohen and L. Taylor: *Psychological Survival* (Pelican Books, 1972); T. Parker, *The Frying Pan* (Hutchinson, 1970).

environments upon individuals, as we have already noted, although there are questions here of considerable importance to psychology, as well as to sociology. This reluctance to investigate what actually happens in penal institutions seems to stem from the belief that such research can only be descriptive and impressionistic—that the problem is not amenable to rigorous research methods. This is surely a mistake. Contemporary developments in other areas of applied psychology (in education, for example, and in the training of subnormal children) have demonstrated the considerable potential of operant concepts in structuring observations of the salient features (from the client's point of view) of a training regime. Skinnerian principles have made some impact upon the design of new correctional programmes (for example, at Karl Holton School in Stockton, California, and at the Kennedy Youth Center in Morgantown, West Virginia), but their value as a frame of reference for naturalistic studies of correctional regimes has—unaccountably—been largely neglected. The effect of the handful of pioneer studies of this kind has been to demonstrate that quite inappropriate reinforcement contingencies are unintentionally presented in most correctional regimes, so that deviant behaviour is actually reinforced, simply because institutions are normally organized to respond to deviant or anti-social behaviour, but to ignore conforming behaviour—a state of affairs that has also been noted in institutions catering for psychotic or subnormal individuals.[11]

There is a danger that the realization that custodial institutions are of doubtful value as agencies of treatment, and the repeated failure of attempts to demonstrate any systematic relationship between the characteristics of offenders and their response to various types of correctional programme will encourage the assumption that individual differences among offenders are of little importance. There are two reasons for thinking that this would be a serious misconception. Even if it turns out to be the case that attempts to treat offenders in custody are wholly and uniformly ineffective, so that individuals do not differ in their response to treatment, this will

[11] E. P. Buehler, G. R. Patterson, and J. M. Furniss: 'The Reinforcement of Behaviour in Institutional Settings', *Behaviour Research and Therapy*, 4 (1966), 157–67; D. A. Sandford, 'An Operant Analysis of Control Procedures in a New Zealand Borstal', *British Journal of Criminology*, 13, 3 (1973), 262–8; D. A. Sandford and D. E. Bateup: 'Learning how to behave: a Review of the Application of Reinforcement to Prison Management', *Howard Journal of Penology*, 13, 4 (1973), 278–83.

not dispose of the strong probability that people do vary in the extent to which they are affected, distressed and perhaps damaged by the negative effects of imprisonment. If this is so, then it is a matter of vital concern to identify the most vulnerable—and also, of course, to discover which features of the regime are most likely to cause trouble. Secondly, it is clear that what one experiences in a custodial institution depends to some extent upon the characteristics of the other inmates—how mature, intelligent, articulate, and aggressive they are, and whether they are diverse or similar in these and other respects. The patterns of social interaction and the behavioural norms that characterize a particular institution are at least partly shaped by the attributes of the individual members of its population. Designing or modifying an institution necessarily involves decisions about its human composition; we need to know much more about the consequences of alternative policies in these matters.[12]

A psychologist in a correctional system is an investigator of individual offenders; he is a researcher; he is also, inevitably, an advisor to those who have to make decisions about correctional matters. Some recent writers on the roles of the Prison Psychological Service give particular emphasis to this function, referring to the selection and training of staff, the industrial potential and work motivation of inmates, the design of security and vigilance techniques, and the planning of prison buildings.[13] One may guess that there is an almost limitless potential demand for advice on administrative matters of this kind, because so little is known about the effects of such practical decisions upon the working efficiency of correctional regimes. But it is doubtful whether it is profitable for psychologists to engage in this advisory role. The special skill of the psychologist lies in his ability to translate a problem into a researchable question, and then to investigate it. He is a scientist, and he relies upon his research techniques, not upon native wisdom or intuitive understanding of the behaviour of others. Deprived of the opportunity to apply his investigative skills, he is no wiser, and probably less experienced, than the governors and administrators who look to him

[12] There is some interesting material in the reports of the Kennedy Youth Center, where some attempt is made to establish differentiated, relatively homogeneous groups for treatment purposes, using Quay's personality measures.
[13] See J. H. Fitch, 'The Socio-Psychological Role of the Prison Psychologist', *Bulletin of the British Psychological Society*, 21, 70 (1968), 19–22; and J. V. J. Donald: 'Psychologists in the Prison Service', *Occupational Psychology*, 44 (1970), 237–43.

for advice. There is clearly a danger that too much of his time will be unprofitably spent in giving advice on matters in which he has no special expertise; there is the risk, also, of blurring the distinction between advice based on systematic research and that which stems only from the armchair. In common with other civil servants and politicians, penal administrators are already inclined to mistake confident opinions for established facts and ought not be be encouraged in this.[14]

The implication of this essay is that it is desirable (and probably in the long run inevitable) that prison psychologists should emerge from their physical and functional isolation in custodial institutions to form a correctional psychological service. It is clearly illogical that the expertise of this large group of specialist psychologists should not be accessible to those who are responsible for the non-custodial measures of probation, parole, community service, and hostel care which already constitute the larger part of our correctional resources, and whose contribution to the treatment of offenders is likely to increase rather than to diminish. We have argued, also, that this change of role would increase the effectiveness of the psychologist's work by extending its scope to embrace the whole correctional process as it impinges upon the offender, in place of the present unprofitable concentration on the custodial phase of the sentence.

This will, of course, entail changes in the organization of psychological services, and probably in methods of recruitment and training. Psychologists will need to establish a new network of collaborative relationships with community-based social workers and probation officers. A substantial part of their work will presumably be with offenders who are not in custody, necessitating the development of new skills in assessing the problems, the handicaps and the satisfactions which men and women encounter in their natural surroundings. The psychologist will have to become at least as knowledgeable about methods of treatment in the community as he now is about custodial provisions.

Whether this newly defined service ought to be manned exclusively by psychologists, or broadened to include men and women trained in other disciplines (thus becoming a team of 'behavioural scientists') is certainly a matter that merits thought. Although it is recognized

[14] The habit of referring to views expressed to Royal Commissions (and to the Advisory Council on the Penal System) as 'evidence' is an illustration of this confusion.

that some of the problems which currently confront the administrations of prisons demand the skills and techniques of the sociologist and the social anthropologist,[15] the Prison Psychological Service is at present mainly composed of psychologists trained in the British tradition of specialization, with a heavy emphasis on the classical areas of experimental psychology (often, it must be said, at the expense of a really adequate grounding in social behaviour and individual differences) with little or no knowledge of the neighbouring disciplines of sociology, social administration, and social anthropology. It is probably feasible to reinforce this initial education, by in-service training, well enough to equip the psychologist for the work he now has to do; but it seems doubtful whether this solution would be adequate to meet the more extensive demands of a general correctional role. (Indeed, it may be thought that the comparative weakness of the prison psychological team in respect of training in social psychology is one of the reasons for its failure—unlike its American counterparts—to develop effective research into the patterns of social interaction that constitute perhaps the most influential aspect of a custodial regime.)

It would be necessary to redefine the responsibilities of the reorganized team in relation to research, and this would also have implications for recruitment and training. Since the establishment of the Home Office Research Unit in 1957 there has been a certain amount of rivalry between the Unit (which contains some psychologists) and the Prison Psychological Service as to whose task it is to undertake psychological research in prisons. It appears that the Research Unit has established its claim to conduct—or at least to control—fundamental research upon prison populations. Perhaps as a consequence of this (though it is difficult to be sure) the research activities of prison psychologists seem to have been limited to a few relatively circumscribed investigations of an 'operational' kind, concerned with the composition of institutional populations and administrative problems within the penal system. The predictable result has been that young psychologists with enthusiasm and talent for criminological research have been attracted to appointments in the Research Unit, while those of their peers who wanted to work with offenders, but were not drawn to research, joined the Prison Psychological Service. Few prison psychologists have training in research methods; indeed, it is officially stated that the possession of a research degree

[15] J. H. Fitch, op. cit.

is not necessary even for appointment to senior posts in the service.[16]

This is a matter for concern. The expertise of the psychologist, as we have already remarked, is research-based. His contribution to decisions about people, processes, or systems derives from his skill in testing the validity of previous judgements, in translating insights and hunches into researchable hypotheses and investigating them. It is a waste of his skill to deprive him of his research role, and thus to force him into the role of armchair expert. If the redeployment of psychologists in the correctional system is to be carried out at all, it is vital that they should be given the responsibility, and the resources, to pursue a vigorous programme of correctional research. This will swiftly affect the value of psychologists' contributions to day-to-day decisions; in the long run it will also have its effect on the quality of recruits to their ranks. And there is no doubt that a well-trained, effectively organized psychological service has a key role to play in the correctional system that is now taking shape.

[16] *The Work of Psychologists in the Prison Service*, Chief Psychologist, Home Office (Prison Department), 1969, p. 9.

10. The Role of Education in the Penal System

W. R. STIRLING

PHILOSOPHICALLY, education and the penal system make peculiar bed-fellows. When Jacques Maritain[1] wrote 'the task of the teacher is, above all, one of liberation', he cannot have had in mind the education centre of a Borstal institution with bars at the window and the teacher with keys at his belt. Yet education has been a statutory requirement in prisons since 1823. Twenty-seven years ago, Sir Lionel Fox, Chairman of the Prison Commission, expressed the hope that 'The Committee' would be able to devise plans by which education in the widest sense would be made more purposive and be more fully integrated into the training, not left as an optional and spasmodic side issue.

In the intervening years there has been a real attempt to give substance to the role of education in the penal system. Since 1953 local education authorities have been responsible for providing education in penal institutions and have been reimbursed by the Prison Department for agreed services. Her Majesty's Inspectors of Education have carried out inspectorial guidance on behalf of the Department of Education and Science. The Prison Department has set up its own structure with a Chief Education Officer, his deputies and regional officers. In penal institutions, tutor organizers have become education officers, most of them full time. Part-time teachers are being supplemented by full-time appointments, yet the part-timers show that there is deep-rooted belief that somehow education has a role to play, for there are easier ways of supplementing an income than by teaching 'inside'.

Despite hope, dedication, and hard work, however, education has continued to be a fringe activity; Dr. Erica Stratta, in her survey of nine Borstals, comments on its peripheral role.[2] Even more to the point, the Prison Department forecasts that 'the education service

[1] Jacques Maritain, *Education at the Crossroads*, p. 39.
[2] Dr. Erica Stratta, *The Education of Borstal Boys*.

will continue to concentrate on providing "out of hours" activities of the kind available in the evenings in colleges and institutions. Day-time activities will continue to be relatively small scale and, in general, for those needing remedial education and those continuing with higher studies'. It felt moved to apologize for the lack of resources available by saying, 'The Prison Department has never had the financial resources to provide more than very limited facilities for education.'

Education obviously does not rank high in the priorities of the Department, and one might well feel moved to ask why it should. The *raison d'être* of the penal system is, by definition, punitive, deterrent and custodial. It must be more concerned with protecting the public from its menaces than in educating them, especially as its 'clients' are already failures of the educative system. A little bit more of what you do *not* fancy is not likely to do you good.

Nevertheless the Gladstone Committee of 1895 gave the system a paradoxical task when it stoutly affirmed: 'We start from the principle that prison treatment should have as its primary objects, *deterrence and reformation*'. Presumably the role of education was subsumed under the reformatory objective and therefore was entangled in the dilemma of whether you can both reform and deter, and enmeshed in its own little skein of whether you can reform and educate.

The penal system has tried to resolve the dilemma by working within a medical model. It is significant that the Gladstone Committee referred to 'prison treatment'. It implied that criminal behaviour is a social sickness which can be quite speedily cured if only we can stumble on the right medicine. At the time it reflected a crude behavioural idea that you can cure a person by some form of deterrent punishment. It belonged, and indeed still does, to the birch ideology—short, sharp shocks, hard labour, and taking one's medicine. It may fulfill deep-seated retributive desires but, as a cure for crime, it has been singularly unsuccessful. It goes against the grain of the treaters' human feelings which have a happy knack of transforming the regime into something different from that intended; witness the history of the Detention Centres since their short, sharp, shocking start. In this context education can only be a salve or a bromide to make a punitive lot bearable.

Education and the curative philosophy come close together today in the more sophisticated behavioural sciences. The behavioural psychologists, Holland and Skinner, in their book *The Analysis of*

Behaviour (1961) provided the premise for an experiment in reform within the California Youth Authority treatment programme at Karl Holton School. It is interesting that the euphemism 'school' is preferred to the more usual one of 'facility'. The entire regime is a programme of behavioural-modification, based on rewarding good conditioned responses. The punitive, deterrent element is minimized, and the environment is structured in accordance with the explicit objectives.

It has certain general features which are significant for education and reformation. It shows that positive behavioural responses are most likely when reform takes precedence over deterrence. It is also symptomatic of the general social climate; it harmonizes with a society saturated in the folk-lore of psychiatry and psychology. Basically, however, it is psychological rather than educational, for it is so heavily weighted with conditioning and induction.

Education, like its historical companion, Greek drama, wears two masks. One *induces* individuals into the social values and conventions of the day and the other *educes* from individuals their full potentiality as persons. Both coexist, both are in tension, and between them stretches a tight rope with existentialism on one side and totalitarianism on the other, with the needs of self and the needs of society. Education aspires to reconcile the two. Sir Fred Clark felt the need for reconciliation strongly and urged the reconstruction of Plato's educative society in a modern context. 'What is novel is the idea of the free development of the individual as a practical possibility within the life of an organized society.'[3] Jacques Maritain expressed the same idea more romantically: 'The education of man is a human awakening—its aim is to guide man, in the evolving dynamism through which he shapes himself as a human person, armed with knowledge, strength of judgment and moral virtues, while at the same time conveying to him the spiritual heritage of the nation and the civilization in which he is involved.'[4]

The odds, of course, are in favour of educational practice falling on the side of society's needs which are far more pressing than Maritain's 'spiritual heritage'. Education is a vested interest from which society expects dividends by transmitting its values and expertise from one generation to the next. It expects its young to conform to its conventions. It is in this inductive conditioning field that educa-

[3] Sir Fred Clark, *Freedom in the Educative Society*, p. 15.
[4] Jacques Maritain, *Education at the Crossroads*, p. 9.

tion and reformative penal practice seem to find common ground. The soil is only made fertile, however, and the harvest a rich one, if certain conditions are met. Reformation needs to have priority over deterrence, it must be accepted that the process is a slow one and that there is a large degree of consensus between public opinion and institutional practice.

The most successful penal educational reformative attempt to date has been the Borstal system. Alexander Paterson recognized that, in the public schools of the late-nineteenth century, he had institutions, embodying socially acceptable virtues, which might be transplanted into the penal system. They had clear-cut objectives based on Arnold's notions of a Christian gentleman and a Victorian transcription of 'mens sana in corpore sano'. He grafted their regime—chapels, houses, cold baths, and all—into the new Borstals and bound it round with a great deal of caring regard and personal relationships. By choosing only the delinquent fringe, with all the signs of educability, he allowed the penal authorities to play down their deterrent punitive role. He manipulated the environment of his Borstals into something approximating to a school, albeit a stern and rigorous Alma Mater. A realistic time-scale was built in through the indeterminate sentence.

Every ingredient of success for the Borstals has been gradually eroded. Their clients are no longer selected, but are criminally comprehensive; the penal system immediately closed ranks and readjusted its priorities, this time in favour of security and control, viz., the bars on the education-centre windows. Pressure of numbers has reduced time to a minimum and 'through-put' is the controlling factor. Most of all, they are institutions out of harmony with the social *mores* and conventions of the day, they belong to the era of public-school East End Missions.

Institutions are only effective as instruments of social conditioning when they are able to receive strong signals from society about its values and conventions. If the signal is weak and their own sensitivity poor, the message is so distorted that it becomes mumbo jumbo and the conditioning influences a rigmarole. Borstals, like schools, have suffered on both counts. Society has no certainty of the values it wants to transmit. We do not need our sociologists to tell us that we live in a pluralist society—it is uncomfortably obvious. Its economic skills change so fast that last year's inventions are today's anachronisms and trade training is short and intermittent, not prolonged and initial. Institutions, by their very nature, soon lose their sensitivity to receive even the strongest signals. They have a habit of looking inwards and backwards, especially if their role is conservationist. They become purveyors of inert ideas and outmoded skills. A schoolgirl in Edward Blissen's book, *The School I'd Like*, puts it nicely: 'Schools usually have one thing in common. They are institutions of today run on principles of yesterday'. Toffler puts it more sensationally: 'Yet, for all this rhetoric about the future, our schools face backwards towards a dying system, rather than forwards to an emerging society. Their vast energies are applied to cranking out Industrial Men—people tooled for survival in a system that will be dead before they are.'[5]

If this is true of schools—and, allowing for generalization and exaggeration, it is basically true—how much more is it true of penal establishments whose doors do not open onto the real world and whose activities are cut off most effectively, as their *raison d'être*, from the community in both time and space. Walls and barbed wire form a barrier behind which time takes on a different dimension. It is difficult to talk of education in schools and colleges as part of an inductive process; it becomes a nonsense when it is part of a penal institution.

Perhaps this is aptly illustrated in vocational-trade training. There are economic determinants behind the whole educational system; schools and colleges exist in one sense to meet the demands of industry and commerce. Education has to do with earning a living. One of the stated objectives of education in penal institutions is 'to help a person . . . acquire a skill, trade or profession and to pursue it successfully'.[6] It is a perfectly laudable objective, and for a small number of inmates it is a realizable goal. It appears to be an attractive proposition. The Educational Service of the Prison Department, knowing it is dealing with the failures of the school system, has looked towards technical education as its mentor. Education officers and teachers are outposts of the technical college world. Vocational courses linked to City and Guilds examinations have been provided and, more recently, there have been attempts to make vocational training more relevant by looking towards the Industrial Training Board schemes, particularly in the construction industry.

[5] Alvin Toffler, *Future Shock*, p. 361.
[6] Home Office Prison Department, *'Education in Prison'* (1969), p. 7.

Yet in practice vocational induction has been disappointing. At the height of the vocational-training programme, it affected only 5·7 per cent of prisoners serving six months or more and 26·7 per cent Borstal 'trainees'; of those trained in the period 1 October 1963– 30 October 1968 only 26·7 per cent found a job in the trades for which they had been trained.[7] The Industrial Training Board's schemes will be faced with exactly the same debilitating factors. The opportunities to provide real-life industrial experience related to real jobs in the home environment of the inmates cannot be replicated within the miniature, essentially non-industrial world of prisons or Borstals. Time is against them; it is either too short, as in the present Borstal time span, or too long, as in the training of long-term prisoners for skills which will be outmoded by the time they are released into a world where retraining every few years is rapidly becoming the norm. The economic climate is against them. Nothing can be more futile than being trained for a job which does not exist, and a certificate of competence will always be a poor substitute for a fully stamped insurance card.

The inductive role of education as a part of a penal reformative system is a forlorn hope because the premise is wrong. You cannot induce an individual to live harmoniously in an open society by incarcerating him in a closed one. Education begins with the individual in the reality of the circumstances in which he finds himself. A. N. Whitehead almost gave a prospectus for education in the penal system when he wrote: 'Education is the guidance of the individual towards a comprehension of the art of life, and by the art of life I mean the most complete achievement of varied activity expressing the potentialities of that living creature in the face of its actual environment.'[8]

Prison education has been most successful when it has seen its role as primarily educative and immediate, not inductive and futuristic. It has taught the backward to read and the bright to become brighter; it has guided individuals like Jim Gilbert in Wakefield Prison towards a comprehension of painting as an art of life. The findings of Dr. Erica Stratta on tests with 1,000 Borstal trainees, using the Raven Progressive Matrices and the Abstractions C.P. Test I, given to 363, showed that, although they lagged behind in attainment, they had considerable intellectual potential.[9]

[7] Home Office Prison Department Report, *Vocational Training for Inmates of Prison Dept. Establishments*, 1971.
[8] A. N. Whitehead, *The Aims of Education*, p. 61.
[9] Dr. Erica Stratta, *The Education of Borstal Boys*.

The population of our prisons and Borstals are not the moronic fringe, but are people with considerable latent talents which can be nurtured and developed. This is the supreme justification for education in prisons. It exists to help individuals grow as people. It is not a strategy for conversion, reformation, or treatment.

The most important role education can play is perhaps to offer to the penal system an alternative to the treatment model. Criminality is essentially an educational process. Criminals are not sick people, but human beings with more than their fair share of human frailty surrounded by strong social determinants. They have learnt a pattern of unacceptable behaviour. Neither the education system nor the penal system can do much about transforming the determinants directly, but they can do something about supporting and strengthening human beings. There are no miracle cures, and when the Prison Department makes the statement that 'there is no evidence that education can cure crime'[10] it is stating a *non sequitur*. There is only the slow working out of time and the recognition and provision of sustaining positive learning experiences to help along the process. The acceptance of such a model offers to those working within the penal system an escape from the debilitating sense of guilt and failure which every batch of reconviction figures elicits. It substitutes realizable objectives for unrealistic goals, and puts their particular role into a time perspective which makes more sense than a hopeless reformation job to be done in six months or six years.

If the task is slow and prosaic, nevertheless education needs a vision to inspire it, and it needs to escape from the constraints of its own thinking. The effect of institutionalizing education into schools, particularly from 1870, has been to reinforce the tradition of scholasticism and to reduce it to something 'done' in classrooms with chalk, talk, and books. Whitehead's 'complete achievement of varied activity' requires a more holistic view of education, one which sees it as the exploiting and structuring of the total learning experience available within a community and the guidance of individuals towards them. This is as much a part of our educational tradition as scholasticism. Plato's Republic did not have schools; medieval chantry schools were a part of a total learning community, and medieval guilds were as much educational as industrial institutions. The rediscovery of community as a basic learning resource is one of the trends of our times, whether it is expressed in the extreme de-

[10] Home Office Prison Department, *Education in Prison* (1969), p. 7.

schooling notions of Ilich and Goodman,[11] the more ordinary attempts of Local Education Authorities to build community schools, or of industry to encourage 'sandwich courses'. It would be reasonable to conjecture that education in the penal system might become sensitive to the trend, and certainly penal institutions are communities in themselves, which are rich in learning experiences, often of the wrong kind!

All would depend, of course, on the willingness of the prison authorities to accept such a holistic concept. How far they will do so is anyone's guess for, after all, Sir Lionel Fox was saying much the same thing a quarter of a century ago. It would mean that education would cease to be peripheral, it would not even be elemental, but central. It would mean a general acceptance that the deterrent, punitive function of the penal system has been totally absorbed by the very fact of taking away an individual's liberty. Everything which followed would be related to maintaining security and supporting people.

It is debatable how far even these two requirements are compatible. If we stop thinking in absolutes, however, there is a pragmatic case for their coexistence. The influence of education will always vary in inverse proportion to the claims of security and will range from open Borstals to top-security wings. The idea that a correspondence course can be a serious breach of security is a fact of life with which educators have to live. Yet much that goes on in prisons in the name of security has more to do with punishment, unpleasantness, and mindless routine than with effective custody. The future role of education is more dependent upon implementing the Mountbatten Report on strong peripheral security and the reappraisal of internal arrangements than with the provision of new education centres. The penal establishment *is* an education centre for good or ill.

The plea for totality, within the constraints of security, needs a reassessment of the purpose of the variety of activities to be found in prison, and particularly of work. Education has always been the poor relation of work in prisons. This is why the idea that a man could be as gainfully employed in the education centre as in the workshops takes some swallowing, and why education in the tradition of the honest Victorian artisan is done after working hours, except, of course, for the backward. If, however, education is seen as permeating 'activities' in the workshops and 'activities' in a classroom, then

[11] P. Goodman, *Compulsory Miseducation.*

participation in either is a matter of equal choice. Work in prisons appears to have three justifications—it fills in endless time as an alternative to sitting in a cell, it 'trains' people for a job outside, it offsets the expenses of custody. The first is true enough, although much which has passed for work does not make time any the less endless, the second is more pious than real, and the third is only marginal. As a competitive force against industry at large, it is a non-starter; the attitude of employers and trade unions will always keep it firmly in its place. It can, however, offer an educative and sustaining experience in its own right; apart from the obvious acquisition of skills, it offers possibilities for social education far more real than those contrived in a classroom, providing that the objectives are stated and the possibilities recognized. Designing, creating, co-operating, punctuality, and being precise, to mention only a few, are intrinsic in the situation once the trammels of 'profitability' are lost. Profitability and even future job expectation might be met, but they would not be a prime purpose.

This is completely at variance with the report of the Home Office on Vocational Training which denigrated the influence claimed for vocational and trade training on behaviour and stated:

These are all intangible values, subjective and unresearched for the most part and it may be that the Department have placed more faith in them than the facts warrant. A preoccupation with them, indeed, may have deflected the Department from fully exploiting the value of vocational training in terms of employment and job satisfaction for inmates on release.[12]

It is quite true that, if behavioural aims are nothing more than pious hopes, then they will realize little. Quite a different expectation is valid, however, if behavioural objectives are explicit and structured. Certainly there is no objective proof that an industrial world, with unemployment as a permanent feature, is willing to absorb ex-inmates in the ranks of the employed because they have been 'trained' inside. Nor is there any tangible evidence that ex-prisoners are eager to work in construction, farming, or laundry work.

G. Venn seems to talk more positively:

Work activity has become more like education and a new and closer relationship between the two has become necessary and possible ... the

[12] Home Office Prison Department Report, *Vocational Training for Inmates of Prison Dept. Establishments*, p. 4.

importance of the job to the individual and the fact that the job is more than ever a function of his education, the changes in the 'meaning' of work and the fact that as it becomes like education, the more education for work becomes mandatory.[13]

This coalescence of work and education is the real significance of the Industrial Training Act, and the reality in prisons is to accept the synthesis irrespective of nebulous employment prospects.

Even within the present work regime there could be significant beneficial changes. In some prisons already prisoners can choose to go to the education centre or to the workshops during the day, which is quite a breakthrough of the time barrier. Monetary reward is, of course, limited to 'real' work, but as the entire pay structure is under review, it would not need a revolution to reward participation equally, whether it was at a bench or a desk. Time is one commodity of which there is plenty in prisons and the more flexible use of waking hours is something which could be immediately realizable. The merging of education and vocational training under a Chief Education Officer is most encouraging. The movement of education, in our holistic sense, to the centre of the scene, would mean that education officers would be key people in the management team. It would require educators with the vision and pragmatism to survey the 'actual environment' and to see in it the learning possibilities. The statement of educational objectives related to the possibilities would need to be clear, yet not overstructured. Learning is not haphazard, nor can it be contrived; there needs to be room for intuition and the casual interplay of minds. The objective might be as particular as learning specific skills and techniques, but they would also need to be concerned with less definable and more complex behaviour such as understanding, creating, co-operating, designing, solving, relating, and choosing would need to rank high in the priorities.

Paradoxically, in trying to meet such educational objectives within the immediate constraints, individuals would have a chance of both coping with the deadening effect of institutionalization and their future social situation, Toffler makes the point that, within a world of change, the most prized qualities are flexibility and adaptability—what he calls 'the individual cope-ability'.[14] It might well be that, in emphasizing the educative aspect of education, the inductive

[13] G. Venn, 'Man, Education and Work' in G. L. Mangum (ed.), *The Manpower Revolution. Its Policy Consequences*, pp. 403, 16.
[14] Alvin Toffler, *Future Shock*, p. 364.

need is best met, always providing that the individual wants to be involved.

Education stands on the principle that you do not instil learning into people, but draw it out of them by offering them possibilities. 'Man is not a block of wood from which you carve a statue which is completely subject to your will', he is a living image shaping, misshaping and reshaping itself.[15]

Whitehead insisted upon 'the guidance of the individual'. Prisons, however, are not particularly good at guiding or of offering choice, although preparing an individual to make acceptable choices is, ostensibly, part of the penal exercise. Yet the possibilities of choice exist in even the most closed situation and it is the task of educators to recognize where they exist and to use them to the full. This is, of course, the old deterrence/reformation, or security/education issue in essence, and it is necessary to reiterate again that the degree of success of education will depend upon the degree to which the regime will permit the making of choices. Motivation is written into the prison scene. The two most powerful motivations are to escape or to do one's time as quickly and as painlessly as possible. The former might well be a stimulating learning experience, but hardly to be encouraged; the latter is a potent motivating force which could be harnessed if the possibilities were offered.

Assuming possibilities, the assessment role of education becomes an imperative. It needs to be done on the spot, to be related to the educational objectives, to be capable of evaluation and to be continuous. A language capable of communicating the assessments and objectives is needed, and the simpler, less jargon-ridden, the better. If education is to be holistic it will involve all and sundry and it needs to be able to communicate with the ordinary folk who will be involved in the process and not merely with an esoteric group of professionals.

Education in the Prison Service has been with us for 150 years; there are all the signs that its relative importance will grow in the next twenty-five. It would be a pity, however, if the possibility of growth was restricted to its present academic-vocational training role. There is big temptation to take the Further Education model to untenable lengths, to build bigger and better education centres and call them colleges, when the real need is to use the indigenous learning experiences of the 'actual environment' and aim to sustain everyone, not only the backward and the bright.

[15] Comenius, *The Analytical Didactic*, p. 108.

This has been a plea that education in the penal system could be comprehensive, that it must be related to people as they are and to the environment as it is. In this sense it is educative and immediate to place and time. Yet education can never be contained by time because it is an integral part of the march of time. It is a continuous process and only makes sense in a perspective of time. The role of education is valid in the penal system only if it turns things 'inside out', if it bridges the gap between custody and non-custody, between prison and freedom. It is not within its competence to do so unless custody is seen as something more than a terminal point, the beginning or end of a line.

The case for a generic sentence embracing custodial and non-custodial elements is powerful. It is only in this framework that education can play its full role. It enables it to be true to itself by being a process in time. It would be integral to a 'through care' situation rather than the expediency of 'after care'.

The major educative role would harmonize with movements towards holistic education beginning to show themselves in the community. The idea of harnessing all the learning experiences available in a community is becoming part of our thinking. Radical alternatives to prison are no longer a voice in the wilderness—the idea is slowly becoming respectable; the intermediate 'treatment' of the Children and Young Persons Act (1969), the community-service proposals of the Criminal Justice Act (1972). The notion of Day Attendance Centres is a distinct possibility. The guidance of individuals towards these and other and more 'varied activities' within the community is only practicable as part of a custodial–non-custodial continuum.

The minor inductive role could stop being pious, futuristic hopefulness; it could be a logical provision marshalling inductive experiences at the appropriate time in the appropriate places. Vocational training could be offered in regional government training centres and directly related to local employment possibilities. The participation in academic study in prison could be directly related to similar ones in local colleges of further education and attendance on 'parole' the bridging mechanism.

Ultimately, however, it is the concept of the educational model which could bring a breath of sanity to our penal system. It affirms quite clearly that you cannot pluck a man out of society, lock him up, treat him, and eject him back into it, resplendent with his railway warrant, £4 in his pocket, and a blank insurance card, and then expect him to sin no more.

The problem with the penal system is that no one believes in it—neither sentencers nor sentenced, neither sinner nor saved. The time has come to admit that the Gladstone dictum of 'deter and reform' is an impossible prescription. It is surely more realistic to concede that it is the task of penal establishments to contain anti-social characters, a task it can do successfully, and to drop the pretence of reformation. It would be the task of education within these constraints to help individuals to survive and, indeed, to grow and to bridge the gap between custody and non-custody as a continual process in time, utilizing the learning resources of the community 'inside' and 'out'. It is only in this framework of continuum that education can guide 'individuals towards a comprehension of the art of life'. Education is not, as the Prison Department would have us believe 'essentially . . . a tool for a job, an aid to living'.[16] It is an individual's total response to his total environment. In the words of Tolstoy 'the only criterion of pedagogy is freedom, the only method, experience'.

In an unfree penal system the role of education must alway be contradictory, not conditioning.

[16] Home Office Prison Department, *Education in Prisons*, 1969, p. 7.

11. The Woman Offender

ANN D. SMITH

PACE the Women's Liberation Movement, women are not the same as men: their physiology is different; their instincts and many of their basic attitudes to life are different; their psychological needs are different. Even allowing for controversy over these factors, however, it is incontrovertible that women offenders—particularly those who are received into custodial establishments—are very different from male offenders.

Numerically alone women present an altogether different problem to the penal system. The total number of women and girls received under custodial sentence without the option of a fine in 1971[1] was 1,521, out of a total reception of 6,518—that is about one in four. These figures compare with 48,037 men and boys sentenced to imprisonment without option, out of a total reception of 135,899 (about $1:2\cdot8$). Thus if crime is predominantly a male activity—the ratio is $8:1$—imprisonment is even more overwhelmingly applicable to male offenders. Overcrowding, so prevalent in the prison system over the last decade or more, is wholly absent from the female side. Whereas any penal policy framed for male offenders is bedevilled by the crisis in the daily average prison population, treatment of women offenders can proceed unhampered by such severely practical problems.

Prison regimes can, and should, increasingly allow for these marked differences. The differences are not confined to the sheer weight of numbers. Many other factors sharply differentiate the female offender from her male counterpart. Reception into prison for women offenders often entails the reception of a mother and her child (or children); sometimes the mother is pregnant and will give birth during her period of imprisonment. Women, moreover, take much less kindly to communal living. Removed from their menfolk and their offspring they chafe under any kind of regimentation. Prisons for women offenders need to be tailored much more to individual

[1] Criminal Statistics for Scotland and for England and Wales, 1971; Statistics for 1972, published at the time of proof stage, show little variation.

treatment and can be less generalized in application, since women are often, in theory, sent to prison for 'treatment' rather than for 'punishment'. Custodial sentences for women are also rare because courts are reluctant to send them to prison, and find, more readily than they do with male offenders, sound reasons for alternative forms of treatment within the community. Courts, moreover, in displaying this reluctance to imprison women, reflect a public attitude which is a good deal less fearful of either female crime or female criminals. The exception is still the group of women—16·3 per cent of those received in prison under sentence—convicted of offences associated with prostitution.

Since the Second World War, especially in Britain, Scandinavia, and the United States there have been increasing signs of interest in research[2] into the criminality of women and into schemes for treatment, custodial and non-custodial, considered particularly appropriate for them. As nearly always occurs, however, by the time such schemes for reform come to be introduced, the situation that inspired them already shows signs of change. Indeed, to look ahead now, when many women are challenging the 'feminine' image of domestication and subordination, it is particularly difficult to forecast who the 'typical' women offender will be by the end of the century, and how society will be dealing with her problems. As woman's role in society changes, so her offences change; perhaps becoming more violent and presenting even a threat to the community. To many concerned with women offenders, however, this possibility makes it only more urgent to ensure that if our society comes to accept that women should be treated as equal to men in some respects, the idea of equality should not be accepted uncritically in penal treatment. The woman offender, in general, is likely to continue to commit offences that are due to the stresses and temptations she faces as a woman. These are not the same as the

---

[2] The interest shown by a group of the Home Office Research Unit in London, under the direction of Nancy Goodman, into problems of women offenders has not only produced two Reports—*Studies of Female Offenders* in 1967, and *Girl Offenders aged 17–20 years*, by Jean Davies and Nancy Goodman, in 1972; but also a news-sheet on current research in Britain and abroad. This has been particularly valuable in stimulating interest in women's problems, since it has circulated not only to research workers but also to those involved practically with the treatment of women offenders within the institutions and in the community. Among research studies concerned with large women's prisons in the United States, Rose Giallombrada, *Society of Women* (1966), and David Ward and Gene Kassebaum, *Women's Prison* (1965), are of particular interest.

stresses faced by men, and will vary according to her age, environment, and physical strength. Even if, with greater opportunity to express her personality and abilities within society, and greater equality with men, she encounters new stresses and temptations, it is all important that society should not forget that when a woman comes in conflict with the law she needs to be treated more than to be punished.

The paper published by the Central Office of Information in London, as recently as 1960, entitled 'The Treatment of Offenders in Britain'[3] gives some idea of the interest taken in women offenders. Women rate one small paragraph in a footnote mentioning 'their small numbers which do not allow such extensive classification arrangements as for men'.[4] In the version of 'Prison and Borstals— England and Wales' published in 1957,[5] although the list of contents included 'sedition prisoners' and 'prisoners under sentence of death' there was no section devoted to women. The third edition certainly included women when analysing the prison population, but they appeared to be so unimportant that, apart from a vague mention of the few prisons set aside for their treatment, it contained only one sentence on reconvictions, a solitary mention of their privileges and a brief paragraph on work in prison; the section on the treatment of convicted prisoners dealt exclusively with men. The paragraph on work for women prisoners noted somewhat complacently that for women the situation was less difficult since the occupations in which they were mainly employed 'are such as most are able to undertake either at once or with a little training'.[6] By 1960, when 'Prison and Borstals' was reprinted, there was still no section on women prisoners, and the quotation under 'principles of classification' showed few signs of progress since the beginning of the century: 'The separation of the sexes is complete; women are retained either in separate prisons or in parts of local prisons which are so far separate, with different locks, that the only place of common use is the Chapel, and they are at all times under the supervision of women officers'.[7] The policy statement continued to stress that the very small numbers of women did not permit 'comprehensive classification'[8] There were, however, signs that the authorities were at last beginning to doubt whether one central prison in London was really sufficient to meet

[3] Central Office of Information, Feb. 1960.   [4] Ibid., p. 14.
[5] H.M.S.O., revised edition.   [6] Ibid., p. 32.
[7] 1960 edition, p. 10.   [8] Ibid., p. 15.

the varied needs of women prisoners. By 1971 the situation had changed radically. The mount of attention given to the future of penal establishments for women and girls in the Reports[9] on prisons for that year show the increasing awareness that problems posed by women prisoners were not remotely the same as those for men. In England and Wales there was particular concern with arrangements for women kept in custody on remand, for units for mothers and babies[10] and all forms of hospital care. In Scotland plans for a new institution for women were beginning to take shape, and it was hoped to provide on an open site near Stirling with very different conditions from those of the old fortress-type prison at Greenock.

The treatment of women and girls in Britain has become much more imaginative since the Second World War. There are signs that a number of radical changes might take place before the end of the century. Security is one of them. In the past far too much emphasis had been placed on the security in women's prisons. Although women might on occasion attempt to escape from institutions or from hospitals in which they were receiving treatment, they seldom remained at large for more than a few days and rarely contributed any threat or danger to the community. Publicity given to the escapes of male prisoners nearly always stressed the threat of violence and the varying degrees of danger which the public might expect, should they meet the escaped prisoner. The attitude towards women prisoners who escaped was very different. Even the hysterical reactions in the press in 1972,[11] when a notorious woman murderer was allowed to walk with her prison officer escort in a London park, was clearly due more to horror at her original offences and anger that her life sentence should have been alleviated by any show of humanity, than fear of the prospect of immediate danger to the community, were she to escape and be free for a few days. Some of the public anxiety was, indeed, fostered by the wholly erroneous press reporting that the perambulation in the park was a prelude to a planned release on licence.

Society has, in fact, begun to accept that there is no need to house women offenders in conditions of maximum security; the majority of women who commit murder or crimes of violence do so because

[9] Prisons in Scotland, Cmnd. 4809, and 'Report on the Work of the Prison Dept. 1971', Cmnd. 5037.   [10] Cmnd. 5037, p. 38.
[11] See generally reports and correspondence in *The Times* and other newspapers, Sept. 1972.

of circumstances which are unlikely to recur, frequently as a result of a domestic quarrel. Such women, if they are likely to be dangerous, need conditions approximating far more to secure mental hospitals than to prisons. It is unfortunate that the plans for new institutions for women still sometimes include expensive schemes for fences, secure windows, and elaborate electric locking devices. These are likely only to increase the sense of claustrophobia which has so often been the source of women's violence in institutions in the past.[12] It is easy to attempt to justify the expense of external security by arguing that such security is necessary to keep people from outside the prison coming in, rather than women prisoners getting out. Such arguments, however, only perpetuate, at the cost of a great deal of money, conditions which will probably be quite out of date by the end of the century. Penal treatment for women does not require the trappings of maximum security, high fences, and large prisons.

This is not to say that society will not have to protect itself from dangerous women. Indeed there are signs that women are now taking an active part in forms of violence in which formerly they seldom indulged. In 1971, 8·9 per cent of all women and girls sentenced were in respect of crimes of violence (murder, other homicide offences, assaults, and cruelty to children). Ten years earlier the percentage was 7·9 per cent when many more women offenders were sent to prison for cruelty to children (69 out of 139 in 1961, 5 out of 136 in 1971). More recent incidents involving the hijacking of aircraft, and plans to intimidate and possibly to destroy individuals or groups of people for political motives have included women.[13] Such forms of political activity are likely to increase rather than decrease in the future in countries with racial tensions and frustrated minority groups whose womenfolk are becoming less and less inclined to be content with mere verbal protest. We cannot predict whether such women who have acted violently within the community and may have received severe sentences from courts, will continue to be violent when they are imprisoned.[14]

As women acquire more mechanical skills, the scope of their

[12] See Ann D. Smith, *Women in Prison* (1962), p. 253.

[13] e.g. the cases involving Lela Khaled, and the Angry Brigade 1972.

[14] About 2 per cent of all women and girls commit violent offences in penal establishments compared with 1½ per cent of men. Although the percentage of violent women committing violent offences among women offenders in the community (13·1 per cent) is higher than that for men and boys (9·3 per cent) it is not always these women who show violence when confined in institutions.

activities is likely to widen. Their share in motoring offences has already risen considerably, although so far their offences in this area continue to be comparatively trivial. As they become physically more active, however, they will be less inclined to play a passive part in violent activities in which formerly they were content to carry the weapons and act as instigators. It is not unusual now to read of young women as well as young men using knives and axes as weapons, taking part in gang fights and 'muggings' and planning attacks on unprotected persons to obtain money.[15] Such activities are not likely to be decreased, any more than the acts of political violence referred to earlier, or participation in mobbing and rioting to express deep-felt social resentment. The next decade will also see an increasing number of women assuming positions of power in the professions and in industry, and facing the temptations of such power, formerly almost unknown to them when they occupied subordinate positions. On the rare occasions when they have held such power in the past, women have not shown themselves to be able to resist the temptations of bribery, corruption, fraud, and embezzlement any more than men.[16] In the struggle for success in an increasingly competitive world one can expect to find many more women coming before the courts accused of such offences.[17]

There is certainly likely to be a need for small secure units for women in Scotland and in England and Wales—and those women confined in these units will probably be young, active, and with considerable physical strength. Many of them, however, may be able to graduate from such conditions comparatively soon, once they are withdrawn from the situation which caused their outbreaks of violence. Others may show signs of mental disturbance, and the provision of a hospital unit as the centre-piece of the new prison complexes in both countries is to be welcomed.[18] Apart from the forms of mental disorder

[15] During the past year courts in Scotland have had to deal with women taking part in all forms of violent activity. Cases of homicide committed by young girls have also occurred, which have created particular problems for those concerned with their disposal; cf. in England, Gitta Sereny, *The Case of Mary Bell* (1972).

[16] Regarding women imprisoned for fraud and forgery, see e.g. Tony Parker, *Five Women* (1965).

[17] In a brief article it would be impossible to mention all the valuable work that has been written recently on women offenders and their treatments. That there should be so much material now available is, however, a sign of the increasing interest taken in Britain and internationally in the participation of women in crime and anti-social behaviour.

[18] On the plans of Holloway see e.g. D. E. R. Faulkner, 'The Redevelopment of Holloway Prison', *Howard Journal* (1971).

already found in women's prisons[19] and, particularly in institutions for young women,[20] more help will be needed for those offenders who have serious problems with drug addiction. It can also be argued that physical conditions and deformities have a considerable effect upon women's criminality, and medical treatment for these is essential for satisfactory rehabilitation.

In the past, fear of contamination led to divisions among offenders of both sexes which were often, quite clearly, artificial. The elderly and middle-aged woman offender was, in fact, far less likely to have an adverse effect on younger women than the criminal expertise of the younger women was to disturb those older than them in years, who often were first offenders. In a small country, such as Scotland, it has been impractical for a long time to make strict divisions between age-groups and it is doubtful whether in the future such divisions will or should be made. It is not normal to divide groups of women according to chronological age, and qualities of caring and unselfishness, which it is essential to instill in them as far as possible, are more likely to emerge in a community which covers all age-groups than when they are strictly separated. When women come into prison as expectant mothers or with small babies they are allowed to keep their children with them. With more open and normal conditions in the institutions it has, indeed, become possible to reassess the age at which it is wise to separate children from their mothers and [21] to question whether such separation is really necessary at all, except in cases where the mother is serving a long prison sentence. This movement away from regimentation and uniformity will almost certainly continue. In England women can now wear

[19] One of the problems that particularly concerned the public during 1972 was baby-stealing. On this subject see T. P. d'Orban 'Baby-stealing' *British Medical Journal* (1972), 635–9. Regarding disturbed women in prison see e.g. Desmond Ellis and Penelope Austin, 'Menstruation and Aggressive Behaviour in a Correctional Center for Women', *Journal of Criminal Law, Criminology and Police Science*, 63, no. 3 (1971).

[20] For examples of studies of Borstal girls, see Home Office Research Unit Reports referred to above, p. 156; note 2; also, e.g. J. B. Price, 'Some results on the Maudsley Personality Inventory from a Sample of Girls in Borstal', *British Journal on Criminology* (Oct. 1968). On delinquent girls in general see e.g. Marianne Felice and David Offord, 'Three Developmental Pathways to Delinquency in Girls', ibid. (Oct. 1972); Jane Gilbert, 'Delinquent and Non-delinquent Girls', ibid.; Cowie, Cowie, and Slater, *Delinquency in Girls* (1968); Helen Richardson *Adolescent Girls in Approved Schools* (1969).

[21] See e.g. D. E. R. Faulkner, 'The Redevelopment of Holloway Prison', pp. 30–1.

their own clothes in prison; clothes of their own choice are provided for offenders who have none.[22]

Work for women in Scotland is still mainly domestic, concerned with cooking, sewing, and housekeeping, and will probably continue to be so. Women prisoners are, however, beginning to undertake much more of the painting, decorating, and general maintenance of the institutions than they ever did in the past, and usually carry out this work under the direction of skilled men instructors.[23] The benefit of women officers and instructors working in men's prisons and men in women's prisons is acknowledged increasingly. This movement away from 'single sex' institutions relieves many tensions which existed formerly, and is another important factor in helping to create a more normal atmosphere and diminish the sense of living in a separate world, which so often hindered a woman's readjustment when she returned to the community. In other countries there are signs that boundaries between institutions for men and women offenders are becoming less strictly observed, and—as in State Mental Hospitals—[24] the two groups join in some forms of work, education, and recreational activities. It is doubtful whether in the foreseeable future prisons will be established in Britain to contain both men and women. Plans for new women's institutions do, however, show a flexibility which should enable them to adapt to for example, changes in the proportions of the various age-groups or an increased need for medical care for particular categories of women. If—as one hopes—society finds other means of supporting inadequate petty offenders and become able to rely more on non-custodial methods of treatment and training,[25] there should be a considerable decrease in the total population of women offenders in institutions, but whether within a hospital or a prison, women will need very much more support than society has so far been able to give, if they are to be resettled satisfactorily in the community and not to become habitual offenders. Not only the women themselves but their families also need help from professionals and from volunteers.[26]

[22] Report of the Prison Department, 1969, p. 21.

[23] See generally Prison Reports for Scotland and England and Wales.

[24] Nigel Walker and Sarah McCabe, *Crime and Insanity in England*, ii (1973).

[25] e.g. Barbara Wootton in 'Community Service', *Criminal Law Review* (Jan. 1973), 19, suggests one form of such 'service' for 'middle-aged women shoplifters'.

[26] Many recent studies have been concerned with the effect of women's imprisonment on their families e.g. Carole Gibbs, 'The Effect of the Imprisonment of Women upon their Children' *British Journal of Criminology* (April 1971).

By the year 2000 it is possible that disregard of individual vanity and acceptance of uniform as a sign of political idealism may have spread to the West. The small communities which already exist, dedicated to the simple life, rejecting material comforts and the affluent society, are likely to increase in number. It is, however, unlikely that within the next decade women will have ceased to wish to acquire the luxuries as well as the necessities of life, by legal or illegal means. During the rest of this century, indeed, women's offences will probably continue to be concerned mainly with petty theft, sexual exploitation, and the diminishing of consciousness through alcohol and drugs.

Greater mobility internationally will inevitably create special problems. Already in Britain and in Europe industries which need extra labour are employing large numbers of workers of both sexes from countries where work is scarce and ill-paid. Such artificial populations, especially when both sexes are not included, bring with them difficulties of language, loneliness, and antagonism which often increase tendencies towards anti-social behaviour. Increase in mobility may lead to greater racial tolerance, but even should this be so—which is by no means certain—such tolerance does not lead automatically to an acceptance of different cultural attitudes to violence, sexual behaviour, and possession of property. The opportunities of conflict in all these areas needs no elaboration. If the men of any community move to work in another country this also creates problems for the women they leave behind and the consequence of increased mobility, even within the 'European Community', should provide ample opportunities for research.[27]

Those who advocate complete equality of the sexes would probably argue that women offenders should be treated by the penal system no differently from men offenders, but courts will still be influenced when pronouncing sentence by the fact that many women are likely to have dependent children and husbands to care for. The

See also Reports of the Advisory Council on the Penal System, *Non-custodial and Semi-custodial Penalties*, 1970, p. 4. On after-care in general see e.g. P. D. Elder, 'House for ex-Borstal Girls', *British Journal of Criminology* (Oct. 1972).

[27] Indeed the intention of this article is mainly to stress how much research will be needed in the future into areas which potentially can cause anti-social behaviour by women, such e.g. different cultural attitudes to 'battered babies'; whether the effect of the 'pill' will be to reduce family tensions due formerly to overcrowding; how far acceptance or non-acceptance of family planning is likely to increase racial and religious conflicts; characteristics of violent women political offenders, etc.

community may well consider that the natural corollary to equality of opportunity is equality of treatment, and that women convicted of serious crimes cannot be expected to be treated differently from men. Even so, in the writer's view, 'equality' of treatment from the sentencing point of view should on no account mean that men and women receive the *same* treatment—but rather that their treatment within the penal systems should become more rational, with regard to their special needs.

12. The Sentencing Process: Present Practice and Future Policy

SIR ARTHUR JAMES

IN expressing an essentially personal and (in fond hope) original view on this subject, one finds inevitably and infuriatingly that it is a view already shared by many, and is largely a redeployment and development of the thoughts of others. The last quarter of a century has witnessed an unprecedented public interest in the punishment of offenders. Not surprisingly, Parliament and the Executive have responded to the problem of providing courts with adequate powers for sentencing offenders by a series of measures in successive Criminal Justice Acts and by the deployment of human and financial resources in custodial and non-custodial settings.

There are voices of protest against the overcrowding of prisons. They urge the courts to turn away from imprisonment, either because, at best, imprisonment is a negative and temporary expedient, or because, from a practical point of view an overstrained Prison Service cannot provide effective treatment. There are voices of protest against the lack of concern for the victims of crime. The courts are urged, no less volubly, to impose longer prison sentences upon those convicted of serious offences. There are other voices counselling the Government—voices less loud in protest but no less authoritative. These are the voices of sentencers and those who have received professional training in, or made a study of the treatment of offenders. They urge in particular a close and continuing review of the sentencing process.

Against this background of interest and exhortation there is some justification for an attempt to state briefly where the courts stand, and to offer some suggestions of the kind of sentencing process we should advocate for the last quarter of this century. If any suggestions are to be made, now is the time. If changes in sentencing practice are to be made it is important, if frustration and disenchantment are to be avoided, that the facilities necessary to put new methods into practice are readily available to match the legislative command.

In sentencing the offender the court is discharging its constitutional function of maintaining the law of the land. One aspect of that function is the prevention of crime. The primary avowed purpose of sentencing offenders is the prevention of crime. It follows that in the court's sentence there should be an ever-present element—the interest of the public. That interest may be so great as to outweigh all other consideration; or it may be so minimal in the particular circumstances of a case as to permit the sentence to be governed by other factors. But the public interest can never be ignored.

The court's function of maintaining the law of the land involves, in relation to sentencing practice, a second and equally important aspect. The court is the guardian of the right of the individual. In respect of an accused person the court's duty is to ensure that he has a fair and just trial of the issue of guilt. In respect of a guilty person the court is furthermore his guardian in respect of sentence. Passed by the court, the sentence is determined free from Executive influence, or from the influence of any other body appointed by, or answerable to, the Executive. Passed by the court, the sentence is pronounced publicly. By being public the sentence is subject to scrutiny and comment—even wrong-headed comment. Passed by the court, the sentence is the court's exclusive responsibility and there is no room for shifting that burden on to others' shoulders. The sentencing process thus carries the stamp of independence, publicity, and responsibility. Should the courts ever cease to sentence offenders and, either as a general rule of practice or as a matter of discretion in particular cases, surrender that function to another body, it would be abdicating its most important role, to the peril of the individual.

These twin functions of preventing crime in the interest of the public and of safeguarding the offender from oppressive or secretive sanctions combine to produce a sentencing process which aims (i) to mark the offence with appropriate punishment, (ii) to provide for society's protection and the offender's needs during the period of the sentence, and (iii) to integrate the offender, as a law-abiding member, into society.

The need for the sentence to include a punitive element, the nature and degree of punishment appropriate, the need for society to be protected from the offender, the needs of the offender during sentence, and the best method of achieving the prisoner's reintegration into the community—all these depend upon the particular circumstances of any given case. Upon these matters the court has to determine the sentence. Once determined, subject to the power in the higher courts to vary the sentence within a limited time of the sentence being passed, and subject to the appellate process, the sentence is immutable by judiciary or Executive.

The three-pronged aim can be pursued by a sentence depriving an offender of his liberty, which seeks to train, educate, and discipline him while in custody and then returns him to society. It can be pursued, on the other hand, by a sentence permitting the offender to remain in society, with or without a variable degree of supervision and guidance, or subject (or not) to a monetary penalty, or to the threat of imprisonment in the event of re-offending. It could also be pursued by a sentence which combines a period in custody followed by a period of controlled freedom: in that sentences of Borstal Training and of Detention Centre Orders have an inbuilt automatic period of licence to follow the period in custody they pursue the aim in this way. On the other hand, the possibility of release on parole licence from custody under a sentence of more than eighteen months' imprisonment forms no part of, and is not reflected in, the length of sentence, although it does possess the advantage of combining a period of custodial treatment and non-custodial supervision.

Balancing the interest of the offender with the interests of the victim of the offence and public following the assessment of the means whereby those interests can best be served is a delicate exercise for those whose anxious task it is to sentence offenders. It has to be carried out both within the limitations imposed by the character of offenders and the legislative prescriptions as to the range of sentences and orders. The sentencing process has to be applied not only to a very large number of individuals but also to the variations in response to the sentence, often unpredictable, which may be exhibited by any one individual. The process has to be applied to offenders ranging in character from the determined, committed criminal, who is intelligent and in full possession of his faculties, to those of low-grade intelligence, the immature, the inadequate, and those addicted to drink or drugs. The practice has to be applied to the old lag and to the first offender, to the elderly and to children. Once the wheels of the criminal process have begun to turn, the stage will be reached, if guilt is established, when the court will be required to sentence the guilty person, no matter whether there is or is not an appropriate method of dealing with him. And in its application of the sentencing process, the court cannot invent sentences; it must pass sentence according to law.

The fewer the weapons in the sentencing armoury, the more restrictions upon the use of what weapons are available, the less flexible and effective is the power of the court. An example was to be found in the mandatory suspension of sentences of six months' imprisonment or less (except in specified circumstances) introduced by the Criminal Justice Act 1967. The mandatory element was removed by the Criminal Justice Act 1972. Another example is the fetter put on the power to sentence to imprisonment persons aged between seventeen and twenty-one.

Present sentencing practice undoubtedly has certain disadvantages. These are the subject of criticism, extending at times to the proposition that the sentencing process should be taken out of the jurisdiction of the courts and placed in the hands of others. These disadvantages are: (i) that the court at the time of passing sentence is not always in possession of essential information relevant to determination of the sentence; and (ii) that at the time of passing sentence it is not possible to predict what the effect of the sentence will be upon the offender, nor what changes may occur which, had they been foreseeable, would have influenced the decision as to sentence.

The first disadvantage arises from the practice of passing sentence immediately following, or shortly after, the finding of guilt, either by confession or trial. At that time the court will normally have a history of the offender in relation to education, employment, and previous convictions prepared by the police. Usually it is the bare outline of those matters. There is insufficient time, and there are no facilities to investigate to the degree necessary to produce a full and detailed report; nor, until guilt is formally established, would it be right in many instances to investigate in depth. At the time of sentencing the court will normally have, in respect of those classes of offender in which social inquiries are likely to yield relevant information, a Social Enquiry Report. Usually it is a pre-trial report. Often it is prepared upon a basis of fact in respect of the offence reported by the accused to the Probation Officer, which is completely invalidated by the evidence given to the court. Normally the court will have at the time of passing sentence, in a case in which it has been recognized that medical evidence may be relevant, a medical report upon the offender's mental or physical health. But not always is the desirability of obtaining medical evidence recognized, and it is not unknown for accused persons deliberately to conceal facts as to personal or family medical history. When such social inquiry reports and medical reports are available, the risk of the court acting on incomplete information is minimized. It has become increasingly the practice of the courts to call for such reports when none is available, and to call for further reports when it appears that the available reports are inadequate. This is so particularly in the case of children and young persons, in which cases, in addition to the type of report already mentioned, educational, welfare, and, if applicable, institutional reports are always considered. When more information is required, or where further investigation is necessary in order to put the court into the best position for deciding the proper sentence, present-day practice is to postpone sentence until either the information is available or the investigation has been carried out.

The first disadvantage can be, and is in practice, largely overcome. Moreover, it should not be thought that every case is one in which reports from specialist sources are of relevance; it is only in a small minority that such reports are of assistance, and the frequency with which the courts are urged to have regard to them in inappropriate circumstances leads to the conclusion that it is unlikely that the need will be overlooked when they are relevant.

The second disadvantage is of more substance. It is a disadvantage which cannot be avoided—no matter whether it is the court or any other authority which passes the sentence—if the sentence is rigidly fixed once and for all at the moment it is passed (or reviewed on appeal). The disadvantage lies in the unalterable character of the sentence. A is sentenced to two years' imprisonment. Six months later the prison authorities are satisfied, for cogent reasons, that imprisonment was the wrong method of dealing with A, in his own interest and in the interest of the public. The court cannot change the sentence. The sentence must remain as two years' imprisonment. B gets eighteen months' imprisonment as his first custodial sentence. After six weeks the initial shock has been such that he is unlikely to risk being sent to prison again. If he serves his sentence, twelve months in prison will have taught him how to tolerate and accept prison conditions, and being sent to prison again will hold less fear. The sentence must remain: the court cannot change the sentence in the light of subsequent events.

When fixing the sentence, the court is required to make an informed, responsible 'guess' at the likely effect of the various available sentences upon the particular offender. Having selected the form of sentence, the court then has to proceed, in the case of a prison sentence, to estimate the length of custody required to protect the public, to elicit the maximum response towards social rehabilitation from the offender, and to serve the necessary punitive purpose. In the event of the court making a probation order or order of conditional discharge, the court reserves to itself the power to intervene in certain circumstances during the time the order is in operation. In the event of a sentence of imprisonment being suspended, the court reserves the power to activate the sentence if the person sentenced offends again during the operative period of the suspension. Apart from those instances, the court exercises no control or oversight over the execution of its sentences, and in no circumstances is the court concerned with the regime under which a sentence is served. Yet it is by the control and oversight and the day-to-day regime that the correctness and efficacy of the sentence are proved or falsified.

To these two disadvantages, inherent in present practice, the critics add a third. The court is not equipped intellectually to perform the sentencing process, in that the process demands specialist knowledge and training in disciplines outside the law and calls for a close knowledge of the regimes under which sentences are served. That the writer rejects this criticism, in so far as it relates to present times, will be read with no surprise. It is certainly necessary for the court to have a clear understanding of what is involved in serving a sentence or, for example, fulfilling the terms of a probation or supervision order. Imprisonment, Borstal training, detention centre orders, care orders—all these sanctions involve different regimes with which the judiciary needs to be familiar. Judges also need to be aware of administrative practices relating for example to release on licence. On the other hand, an efficient sentencing practice does not require the sentencer to be a doctor, psychologist, or criminologist. Ability to understand, to evaluate and, in the appropriate circumstances, to give effect to the evidence of such experts is what is required. The established training programme for new magistrates, the conferences arranged by the Magistrates' Association branches, and the seminars and conferences for Recorders and Judges, arranged under the direction of the Lord Chancellor and Lord Chief Justice, have ensured, and continue to ensure, that the sentencing process is in the hands of those qualified to carry it out.

Looking ahead then to the last quarter of this century, the writer concludes that there are good cogent reasons for leaving the courts as the sentencing authority. Such disadvantages as can be pointed to in the present practice do not seriously detract from the cogency of those reasons. But if the sentencing practice is to be that of the court, there are undoubtedly a number of changes that should be made.

The first suggestion is designed to provide for more efficacious sentencing. At present the sentencing process has to be applied in situations which are not appropriate to a criminal process, and for which the law makes no provision by way of appropriate sentences. The inadequate personality, who for his lifetime will need close community support and whose offences are no more than a nuisance to society, does not fit into a sentencing process designed for criminals. The addict to alcohol, for whom all known treatment has been tried and failed and whose offences are those of minor criminal damage committed when drunk or petty thefts to get drink, likewise is unfitted for criminal process. Other examples come readily to mind.

In seeking to provide for such cases the court cannot provide an effective remedy. The sentence of the court is bound to fail. What is needed is a step in the investigation of the offence to separate out those offenders who can safely be dealt with outside the criminal process. If offenders with 'social problems' whose offences are committed because they have those problems can be dealt with by non-penal treatment, then the practice of the court can be concentrated within its proper sphere, and operated without the pressures created by a mass of inappropriate material.

The present power to postpone sentence for the purpose of further inquiries being undertaken or information obtained could usefully be replaced, in the case of both offenders under twenty-one years of age and first offenders over that age, by a mandatory requirement that sentence be postponed for a period not exceeding six weeks to enable a comprehensive report to be presented to the court. Whether the convicted person should be remanded in custody or on bail would be decided according to the particular circumstances of the case. During the remand period the convicted person would be under the obligation to submit himself to examination of his physical and mental health, intellectual level, education, record of employment, and his family and social relationships. As soon as the comprehensive report of such examination is ready, the case would be relisted for hearing, although the full period of remand may not have expired. By this postponement the court will have not only the advantage of a full and detailed report but also one which is based upon a post-conviction situation. By section 22 of the Criminal Justice Act 1972 a court may defer passing sentence. This new provision recognizes that there may be a change of circumstances after conviction which could influence the sentence. It provides for a departure from the practice of proceeding to sentence immediately upon, or shortly after conviction. The suggestion is an extension of that departure, in that it is designed to cater not only for post-conviction changes but also for the provision of full information as to circumstances before and after conviction.

Thirdly, it is suggested, that, while the court should retain the decision as to the sentence, a greater measure of freedom ought to be given to those whose duty it is to supervise the performance of the sentence. This freedom would be exercised within the framework of the sentence, and would be related to the regime imposed upon the person sentenced. In its application the measure would have its greatest importance in respect of juvenile offenders, whose attitudes are less likely to be fixed and who are more likely to be persuaded by education and advice. There is no reason, however, why the device of postponing sentence should not be applied to adults, though the application is likely to be less frequent. It is the persons who have the day-to-day supervision and training of those serving custodial sentences that are best able to judge the response to, and progress under the sentence. These are the best judges of when a person in custody is best fitted for, at least, a trial period in non-custodial conditions, though the term of the custodial sentence may not have run its course. This is a matter upon which the court cannot judge. The working of the parole system is to a degree an example (operating in the restricted field of imprisonment for at least eighteen months), of the variation of the regime by the Executive authority.

But the effect of, and the response to, the sentence are not the only relevant considerations. To give to the Executive unrestricted power to vary the regime, under a custodial sentence, from a custodial to a non-custodial setting would undermine the very reasons for which the court is the sentencing authority. The court should retain the right to prescribe that part of a custodial sentence which the offender *must* serve in custodial conditions. The court cannot properly divest itself of its constitutional duty to protect the interest of the public. It must retain the right to pronounce a sentence in the form of 'X years' imprisonment, of which at least Y months shall be served in prison'. In turn there should be a limit to the minimum custodial period which the court has power to prescribe. It is suggested that one-third of the sentence should be the most which the court should prescribe as the minimum period which must be served.

Any sentencing process, which permits a person subject to a custodial sentence to be released on licence into the community by Executive action, must make provision for the recall of such a person into custody in the event of a breach of the terms of the licence, or, in the event of it being expedient that he should be recalled. Again the working of the parole system affords an illustration of this. In relation to this aspect the function of the court would be to adjudicate upon any application made for the recall to custody of a person on licence and, in circumstances in which a person has been taken back into custody without an order of the court, to adjudicate upon any complaint by such person against his recall. In circumstances in which a person is recalled after being on licence for three months or more, it would be the duty of those effecting the recall to inform the court of the fact of recall, and to make application to the court for an order confirming recall.

Any changes giving effect to these suggestions would involve much detail in procedure, inappropriate for discussion here. The essential purpose of the proposals are: (i) to place in the hands of the social services the cases which are essentially social problems and not properly matters for sentence in the criminal courts; (ii) to ensure that sentence is passed after mature consideration of the fullest information obtainable; (iii) to secure that the sentence is decided by an independent judiciary, that it is pronounced publicly, and that responsibility for the decision is placed firmly on the judiciary; and (iv) at the same time to secure that there is a flexibility in the working out of the sentence which makes provision for changes of attitude, changes of circumstances and, where it is shown to be necessary in the light of after events, the correction of error in the choice or length of sentence.

13. Sentencing Structure: a Paradigm for the Future

LOUIS BLOM-COOPER

THE courts are first and foremost the protectors of individual liberty against Executive action. Inherent in the system of criminal justice is the notion that trial judges (subject to supervision on appeal) ensure that due process of law is observed, and that no one shall be deprived of his liberty unless properly convicted of an imprisonable offence, and then only to the extent appropriate to the offence and to the offender.[1]

The other, equally important, role of courts is to seek to protect the public from those offenders who are a danger to society.[2] (I do not pause to consider what might be defined as 'dangerousness', although it is worth observing that some offenders are not as dangerous as they are made out to be: dangerousness may be a label or a self-fulfilling prophecy.) This is, or should be, achieved primarily by the prosecution of offenders to conviction which provides the justification for some form of social intervention. Protection of the public, through the effect of penal sanctions, is ancillary to the primary right of intervention by the fact of conviction.

The court of trial is not in any position appropriately, and certainly not accurately, to protect society by determining how long the offender should stay in prison, for the main reason that the court cannot project itself into the future and predict the offender's behaviour with anything but crude guesswork. The court can protect society by decreeing that the offender should be put away at the moment of passing sentence. Any sentence of imprisonment of any duration beyond the day of sentence may deprive the offender of his liberty

[1] *Elko* v. *Government of Nigeria* [1931] A.C. 662, 670 and *R.* v. *Governor of Brixton Prison, Ex parte Ahsan* [1969] 2 Q.B. 222, 232. They cannot, and do not grant writs of habeas corpus as a means of appeal against conviction or sentence by a court of competent jurisdiction, but the High Court would grant habeas corpus if it were satisfied that the prisoner was being held by the Executive after the term of sentence passed on him had expired: Re *Wring* [1966] 1 W.L.R. 138.

[2] *Practive Direction* (*Corrective Training: Protective Detention*) [1962] 1 W.L.R. 402, 403.

for a period of time either extending beyond the limits required to maintain public protection, or to reflect the criteria of punishment. The instant decision of the court can take account neither of the offender's instant reaction to the conviction, nor of his subsequent behaviour, nor of any subsequent behaviour in conditions of captivity. Nor, more significantly for society's protection, can the court predict the offender's behaviour when he is released, either on licence or under supervision; and even less when release is unconditional.

The court can, at best, only guess as to the offender's behaviour either in custody or at liberty. It can thus properly make a 'once and for all' decision at the moment of sentencing only on the basis of the offender's criminal responsibility for the offence of which he has been convicted, and make some general assumptions about his future criminal propensities with reference to his previous criminal record and to his social and medical history. Upon those assumptions the court might make a prognosis of future conduct.

Indeed the courts have stated that it is even wrong in principle that the length of a sentence should be determined by what the court would do if the offender were to re-offend.[3] If a sentence is intended to be remedial (and there is a large question mark over the concept of a remedial sentence) a court cannot, with any degree of confidence, make a decision about either the offender's treatment needs, or, more particularly, his response to differential treatments. An individual's needs and circumstances change; any meaningful treatment programme must constantly be modified in the light of changing circumstances. This poses the crucial question whether the courts should ever make a single binding decision determining differential treatment, subject only to minor modification subsequent to sentence; or whether day-to-day treatment decisions should be made by those responsible for administering the treatment.

LIMITS OF PUNISHMENT

The conclusion to which I have come is that any sentencing structure within which the courts should operate should be vitally concerned to build in safeguards against Executive interference with individual liberty rather than with ensuring precise, or even imprecise periods of custody for the offender, determined by the court of trial once and for all immediately after conviction. Courts should assign

[3] *R.* v. *Lycett* [1968] 1 W.L.R. 1245, 1246.

priority to considerations of justice rather than to questions of the offender's treatment.[4] It is grotesque to pretend that criminal courts in the sentencing process are protectors of individual liberty, particularly when they reject a non-custodial disposal and impose a sentence of imprisonment. Then they are depriving the offender of individual liberty in the cause of social order.

The courts may mitigate the degree of interference with liberty only by imposing sentences of a duration shorter than would ordinarily be passed according to the tariff principle. Sustained protection of the public, moreover, lasts only so long as the offender is incarcerated. To the extent that the offender loses his liberty, the courts have put a temporary stop to the offender's criminal proclivities. One of the methods used to prevent an offender from repeating his crime is incapacitation. In the past this took the form of cutting off his hand (if he was a thief), or of tearing out his tongue (if he was a blasphemer). Its present form is restricted to temporary loss of liberty. Incapacitation cannot be permanent unless the prisoner is incarcerated for the rest of his natural life. Our sense of justice demands that prisoners, with the few exceptions of those who die in prison, should return to society—and sooner rather than later.

The courts, moreover, pursue a chimera in attempting to equate degrees of criminal responsibility with periods of time during which the convicted offender must be deprived of his liberty. What the court can attempt is some measurement of harmful conduct which justifies social intervention. But the different forms of social intervention employed in a coherent treatment programme can be measured only by those who manage the programme. The tariff by which courts currently sentence offenders is little more than a crude gauge of punishment for offences scaled according to moral values attached to particular crimes. Courts do not pass a custodial sentence in preference to a non-custodial one because of a belief in the peculiar efficacy of institutional regimes to change the offender's social behaviour. The main reason for selecting custody is to remove the risk of repetition of the crime in the immediate future; a desire to discourage others who might emulate the offender; or even to assuage public attitudes towards crime. The sentencers may of course hope that the regime of the institution will help to alter the offender's behaviour while in detention and on his return to the community.

4 See Bishop, 'Some Aspects of European Penal Systems', p. 99–100, *supra,* who argues that the same priority is being demanded of penal authorities by prisoners.

But such treatment considerations are secondary. Reform is incidental to, and not the objective of punishment. The fact that custodial sentences are awarded for purposes unconnected with treatment, therefore, should be taken to its logical conclusion, that considerations of treatment have no part at all to play in the sentencing process.

Once the courts stick to their exclusive role of sentencing according to punishment criteria and eschew any desire to determine the nature and degree of social intervention on the offender, they maintain their constitutional position as law enforcers rather than of upholders of public order. 'Law and Order' is a politically modish phrase which is an unfortunate collocation of words containing two quite distinct and separate notions. The courts are responsible for declaring what the law is: the Executive for the maintenance of order. Order may (and one hopes does) spring from law. But to couple the two together so as to suggest that they are the province of a single agency, be it court or Executive, is to give a totally misleading picture. The two perform complementary and constitutionally distinct functions.

The court's true function of sentencing should be to determine whether the offender's social history and delinquent behaviour warrants social intervention. It is the distinction between social intervention and non-intervention (whether the offender should be sent home, or whether the services or control of the penal system should be applied) rather than between custody and non-custody that is crucial at the sentencing stage. Social intervention in this context includes supportive treatment from the corrective services of either or both a custodial or non-custodial nature. Social intervention also involves deprivation of liberty and/or leisure. Once a court determines that a fine, discharge, or deferred sentence is inappropriate—these disposals being non-custodial and involving no interference with leisure—a single sentence of supervision and control should be the only remaining appropriate sanction.

Sentencing is the most delicate, difficult and distasteful task for a judge. It is not made any easier by the fact that the two functions of punishment and treatment are at present conferred primarily on the single agency—the court—incapable by definition of performing the latter role. The most glaring defect in the present system of sentencing is the blurring of treatment decisions with decisions designed to reflect requisite degrees of punishment—what may be described as the osmotic effect of the current sentencing policy of the courts, in which punitive reactions are intermixed with a vague belief that treatment is available in prisons, and a hope that the offender will actually receive it. If it were the proper function of the court to ensure treatment, there would need to be some system whereby the court's expectations were checked.

LIMITS OF TREATMENT

Coercive measures (as all forms of social intervention are in varying degrees) do not lose their character merely by our calling them treatment. Indeterminacy of sentence is objectionable because release is dependent upon the efficacy of the treatment as determined by the 'treaters'. Even if we knew (which we do not) what treatment worked with what kind of offender, indeterminancy would still place a high degree of arbitrary action in the hands of persons not readily subject to judicial control. Put rather graphically and dramatically, indeterminacy would put offenders under the control of smooth men in white coats whose business it would be (like the 'Straighteners' in *Erewhon*) to adjust them to the desired degree of conformity. This is also an argument against the establishment of any sentencing authority to replace the judiciary. (There are, additionally, severe practical problems about setting up sentencing panels.)

Every offender, whom the court determines should be subjected to a period of custodial treatment, has sooner or later to take his place back in the community. Every penal action, therefore, should be relevant to the offender learning to live at liberty without re-offending. The emphasis of social intervention should be on treatment within the community with short-term custody or longer-term institutional training available only as constructive aids to such treatment.

If it is objected that, on questions of treatment, no better results can be expected from decisions taken by an executive authority than from sentencing by the judiciary, the answer is that at least these decisions will be made by people with some of the necessary resources at their disposal. Such a process would at least be 'on-going' instead of being 'one-off'. The judiciary, can never, by definition, either provide, or be provided with an equivalent expertise. However much the process of assessment and prediction can be refined through more and more elaborate social inquiry reports, there will always remain the inherent obstacle that a court of trial will not be able to judge the effects of the post-conviction period on the offender's behaviour. There is under the present system in any event very little feedback to sentencers of the effect of their sentences, although in 1961 the Streatfeild Committee on the Business of the Criminal Courts strongly advocated liaison between the Prison Service and the judiciary.

With these guiding principles in mind, it is possible to outline the specific proposals for a sentencing structure which transfers decisions of treatment from the courts to persons who can make those decisions in the light of a continuing assessment of the offender and his response to treatment. What is proposed is in no way intended to take away from the courts their exclusive power of sentencing offenders: what is sought is a sentencing structure to ensure that the exercise of that power does not impinge upon, let alone determine the appropriate treatment of offenders.

Professor Rupert Cross in the twenty-third series of the Hamlyn lecture stated: 'I attach great importance to the preservation, under our system, of the courts' power to fix the maximum of a man's sentence . . . To give the Executive power to modify a sentence . . . is another matter; it promotes the liberty of the subject instead of curtailing it.'[5] Curtailment of liberty may be the necessary concomitant of a criminal conviction. Any anticipation of the prescribed date of release, on the other hand, is properly the province of the Executive.

Some people object that any unlimited Executive discretion to release might mean that offenders remain inside a penal institution for longer than is warranted in terms of their criminal responsibility. That objection certainly influenced judicial attitudes to the philosophy of Borstal training in the inter-war years, when it was preached that the only objective was reform, which required a period of detention longer than the courts might be prepared to countenance were they to apply the normal tariff of imprisonment. That this is a real danger cannot be doubted. A sentencing device needs to be built in so as to control the amount of time an offender can be made actually to stay in custody, as is done at present. This can be done primarily by the simple technique of requiring the court to stipulate the maximum period of any offender's time spent in prison.

The contrary objection that the Executive might release offenders too soon either for judicial liking or for public comfort is less rational. Experience of the release of 'lifers', before parole came into the penal picture, leads one to think that, if anything, administrators are too cautious, and that few, if any, 'lifers' were released prematurely.

[5] *Punishment, Prison and the Public* (1971), p. 92.

Administrators, no less than judges, will make mistakes; but it is inherent in any system that has a deep concern for individual liberty that risks must be taken, and that occasionally even the risks will prove to have been wrongly calculated. But at least they will be based on all the relevant evidence available, at the moment before discharge. Courts, fixing in advance a precise date of release, can hope to do the job at best only on the basis of an uninformed hunch.

The ideal sentencing structure then must be one in which the court provides an exclusive sentence of social supervision and control. The court would then be free to make either a custodial supervision-and-control order, or such an order with no custodial component. In the former case the court would prescribe the maximum time for which the offender could be kept in prison. If the court adopts the latter course, then the Executive authority can decide what kind of non-custodial treatment to apply—hostel, probation, community service, day-training centre, etc. If the order contains a custodial element, the authority would still primarily treat the offender within the community in such a manner as it thought fit, subject to its power to execute the whole or part of the prescribed custodial period at any stage during the currency of the order.

CONCLUSION

Criminals, not unexpectedly and with some justification, are fed up with the courts. Much of the simmering discontent within penal establishments stems from the sense of injustice perpetrated by a legal process that has shown itself increasingly punitive in its reaction to crime. Criminologists, too, are becoming exasperated by what appears to be the courts' singular unawareness of the fact that they are very largely responsible for the soaring inflation in the prison population, and have so far shown little inclination dramatically to reverse the upward trend of increasing numbers of offenders sent to prison.

Proposals for substituting sentencing panels have been aired from time to time, but only half-heartedly. There is, rightly, no great enthusiasm for substituting so-called experts for the judiciary, who, however inexpert by comparison, do at least perform their work in public, subject to the appellate process and to press scrutiny. Opposition to executive decisions about the release of offenders stems from those unfamiliar with the penal system. Experience on the Parole Board has shown the responsible attitude of those exercising release powers. The Parole Board in fact provides uniquely a useful pointer, by injecting a strong judicial component into its membership, and has thereby evoked a confidence that augurs well for extending the procedure.

If we are driven to the conclusion that treatment decisions (including how much of a custodial sentence should actually be served) should be made by penal administrators, it is imperative that any such decisions should be subjected to independent review along the lines of the Parliamentary Commissioner for Administration before some independent but publicly accountable body. We must not throw the baby out with the bath water. Instead of jettisoning the judicial process of sentencing, as having failed to achieve a rational penal policy, we should inject a strong judicial element into penal administration. Just as the experts (through social inquiry and medical reports) have increasingly been used to guide and advise the judiciary in the recent past, so now the experts in the penal system need to be guided and advised by the judiciary. Both are needed to ensure a system in which the need for treatment (primarily within the community) is tempered by the dictates of justice.

14. General Deterrence

SIR BRIAN MacKENNA

SENTENCERS do not waste their time if they occasionally consider the proper aims of punishment. The aims, if any, which they are consciously pursuing may affect the sentences they pass, and if they do, these aims will have a practical importance. If the sentencer believes, as some appear to do, that punishment for crime is its own justification, whatever its effects, he may give one kind of sentence. He might possibly give another if he believed that punishment was justified only by its good effects, and that the right punishment was the one most likely to produce them. Though sentencing is a 'hit and miss' affair, it would be strange if the choice of target were completely irrelevant.

Without more ado I shall describe my own idea of a defensible sentencing policy. It has the single aim, broadly stated, of preventing crime—'reductivism'—to use Professor Nigel Walker's word.[1] Other things being equal, the right sentence is the one most likely to prevent or reduce crime. The other things to be considered are:

(i) The expense to the State, direct and indirect, of carrying out the sentence, and

(ii) the suffering and deprivations of the man who must endure it, which ought not to be excessive.

The sentence should not be greater than the offence deserves. It is no objection to this limitation, as I see it, that it accepts in part the retributive idea of a just sentence for an offence, 'no more and no less'. It is only the 'no less' that is repellent in that idea. I would admit as apparent exceptions to the limitation those cases where the offender's previous record, taken with his current offence, proves him to be a person particularly likely to offend again.

Though heavy sentences may conceivably be more effective in reducing crime than lighter ones, the marginal reduction may not be worth the extra costs, whether these are payable by the State, the offender, or others. A sentence which is heavier than it needs or ought to be for the reduction of crime, is, to that extent, a bad one.

[1] *Sentencing in a Rational Society* (1972) p. 3.

My single aim excludes others, such as 'retribution', 'expiation', 'atonement', *et hoc genus omne*. These may be the effects of a sentence chosen for the purpose of reducing crime, and if they are pleasing to the sentencer or others who believe them to be desirable, so much the better, but I would not allow the sentencer to pass a sentence, in order to achieve these effects, different from what he thinks necessary for the reduction of crime.[2]

A sentence can reduce crime either by its good effects on the offender or on others.

First as to its effects on the offender.

(i) He may be reformed by the treatment he receives while undergoing his sentence.

(ii) He may be deterred from committing other offences by fear of suffering the same or some worse punishment if he offends again, which is individual deterrence.

(iii) If he receives a prison sentence, he will, during the period of his detention, be incapacitated from committing such crimes as can be committed only by men at liberty.

These are permissible objects in choosing the right sentence for the offender.

Where reform is the sentencer's object, it will usually lead him to choose a sentence of probation. Because of the likelihood of corruption in prison, a rational sentencer will seldom send a man there with the object of reforming him, though there are some cases where he may sensibly do so. There is the mentally disturbed offender who may be a suitable candidate for the psychiatric prison at Grendon. There is the drug-taker or the alcoholic whose chance of rehabilitation may be better in prison than elsewhere, but as these men will not be effectively treated until they wish to be cured,[3] and as there is no reason for thinking that a prison sentence induces that state of mind, this is an unimportant exception to the general rule that prison is not a place where men are likely to be reformed. Where there is a chance of reformation, the nature of the treatment can be allowed to fix the

---

[2] Again it is all to the good if the sentence has the effect of protecting the offender against reprisals by those whom he has injured or by the public generally, and if those reprisals would themselves be criminal, it could even be argued that the heavier sentence, which makes them unnecessary, has in this way the effect of reducing crime and is justified. But the question hardly arises in England.

[3] The point is reinforced by Dr. Prewer in his essay, 'The Contribution of Prison Medicine', Chapter 8 above.

length of the sentence, which may be longer than would otherwise be the case, provided there is no serious disproportion between the sentence on the one hand and the offence taken with the offender's record on the other.

As to individual deterrence, it is reasonable to suppose that probation orders, fines, and orders of community service have less effect than prison sentences. So, after these lesser punishments have been tried without success, it may be sensible to choose imprisonment as the last alternative. It will teach the offender that the law has this sharper weapon to use against him. It will bring home to him the difference between life in prison and life outside which he may not have sufficiently imagined. A short sentence will be better for this purpose than a long one. The sense of deprivation, keenest in the first days of imprisonment, may grow duller in time. The prisoner may get used to prison conditions if he stays there long enough, and in any case the longer the sentence the greater the risk of corruption, or of the prisoner being alienated from society. (I once asked a Deputy-Governor what was the ideal length of a first prison sentence. He said twenty-four hours.)

There are in theory two reasons for giving a recidivist longer sentences each time that he offends. One is that he may be more effectively deterred: if twelve months was not enough last time, two years may do the trick this time, and so on. To my mind this is not a very sensible reason. The recidivist is probably immune from the deterrent effects of punishment, even on an increasing scale, either because at the moment of committing the offence he does not think far enough ahead, or because he believes too optimistically that he will escape detection or conviction, or because prison has no fears for him, or because there is in his case no practical alternative to a criminal way of life. The other, and the better, reason for imprisoning such a man is to keep him out of harm's way. By his continued offences he has proved himself to be a danger to the community, perhaps an intolerable one.

So much for the effects of the sentence on the individual offender.

The sentence that the offender receives may put others in fear of similar punishment if they offend, and this fear may be effective to deter them. The sentence may benefit them in other ways than by instilling fear. It may teach them a moral lesson. They know that they ought not to do deeds disapproved of by society. Society, in the person of the sentencer, has shown by its sentence that it disapproves of the offender's conduct, and if the sentence is a severe one, that it strongly disapproves. Thus the sentence teaches them that they ought not to do such deeds. These good effects of the offender's punishment on others, whether arising from fear or more exalted feelings, are described as general deterrence, and are the subject of this paper.

The distinction between general and individual deterrence is in some ways artificial. Every sentence that deters the individual offender will have some deterrent effect on those who hear of it and are sensitive to its deterrent purpose. Every extra punishment given to the individual to increase its deterrent effect on others may increase that effect on him, if it does not make him more hostile to authority or habituate him to prison.

The sentencer who considers what sentence is required to prevent the individual offender from offending again, and passes it, has not been influenced by the object of general deterrence. He would have been only if he had passed a heavier sentence than that required by the needs of the offender and had done so because he thought it was necessary to deter others.

A great many sentences are passed with this object of general deterrence. Where a sentencer gives a long sentence for a serious offence to an offender whose record does not show him to be a likely recidivist, his object, if not retribution, must be general deterrence. So far as our sentencing tariff has been settled on considerations of deterrence and not of retribution, sentences passed in accordance with it are determined by this object.

To give an offender this extra punishment (i.e. a punishment more than his own needs call for) is, I believe, morally justifiable, but only subject to conditions of which there are at least two:

(i) There should be a reasonable prospect of crime being reduced proportionately to the costs of the extra punishment which are payable, as I have pointed out, not only by the man enduring the punishment but also by the State which incurs the expense of housing, guarding and maintaining him and in many cases of supporting his family.

(ii) The total punishment should not be disproportionate to the offence.

The amount of extra punishment given by the courts at present for the sake of general deterrence must in total be very large indeed.

Some idea of its dimension can be got by considering the sentences passed by the higher courts. A table in McClintock and Avison's *Crime in England and Wales* gives the number of sentences passed by these courts in 1965 under five headings, up to one year, over one year and up to three years, and so on.[4] I estimate that the longer sentences, those of over one year, account for some 16,000 man-years compared with 4,500 for the shorter ones, of under one year. If all the long sentences had been of under one year the total man-years of all sentences passed in 1965 would have been less than 10,000 instead of the actual figure of over 20,000.[5] A substantial part of the difference is attributable to general deterrence.[6]

In the table on which I have based my calculations McClintock and Avison compare the figures for 1965 with the figures for 1955 which are in some respects lower, and make this comment:

It is, however, the gradual increase in the number of very long-term sentences—possibly relating to the curtailment of capital punishment and probably a reaction of the courts to the increase in serious crime—which is building up a significant problem for the prisons in terms of security, in terms of prison morale, and in terms of effective prevention of recidivism.

Should this extra punishment for general deterrence be increased, so that the crime rate may conceivably be lowered, or should it be reduced on the ground that less cost would be incurred at the lower level and that the crime rate might not be worsened?

[4] Table 9.3 at p. 259.
[5] These are my calculations. The Table gives the following figures of sentences:

Up to 1 year . .	6,030
Over 1 year and up to 3	5,420
Over 3 years and up to 5	682
Over 5 years and up to 10	205
10 years and over .	99

I have assumed average lengths of sentences of 9 months, 2 years, 4 years, 7 years, and 12 years in each of the 5 classes respectively. On these assumptions the figure of man-years for the longer sentences is 16,121 and for the shorter ones 4,522. The number of longer sentences is 6,406 and if these offenders had been given 9 months each the figure of man-years for them would have been 4,800. This added to 4,522 gives a total of 9,326.

[6] Professor Andenaes in his paper 'General Deterrence—Illusion or Reality', 43 *Journal of Criminal Law and Criminology*, 176, quotes a Danish physician, Tage Kemp: 'I shudder when I think what this essentially fictitious concept has cost us in terms of thousands of wasted man-years of imprisonment and how many lives have been ruined which could just as well have been saved.' The concept may not be so fictitious as he thought, but his idea that the cost is high is surely right.

To help in answering this question there is plenty of theorizing, much of it by the sentencers themselves, but little real evidence.

The extreme views on either side are neatly stated in this passage from a new American book on deterrence, the best thing written on the subject in our language.[7]

If penalties have a deterrent effect in one situation, they will have a deterrent effect in all; if some people are deterred by threats, then all will be deterred; if doubling a penalty produces an extra measure of deterrence, then trebling the penalty will do still better. Carried to what may be an unfair extreme, this style of thinking imagines a world in which armed robbery is in the same category as illegal parking, burglars think like district attorneys, and the threat of punishment will result in an orderly process of elimination in which the crime rate will diminish as the penalty scale increases by degrees from small fines to capital punishment, with each step upwards on its predecessor. Other officials, however—frequently those engaged in correctional work, the discouraging end of deterrence—will sometimes take a different but equally unitary view. Since human behaviour is unpredictable and crime is determined by a variety of causes, deterrence is a myth.[8]

The first of these opinions is held by many of our sentencers, as appears from the homilies which they address to the prisoners when passing sentence. 'There is far too much of this kind of thing going on and the courts are determined to put an end to it.'[9] I have noted one particular instance in 1961. The Chairman of Nottingham Quarter Sessions was about to pass sentences of eight years and under on four young burglars. After expressing the court's disquiet at the number of serious offences committed by the accused, he said:

... I do not hesitate to say that if the severe sentences which we are about to pass in this case do not have the effect of checking this kind of conduct, we shall not hesitate to pass even more severe sentences. That this kind of thing can be allowed to continue in a civilized community is simply intolerable.

The Court of Criminal Appeal approved these sentiments of the Chairman:

There is no doubt that an orgy of crime of this sort such as he described does indeed call for severe punishment, and if the Court of Quarter

---

[7] Zimring and Hawkins, *Deterrence, The Legal Threat in Crime Control* (University of Chicago Press, 1973).

[8] Ibid., pp. 19–20.

[9] I remember a writer in *Punch* many years ago quoting one of these homilies and asking what the judge thought would have been 'the right amount' of this kind of thing. The question was not unanswerable: the amount not reducible in present circumstances by any sentence that could reasonably be given.

Sessions finds itself compelled to deal with an outbreak of crime on this scale, then in order to punish the criminals and to deter others from following their example, it is of course essential that punishment should be severe. We endorse wholeheartedly the principles expressed by the learned Chairman.[10]

I sympathize with the Chairman's attitude. The rise in crime is a terrifying thing, and no judge likes to think that he is powerless to check it. The law has given him almost unlimited powers of sentencing. He can exercise these powers and hope for the best. Even if the rise in crime continues, it might, he thinks, have been even worse if he had not passed his heavy sentence. There is, at least, no proof that this would not have been so. I sympathize, though I do not approve. I see the problem in this way. The Chairman's threatened audience included some who would never burgle, even if they were sure of going unpunished. It included others who would burgle, whatever punishment was threatened, even if it were death. There was a third class of potential burglars susceptible to threats of punishment. It was this class that mattered. Did it include any man who would not have been deterred by a lesser sentence than one of eight years—say by one of five—but would have been deterred by eight? Did it include any man who would not have been deterred by eight, but would have been by a still higher sentence—say by one of ten? If, as I suspect, it did not, nothing was gained in the way of deterrence by raising the level of punishment. Even if some would have been deterred by the heavier punishment who were not deterred by the lighter, the question would still remain whether their obedience had not been purchased at too high a price.[11]

Do these exceptionally heavy sentences serve any useful purpose?[12] May there not be reason to suspect (as I do) that even the range of our normal sentences is unnecessarily high? Have we not experimented often enough by increasing our sentences? May there not be

[10] *R.* v. *Dunn and others*, Nos. 50, 51, 70, and 93/1961, per Ashworth J. The court reduced the sentences because the offenders were young men with comparatively good records. If such long sentences would have been appropriate for them, the right sentence for an old lag would have been impossibly high.

[11] 'He who invests in increased severity, has to expect diminishing returns', Andenaes, 'Deterrence and Specific Offences', *University of Chicago Law Review*, 38 (1971), 553.

[12] A number of them have been passed from time to time. If they had been effective, our books should be full of instances of their being followed by a reduction in crime, even if only a temporary one. But there are very few such instances. The Liverpool garrotters and the Notting Hill rioters do service suspiciously often to justify the heavy sentencer, and even these instances have been questioned.

a case (as I believe there is) for experimenting in the other direction, by moderately lowering the high level of punishment for serious crime?

In our present state of knowledge these are difficult questions to answer. Criminologists confess that we are inexcusably ignorant. Professor Andenaes ends his paper on the Morality of Deterrence with this passage:

One conclusion ought to be beyond controversy. As long as society feels obliged to use punishment for general preventive reasons, it is important for researchers to attempt to evaluate the accuracy of the assumption that law-makers, courts and law-enforcement agencies make about general prevention. This is a badly neglected field of research. It may be necessary and ethically justifiable to base policy decisions on commonsense reasoning, as long as no other alternative exists. But it is morally indefensible to continue to punish other human beings without making real efforts to replace speculation with scientific fact.[13]

Professor Norval Morris had made the same plea some years before in his inaugural lecture as Professor of Law and Criminology in the University of Chicago:

When I listen to the dialogue between the punishers and the treaters, I hear the punishers making propositions based on the assumption that our penal sanctions deter others who are like-minded from committing crime. And I hear the treaters making propositions concerning the best treatment for a given offender or class of offenders which are based on the assumption that our penal sanctions do not at all deter. There is rarely any meeting of the minds on the issue central to the discourse. And it is not as if such knowledge is unobtainable; it has merely not been sought with anything like the energy and dedication that has been given to the expensively outfitted and numerous safaris that have searched for the source of criminality. The polar argument becomes a bore; a modest beginning on the search for more knowledge becomes a compelling need. We have endured a surfeit of unsubstantiated speculation, continuing quite literally since man first laboriously chipped out his penal codes on tablets of stone, or scrawled them on chewed and pounded bark.[14]

There has been a great deal of 'commonsense' theorizing, going back to Bentham and perhaps beyond, but so far as I have been able to discover in a few days' reading at the Cambridge Institute of Criminology not much in the way of practical studies. I shall summarize what I have read. I offer these fruits of my reading for

[13] 31 *University of Chicago Law Review* (1970), 664.
[14] 'Impediments to Penal Reform', 33 *University of Chicago Law Review* (1966), 631–2.

two purposes, to persuade sentencers that an experiment of lower sentences would not be obviously foolish and (by the very meagreness of the fruits) to encourage criminologists to do more by way of research.

ENGLAND

There is some material in the Introduction to the 1928 Criminal Statistics of England and Wales where the writer compares our sentences and our crime rates in 1911 and 1928, showing that the crime rate had fallen in this period though the sentences had become less severe. He ends with these words:

> If one summarizing conclusion had to be hazarded, perhaps it would be that the community's efforts to deal with offenders leniently and yet with discrimination, with various enactments and practices which were devised by that older generation, have succeeded with that generation for, among that generation, serious crime and petty offences alike have, in general, decreased but that whether the same methods hold good, or will continue to be good, with the new generation is another matter.[15]

More recently there is the material supplied to the Royal Commission on Capital Punishment 1949–53, published in its Report[16] and discussed by Professor Nigel Walker in *Crime and Punishment in Britain*.[17] I quote a passage from the Report itself:

> It would no doubt be equally difficult to find statistical evidence of any direct relationship between the severity of any other punishment [than capital] and the rise or fall of the crime to which it relates. Too many other factors come into the question. All we can say is that the deterrent value of punishment in general is liable to be exaggerated, and the effect of capital punishment specially so because of its drastic and sensational character.[18]

In the 1960s Mr. Willcock asked a large number of youths 'what thing would worry them most about being found out by the police'. Only 10 per cent put punishment first.[19]

In the connected field of individual deterrence there are Dr. Hammond's studies showing that fines are more effective than prison with first offenders, though not with others.[20]

---

[15] *Criminal Statistics, England and Wales 1928*, lxii.
[16] Cmnd. 8932 (1953).   [17] Second edition (1968), pp. 236–41.
[18] At p. 24, para. 67.
[19] Nigel Walker, *Sentencing in a Rational Society* (1972), pp. 63–8.
[20] Ibid., p. 94.

I did not find any study that compared the effects of long prison sentences for serious crimes and shorter sentences. There are, I do not doubt, some judges whose sentences are lighter than the average, and others whose sentences are heavier. If it were possible to compare the after-histories of the men receiving these sentences, and to do so on a scale that would eliminate chance differences, something might be learnt, and that learning might have its use even for general deterrence. Nor did I succeed in finding any comparison of the sentences given in England with those given in other countries. There are, I realize, difficulties of definition, and Englishmen of course are not exactly the same as other men, but after allowances have been made for these differences something might be gained from this comparison.[21] It could begin with Scotland and Ireland and might after a time venture beyond Calais. I have myself, with the help of a dictionary, glanced at the 1969 statistics for Holland, choosing rape as an example, where the difference (if any) of definition was not likely to be serious. The figures seemed to show that the Dutch punishments are much lighter than the English.[22] From an observation of Professor Andenaes I should infer that Scandinavian punishments too are lighter than ours. He said: 'A penalty of 3 years' imprisonment in Norway marks the crime as very grave, quite unlike the situation in the United States.'[23] McClintock and Avison's Table, to which I have already referred, shows that in 1955 44·3 per cent of the sentences passed by our higher courts were for over one year and up to three years, and that 11·9 per cent were for over three

[21] The Gowers Commission on Capital Punishment was, I think, unnecessarily discouraging: 'Any attempt to [draw valid comparisons between different countries in the matter of capital punishment] may always be misleading . . . owing to differences in the legal definition of crimes. . . . in the methods of compiling criminal statistics, in moral standards and customary behaviour, and in political social and economic conditions, it is extremely difficult to compare like with like, and little confidence can be felt in the soundness of the inferences drawn from such comparisons', at p. 22, para. 64.

[22] If I have understood the language correctly, the figures were classified under two headings, one where the offender had committed the crime once and the other where he had committed it more than once. Under the first heading 63 had been convicted and 56 imprisoned, of whom only 3 had received sentences of more than one year. Under the second heading 19 had been convicted, of whom only 5 had received sentences of more than one year. In England and Wales in 1963 (Cmnd. 2525, Tables III and V), 114 were convicted of this offence of whom 6 were sent to Borstal and 81 imprisoned. Of those imprisoned 72 received sentences of over one year's imprisonment and 37 sentences of over three years.

[23] 'The General Preventive Effects of Punishment', 114 (1966), *University of Pennsylvania Law Review*, 966.

years. The corresponding figures for 1965 were 43·6 per cent and 7·9 per cent.[24]

GERMANY

Rusche and Kircheimer compare the criminal statistics in three countries at different periods to see whether crime rates went up with leniency of sentencing or down with severity.[25] Dealing with some English figures they say: 'A comparison of the various figures leads to the conclusion that the lenient policy did not have a negative effect on criminality.'[26] They say the same about French experience: 'In conclusion, the French figures also provide no basis for assuming that the policy of punishment affects criminality.'[27] About the German figures they say that a careful study had 'conclusively proved that German penal policy has had no influence on the crime rate' either before or after the 1914 war.[28] They conclude generally:

Our investigation has thus substantiated on a still broader basis the conclusions that Ferri had reached at the end of the 19th Century on the basis of Italian experiences, that the policy of punishment and its variations have no effective influence on the rate of crime. Changes in penal praxis cannot seriously interfere with the operation of the social causes for delinquency.[29]

U.S.A.

In 1957 Professor Beutel compared the figures in two adjoining states for the offence of passing dud cheques. In one state (Nebraska) the maximum penalties were much higher than in the other (Colorado). 'All available figures', he wrote, 'tend to show that the differences in the cheque law do not affect the number of bad cheques in the two States. If anything there are fewer short-cheque losses in Colorado where the penalties are more lenient.'[30] But Zimring and Hawkins point out that the Nebraska law was rarely enforced.[31]

In 1966 the State of Pennsylvania greatly increased the maximum

---

[24] *Crime in England and Wales*, p. 259.
[25] *Punishment and Social Structure* (1939).
[26] Ibid., p. 197.   [27] Ibid., p. 200.   [28] Ibid., p. 200.
[29] Ibid., p. 204. This may be true for serious crime where the level of punishment is in any case fairly high. I doubt if it is true for offences against traffic regulations, including drunken driving. Punishment seems to have been effective in Scandinavia to stop drunken driving, and here in England the breathalyser making detection easier, and mandatory disqualification, have had a good effect.
[30] *Some Potentialities of Experimental Jurisprudence as a New Branch of Social Science* (1957), p. 355.   [31] Op. cit., p. 197.

penalties for rape and attempted rape. This was the consequence of a bad case of rape committed on 3 April 1966. After a few weeks of excited discussion, the new law was passed on 12 May 1966. A comparison was made of the number of offences committed in Philadelphia during the months of April to September 1965, with the number committed during the same months of 1966. There was no real difference: 292 offences in 1965, 280 in 1966. In an attempt to ascertain the immediate effects of the discussion which preceded the passing of the law and of its imposition, figures were taken for three periods in 1966, 1 March–3 April, 4 April–12 May, and 13 May–31 July. They were 22, 24, and 67 respectively. The writer stated his conclusion: 'We bring this investigation to a close by noting that Philadelphia found no relief from forcible and attempted rape either during the excitement leading up to the imposition of stronger penalties for this offence or after the imposition itself.'[32]

Zimring and Hawkins describe two similar American studies which I have not seen, one by Gibbs,[33] the other by Tittle.[34]

Gibbs's study deals with homicide and compares the crime figures for a number of states where the penalties differ. Tittle makes a similar comparison for homicide, rape, burglary, robbery, sex offences, and thefts of motor cars. When the comparison was made on a nationwide basis, without regard to regions, it appeared that the crime rate was lower in those states where the penalties were high. But when the states were grouped in regions, no substantial differences were found between the states with high penalties and those with low. Zimring and Hawkins make this comment:

Thus, regional differences in crime that are unrelated to severity of punishment appear to have been responsible for the nationwide correlation between punishment levels and crime. A more detailed statistical analysis of similar data is in progress and the preliminary findings suggest that greater sentence severity is associated with lower crime rates while not isolating as yet the question of general deterrence.[35]

The material I have examined, so far as it goes, does not tell against the experiment I would make of lowering the level of

[32] Schwartz, 'The Effect in Philadelphia of Pennsylvania's Increased Penalties for Rape and Attempted Rape', *Journal of Criminal Law, Criminology, and Police Science*, 59 (1968), 509–15.

[33] 'Crime, Punishment, and Deterrence', *South Western Social Science*, 48 (1968), 515.

[34] 'Crime Rates and Legal Sanctions', *Social Problems*, 16 (1969).

[35] Op. cit., pp. 219–20. A footnote on p. 220 refers to an unpublished work, Ehrlich, 'Participation in Illegitimate Activities').

penalties for some at least of the more serious offences, though I recognize that there are obstacles to the making of the experiment, which will not easily be overcome, particularly at the present time when recorded crime rates are rising.[36]

One obstacle is the belief, which dies hard, that the sentencer should have the retributive aim of punishing the offender, whatever may be the effects of the punishment. How is such a man to be persuaded to pass a lower sentence in the hope that that may be sufficient to deter, if he believes it is a good thing in itself to punish the offender and has an intuition that a heavier sentence is needed for this purpose? Perhaps our penal code, when it comes, will define the aims of criminal punishment and will exclude retribution once and for all.

Another obstacle is the belief that our sentences should be such as the public will approve, and that the public will not approve of shorter sentences. This argument would be a stronger one if retribution were the aim of punishment. The common man's intuition of the 'deserved' punishment is as good as mine, and may indeed be better. But if the aim of punishment is the reduction of crime there is no reason for preferring the common man's view to the judge's. I would add this word of caution. While the sentencer should lead and not follow, the changes he introduces should be moderate and not such as will shock public opinion.

A different argument brings in the public interest in another way. As I have pointed out earlier, one of the objects of punishment is to strengthen the public's moral inhibitions. Society, in the person of the sentencer, shows its disapproval of the crime by the sentence which it passes, and in this way teaches a moral lesson. If the punishment is reduced, may not the lesson lose its sharp point? I should hope not. If we keep the level high enough to frighten those who are open to deterrence, we should still be able to teach that moral lesson, which is the other object of general deterrence. It is desirable, for practical as well as moral reasons, that grave offences should be punished more severely than trivial ones, but this purpose can be served even if the general level of punishment is reduced. I cite Professor Andenaes yet again:

Punishment is an expression of society's disapproval of the act and the degree of disapproval is expressed by the magnitude of the punishment. A

[36] Since this paper was written figures have been published which show a fall in the rate during the first quarter of 1973.

serious crime must be answered with a severe punishment, a minor mis-
demeanour with a lenient reaction. But here it is rather a question of the
relative severity of the punishment than of its absolute magnitude. The
humanizing of penal law in the past generations has led to a marked
lowering of the general level of punishment. What was punishment for a
minor crime a century ago is today punishment for a major one. So long as
the development does not take place faster than the public has a chance to
adjust its ideas on appropriate punishment, it need have little effect on the
ability of punishment to express society's disapproval. It is the same as
with marks at school: the same marks can be expressed on a scale from
1 to 2 as on a scale from 1 to 6 or on one from 1 to 100.[37]

There is no country in which changes in the level of punishment
can be made more easily than in England, where the sentencer's
discretion in this matter is, except in the case of murder, unlimited.
In the background there is the Court of Appeal, whose power to
reduce sentences is also without limit.

I end with another quotation from Professor Norval Morris's
inaugural lecture, whose inspiring words, though addressed to an
American audience, have, I believe, a message for the English reader:

The diminution of gratuitous human suffering, gratuitous in the sense that
no social good whatsoever flows from it, that it in no wise diminishes the
incidence of crime and delinquency, remains an important purpose of
penal reform. One does not have to travel far from this place to find
thousands of convicted persons, adult and juvenile, subjected needlessly to
such suffering and for grossly protracted periods. Moreover, most of such
suffering is more than useless; it is harmful to us. It tends to increase the
social alienation of those we punish beyond our social needs, and it is
highly probable that we pay a penalty in increased recidivism and increased
severity of the crimes committed by those who do return from such
punishment to crime.[38]

[37] 'General Prevention—Illusion or Reality?', 43 *Journal of Criminal Law and
Criminology*, 192.
[38] *University of Chicago Law Review*, 33 (1966), 629.

15. Winners and Losers: a Perspective on Penal Change

JOHN P. CONRAD

As in most human endeavours, even in penology, there are moments of illumination which epitomize a problem and the frustrations attendant on its unsolved condition. Such a moment occurred for me some years ago at a meeting of an executive staff of which I was a member. The Director of Corrections, a forthright man who wished to be known for activism and stout commonsense, was presiding over a long-range-planning seminar. A plan, he explained, was to be directed at an objective. The objective of the Department of Corrections was to change criminals into people like us.

The crucial question, therefore, was: 'Why aren't they like us?' At first blush, the answer seemed to be contained in the contrast between us, these confident and successful men in a board room in the state capital, and those prisoners in chambray and denim in correctional facilities and camps scattered around the state. They weren't like us because they were in prison and we were not.

The Director had a longer answer, drawn from the well-kept statistics of our Research Division. Our prisoners weren't like us because their educational levels were far below the average for the communities in which they lived. They had no marketable skills. They were rejected by society because of their past behaviour. The rates of recidivism approached 50 per cent, no matter how we varied administrative and sentencing policies. Surely this record demonstrated that the solution lay in the community, not in the cell-blocks.

Analysis of experience pointed to the need for a new policy. We should reduce the length of stay in prison to the minimum that the law and the parole board would allow. We should create community correctional centres. We should reduce parole caseloads to enable the staff to do a realistic job of supervision. We should develop a work-release programme to put prisoners to work outside the walls.

Many good things followed the adoption of this policy, and some untoward events, too. Length of stay in prison was reduced; parole staff was increased and intensively trained. Community correctional centres proved to be more difficult to popularize, but determined negotiations resulted in the creation of several such establishments. The rates of recidivism have declined significantly. All this has resulted in empty prisons and the scrapping of a building programme which seemed destined to add a new fortress to the system every two or three years for the indefinite future.

The applause due such a record of success has been muted. The prisoners remaining in custody are reputed in the press to be an angry, mutinous lot, kept under the system's control by violent coercion. Tragic and spectacular events have shaken confidence in the system's administration despite all its solid accomplishments. Criticism persists vociferously from both ends of the political continuum, but the alternatives advocated by the extremists are unattractive. The public cannot be persuaded that the problems of the prisons will be solved by emptying them, as the radical left would like, or by imposing even more severely repressive regimes, as the radical right urges.

I am encapsulating the recent history of Californian penology. In the early years of my career in the California prisons, our system was renowned for an innovative and professionalized correctional programme. Over the recent past, our verifiable successes have been overshadowed by events of worldwide notoriety and a literature of denunciation. In this contribution, I shall consider the meaning of the Californian experience for the prospects of crime prevention and rehabilitation. I shall try to sort out the useful issues for policy-makers to settle by returning to the Director's question: 'Why aren't they like us?'

THE LOSERS

A plausible claim could be made that at last California has a penal programme which is effective and increasingly so. More felons are surviving on probation and parole. Fewer felons are committed to prison. The crime rate continues to rise for the total population, but the recidivism of felons does not. The system must be doing something right, a point which is insistently made by its administrators.

But in spite of an apparatus for criminal statistics which is without a rival for continuity and comprehensiveness (except, possibly, the Criminal Statistics for England and Wales), there are no data that

confirm that the system or its programmes have any influence of a
positive nature on the offenders in its charge.

It is possible that some inmates of the prisons have found the
experience so unpleasant that they are intimidated from the commission of further crimes. It is possible that some unemployable or
marginally employable inmates have acquired skills which have
fitted them for conventional economic survival. It is even possible
that counselling has sufficiently modified the attitudes of some
inmates to a degree that has enabled them to conform to the requirements of citizenship regardless of adversity. It is conceivable that the
influence of parole officers has made the necessary difference in
social adjustment for some offenders.

All these intended processes may be occurring, but there is no
research to support the belief that any of these scenarios of rehabilitation are taking place. What evidence we have that bears on any of
these expectations of the system suggests that they are not fulfilled.
The critical reviews of the evidence by Bailey[1] and Martinson[2]
produced almost nothing to confirm the existence of rehabilitative
processes in any of the penal programmes that have been attempted
under research conditions in any correctional system. The analytic
observation of parole process by Studt[3] did not uncover any inter-
active patterns between parolees and the officers supervising them
that convincingly accounted for any change in the conduct of
offenders under control. In the elaborate experiments of Warren and
her associates,[4] there is some evidence suggesting that extramural
rehabilitative programmes succeed with some types of offender. These
conclusions have been called into question by Lerman,[5] and ten
years of effort have not convinced the doubtful. The elaborate *post
hoc* analysis of the outcome data of the Pilot Intensive Counselling

[1] Walter C. Bailey, 'Correctional Outcome: an Evaluation of 100 Reports',
Journal of Criminal Law, Criminology and Police Science, 57.2 (June 1966),
153–60.
[2] Robert Martinson, 'Correctional Treatment: an Empirical Assessment'
(Columbus, Ohio: The Academy for Contemporary Problems, 1972: available in
photocopied typescript).
[3] Elliot Studt, 'Surveillance and Service in Parole: a Report of the Parole
Action Study' (Los Angeles: Institute of Government and Public Affairs,
University of California at Los Angeles, 1972).
[4] Marguerite Q. Warren, 'The Case for Differential Treatment of Delinquents',
The Annals of the Academy of Political and Social Science, 381 (January 1969),
47–59.
[5] Paul Lerman, 'Evaluation Studies of Institutions for Delinquents: Implications for Research and Social Policy', *Social Work* 13 (July 1968), 55–64.

Organisation (PICO), by Adams,[6] indicated that some offenders vaguely defined as 'amenable' to treatment profited from the experience, but neither in California nor elsewhere does there seem to be any confirming replication of this virtually unique finding. The recent report of Kassebaum, Ward and Wilner[7] not only explodes the notion that lasting effects are achieved by group counselling in the California model, but it also explains the disappointing results. Neither the interest nor the loyalty of those exposed to the programme was engaged, nor did it succeed in changing attitudes while it was in progress.

There is much more evidence of the futility of correctional treatment, not only in California, but also in the even more affluently programmed United States Bureau of Prisons. Not even a halo effect has been reported for the thoroughly researched and lavishly supported innovations at the Kennedy Youth Centre maintained by the Bureau of Prisons. The work of Glaser,[8] ten years ago, succeeded in showing that recidivism was not as serious in the Federal system as had been supposed, but it did not establish that the actual programmes administered to offenders had any significant impact.

The English studies show that penal treatment has been no more successful. Hood's impressive assessment of the Borstal system showed that, however successful it may have been in the great days of Paterson and Llewellin, it has sadly declined in recent years.[9] The studies of probation by the Home Office Research Unit has cast doubt on the rehabilitative value of the process, although there is still reason to suppose that useful services are being performed in arranging for the re-establishment of offenders in the community.[10]

Professor Rupert Cross concludes his impressive summary of all this disappointed effort with the assertion that we have entered an

[6] Stuart Adams, 'Interaction Between Individual Interview Therapy and Treatment Amenability in Older Youth Authority Wards' (Sacramento, California Board of Corrections, 1961). Reprinted in Norman Johnston, Leonard Savitz, and Marvin E. Wolfgang, *The Sociology of Punishment and Correction* (2nd ed.), pp. 548–61.

[7] Gene Kassebaum, David Ward, and Daniel Wilner, *Prison Treatment and Parole Survival* (Wiley, New York, 1971).

[8] Daniel Glaser, *The Effectiveness of a Prison and Parole System* (Bobbs-Merrill, Indianapolis, 1964).

[9] Roger Hood, *Borstal Re-assessed* (London, 1965).

[10] Roger Hood and Richard Sparks, *Key Issues in Criminology* (World University Library, London, 1970), pp. 186–8.

age of penological pessimism.[11] Evidence that nothing has been tried that succeeds in influencing offenders to mend their ways does not prove that such a goal is an impossibility, but it certainly suggests that the burden of proof is on the proponent of rehabilitation. We have little reason to hope for a magic bullet which will cure criminals of their criminality. I shall contend in the remainder of this article that the obsession with the idea of cure is a misconception of the entire problem which has seriously obstructed its solution.

To proceed from empiricism to sociological theory, the penological pessimism is deepened by the analysis of power and compliance by Etzioni. In his elegant analysis, initiated in the *Theory of Complex Organizations*[12] and pursued further in *The Active Society*,[13] Etzioni propounds a typology of power structures and a derivative typology of compliance. Without presenting the entire theoretical position, it may be enough to draw from it the proposition that where coercion is the basis of compliance, the response will be characterized by alienation. In Etzioni's view, the archetype of the coercion–alienation model is the prison. To anyone experienced in the relationships established between prison-staff members of any category and the prisoners themselves, Etzioni's conclusions are chillingly plausible. The failure of all those programmes to achieve significantly widespread rehabilitative goals is persuasively attributable to the attempt to help with one hand while the other restrains. We are not far from closure on the question of penal rehabilitation. It was a gallant attempt, nobly motivated, but the measured results so far support the position that coercion is incompatible with socialization.

Then how are we to account for the statistically improved results of the Californian system? The easy answer is that before our Director made all those policy changes, far too many offenders were locked up for far too long. Through the legislative device of Probation Subsidy,[14] it was discovered that in addition to the reduction of time in prison for   many offenders, even more could be entirely diverted from prison by placement on probation. Between 1968 and

[11] Rupert Cross, *Prisons, Punishment and the Public: The Hamlyn Lectures* (Stevens & Sons, London, 1971).

[12] Amitai Etzioni, *Theory of Complex Organizations* (The Free Press, New York, 1961), pp. 12–22.

[13] Amitai Etzioni, *The Active Society* (The Free Press, New York, 1968), pp. 370–5.

[14] Robert L. Smith, *A Quiet Revolution* (U.S. Government Printing Office, Washington, D.C., 1972).

1972, the population of male felons in the Californian system fell from 22,410 to 15,382,[15] or by nearly one-third. If rehabilitation did not account for this dramatic change, what lessons are we to draw from this impressive experience?

The long answer can now be addressed to the Director's question. For the most part, these people *are* like us, except that they are losers. There is no common set of traits which distinguishes them from us, no mysterious pathological process which drives them into crimes which we do not commit. Some of them are mad, some are stupid, but there are plenty of madmen and dullards among us who have committed no crimes. There is no condition common to criminals which requires a special cure for criminality. Some can profit from psychiatric care, just as some winners can, but the majority will not. Some of them will become more employable by education or vocational training, but most of them are employable enough in a free labour market, assuming that the labels of deviance could be expunged. There is nothing fundamentally wrong with them except their common history of defeat.

They are losers, and ours is increasingly a society of winners. The social gains of the last fifty years have created a system which will take care of most of us. Children are socialized for secure and regular employment when they become adults. Some will make no more than an austere competence, but they will be secure. They will not be motivated to take measures, legal or illegal, to improve their condition. Most of us move up and down an economic ladder, never falling off. Unemployment insurance, pensions, health benefits, and other economic cushions are not merely available; they are unavoidable safety nets should we fall off the ladder. These cushions against social misfortune may become more ample and probably they will, but even in their present form the social-security structure is sufficient to protect most of us from disasters which used to be common. Once the youth has emerged from the competitive arena of adolescence and into this comfortable system, powerful incentives keep him on a track which is straight, narrow, and crime-free, if often dull and square. We survive—and in reasonable comfort.

What is new in the world is this society of winners. The situation

[15] California Department of Corrections, 'California Prisoners, 1969' (Sacramento: The Human Relations Agency, publication date not indicated). See also, 'Characteristics of Felon Population in California State Prisons' (31 Dec. 1972). Mimeographed tables distributed by the Health and Welfare Agency, State of California, 26 Feb. 1973.

is unprecedented in the history of the human race. No nation had a majority of winners as recently as a century ago, or during the most golden of previous ages. To be a loser was the general lot; submission to impersonal exploitation and early death made up the destiny of the ordinary man. Misfortune still characterizes the prevailing human condition in most contemporary cultures. But in the industrial or post-industrial society, few of us live on this edge of disaster, and we know it. For as long as we comply with the simple requirements of the system, we shall continue to be winners, and some of us will win heavily.

Even in rich California there are still hundreds of thousands of losers. No statistics will tell us how many, but there are enough to impose uneasy and unwelcome burdens on the winners. Some losers survive in resignation on the welfare caseload. Some eke out a usually honest living at casual labour. Some are clients of the mental-health apparatus. And some are criminals. There is much shifting from sector to sector amongst this population of losers, but we shall never know how much.

Losers are the people who never made their way into the society of winners. Racism, class discriminations, the culture of subsistence, and other adversities of contemporary poverty have combined to create a structural underclass from which it is increasingly difficult to escape.

It is not agreeable to concede the existence of an underclass in a democratic state, but we must know more about it. We know that there are routes by which losers and children of losers escape into the conventional mass of the rest of us. Not much is known about this route or how often it is travelled. Nor do we know much about the lives of those who survive in the underclass without resort to criminality; we do not even know how many such people there are. Social workers who have been assigned to the public-welfare caseload know that there are many lives of inaudible resignation among these losers. Except that they are charges of the public treasury, they are no trouble to the winners. Their fellow-losers, the criminals, frighten us into action. Partly because of our fear, partly because of our inability to understand the loser, we resort to action which is expensive, ineffectual, and aimlessly cruel.

THE LESSONS OF THE RECENT PAST

The collapse of the claims of rehabilitation and the discovery that we do not need incarceration as much as we had thought should lead to some useful conclusions. The question we can now answer in part has to do with all those empty prisons in California. If we have made no discoveries that assure us that offenders can be rehabilitated by treatment, then we can only attribute our success in diverting them from prison to a recognition that a large fraction of those formerly confined did not need so much control. They were certainly not improved by the experience of prison, and if they can now be safely managed on probation and parole then the public received no significant protection. The only purpose that could have been served by their removal from society was the deterrence of potential offenders. It does not appear that the objective of deterrence has been seriously impaired by the radical decrease in the Californian prison population. The theory of deterrence is extraordinarily difficult to test by strict and conventional experimental methods. But it appears that we may have overrated the deterrent influence of the prison if the Californian data during this exceptionally turbulent period provide us with clues.

Eventually there will be studies of probation and parole which will complement the massive literature on the prison. Until such a body of knowledge accumulates, we can reasonably doubt that rehabilitative processes occur as a result of the influence of the system. The successes of probation and parole are difficult to attribute to purposive expertise. Some successes may be accounted for by a probation officer's efforts in mobilizing community resources in behalf of offenders. A successful referral to a sympathetic and effective employment counsellor calls for no special skill, but it will lead to a job for a loser and a statistic of non-recidivism. Probably more often, these goals are really attained by the offender's own efforts to survive without resort to crime. Survival in the underclass may take many forms, running from a legitimate job through various unconventional forms of gainful effort and sometimes dependency on other losers. As I have suggested above, we don't know much about survival in the underclass but we know at least that the loser has an alternative to crime. What doesn't hurt us, we don't know.

The knowledge that with the meagre resources available to the probation officer and his clients so many offenders contrive to live inoffensively should suggest to us that more resources might increase the statistics of non-recidivism. More alternative choices to crime will reduce crime; the more attractive the choices, the more crime will decrease. Losers are like the rest of us except that they have lost consistently and often. Access to career incentives like those that motivate winners will transform them into winners.

The reverse is true. An unbroken losing streak will transform the winner into a loser, too. We all need the comforting reassurance from fate that our efforts will be rewarded. Without this reassurance, we shall not necessarily resort to crime, but experiences at least as bleak are in store for us. It is an overlooked irony that Western society operates on the assumption that we are all economic men dependent on incentives for motivation, except for the poor, to whom conventional incentives are all but inaccessible. We proceed from these assumptions to the cruel conclusion that only the fear of punishment maintains the social control of the poor which is required for civic stability.

I shall be accused of oversimplification. Not all criminals are losers. Some are diseased personalities, tormented and miserable men and women in need of much more than access to the conventional socio-economic system. Sometimes they will respond to psychiatry, sometimes we will have to reconcile ourselves and them to longer-range social controls. Some criminals are defectors from the society of winners, demonstrating that a surfeit of carrots will create in some an indifference to the inducements which lead the rest of us to conform.

The rough division of the world into winners and losers results in a much needed simplification. We can now dispose of the troublesome quibble that some mysterious cause of crime must be sought to account for those two hypothetical unfortunates who are essentially similar in all respects except that one is a criminal and the other is not. We can now see that this perplexity is an irrelevance. We are concerned with losers, not with criminals. If we can provide realistic exits from the underclass, we shall make the inroads on the crime problem that we desire. The problem of the underclass is much larger than crime. To deal with crime as though it were a separable problem is a wasteful exercise in futility. This is the lesson that we can learn from those empty prison cells in California and from those successful Californian probationers.

Readers familiar with the work of Cloward and Ohlin[16] will readily equate the society of winners with the opportunity structure which occupies the central position in the theory of delinquency proposed

[16] Richard Cloward and Lloyd Ohlin, *Delinquency and Opportunity* (The Free Press, New York, 1960).

by these authors. In their version of the problem, when access to the conventional opportunity structure is restricted by circumstance, delinquency presents an alternative route to satisfaction. The influence of reference groups on the choices of disadvantaged youth will reinforce delinquent behaviour. The phenomenon of the juvenile gang thus accounts for the socialization of the individual youth to criminal roles.

This perspective is obviously compatible with my position. The emphasis on the condition of losers as the principal source of offenders leads us to an appreciation of the magnitude of our problem. The losers who become criminals are drawn from a larger universe which must be addressed if we are to prevent delinquency. So long as society includes a large population of losers, there will be criminals. Juvenile gangs may be broken up, the flow of the narcotics traffic may be dammed, and ferociously repressive sanctions may be enacted, and imposed, but if there are losers some of them will choose crime because they have nothing to lose by that choice.

In the long range, then, our hope for the prevention of crime must depend on the inroads we can make on the structure of contemporary poverty. If law-abiding careers are sufficiently available, most delinquents can be diverted to them. A society which cannot provide careers with consistent incentives cannot expect that losers will have reasons to refrain from law-breaking during their active years.

So far, this analysis leads to a counsel of despair. Throughout history, mankind has struggled with the inequities of the human condition. No society has succeeded in removing them. The great industrial societies have increased them. Disenchanted with the State as a vehicle for the achievement of social justice, the political and economic élites are leading us to a new version of *laissez-faire* in the hope that stability can thereby be achieved. Unemployment, urban disintegration, and increasing inequality are seen as conditions to be tolerated with the minimum intervention necessary. Increased reliance on the police, the heavy sanctions of the criminal law, and the use of the prison for the incapacitation of the recidivist are recognized as the necessary consequences of our tolerance of poverty.

It is tempting to predict early disaster as the consequence of this turn to the socio-economic right. There are several reasons to expect the failure of such a prediction. Our populations are ageing; crime rates will decline as the proportion of young people in the population is diminished. Improvement in economic conditions will improve life on the social margins for as long as such improvements can be maintained. Increasing attention to the effectiveness of police operations is bound to lower the volume of crime; we have no reason to doubt that repression can reduce some kinds of criminal behaviour for considerable periods of time.

The passage of time will tell us how well this fundamental change in social policy will serve us. Meanwhile, the volume of crime will still be great, the numbers of criminals to be reinstated in society will increase, and the costs of the criminal justice system will mount, regardless of the austerity with which it will be managed. Can a rational penal policy be devised in such a context?

A POLICY OF ENLIGHTENED EFFORT

The lesson we should have learned from the failures of the prevailing criminal policy is that the burden of crime will not be relieved by measures directed at crime alone. Until we can raise all children to become citizens, some will become criminals. Until we have reasonable alternatives for the criminal when he is sentenced, most criminals will sensibly choose to continue in their criminal ways. We also know from these disillusioning years that no utopian change is in prospect for our larger society which will radically reduce our population of losers. These are obvious lessons which society should not have had to learn so painfully. Their application comes hard, but it will not be impossible to devise a much more effective criminal justice system from the ruins of the present.

Keeping in mind that programmes directed at increasing the prospects of losers to become winners will ultimately reduce crime, criminal policy-makers should encourage their adoption. Preoccupied with the specifics of operations and management, those responsible for the administration of justice do not often take steps to participate in wider social planning or to establish in the public mind the connections between social justice and the prevention of crime. Advocacy of social amelioration as the fundamental requirement for public safety should be well within the expected wisdom of legislators and judges. That such insight is so uncommon indicates a considerable deficiency in the preparation of our leaders for their responsibilities.

If the prevention of crime depends on fundamental readjustments of the social system beyond the reach of criminal justice, much can still be done about the criminals we have by applying the lessons of our experience with losers. The guidance to be derived from the disappointments of the recent past can be reduced to five maxims:

(1) To the greatest extent possible, the first offender must be kept out of the criminal justice system. His offence must be seen as a signal that some kind of services are needed if he is not to become a liability to society. If services can be provided, they should be offered on the same basis as they are available to ordinary citizens. If no services are needed, the offender should be sent home to reflect on whatever lessons his apprehension may have for him. There is no reason to believe that further exposure to the majesty of the law will accomplish any valuable result for either him or the society whose laws he has transgressed.

(2) Recidivists should be placed under the minimal control required for the protection of the public. The imposition of any sanction should require that the sentencing authority must consider and reject all lesser sanctions as demonstrably inadequate.

(3) The degree of social control imposed is directly proportional to the difficulty that will be encountered in the social reinstatement of the offender. Where prolonged removal from society is required, prolonged surveillance will be needed in the process of reinstatement.

(4) Treatment under coercion is axiomatically ineffective. Therefore, help should be readily available to an offender at all stages of his control by the criminal justice system, but always and only at his own volition. Acceptance of help should never be a condition of the disposition, nor should its success be a condition of the offender's release from control.

(5) Decisions about the disposition of any offender should be guided by the examined results of decisions imposed on similar offenders in the past. Changes in social conditions will change the requirements of control. Sentencing authorities should determine requirements by reference to interpreted summaries of statistical trends.

A system governed by these maxims would begin with classification services to sentencing authorities. Discretion at all levels must be informed discretion, especially where the imposition of sanctions is the issue. The system would no longer rely on specialized correctional services of supervision, counsel, and control. Assistance would be obtained by referral to the professional and social resources of the community on the same terms as these resources are delivered to ordinary citizens. When surveillance is needed, it would be provided by the police. There will continue to be prisons for the restraint of dangerous adult offenders, but these prisons should be managed to provide the prisoner with a maximum freedom of choice and movement consistent with the public safety, the safety of other prisoners, and his own. Finally, accountability should be maintained throughout the system, governed by continuous review of results and supervision by the courts.

The policy of enlightened effort is grounded on the assumption that criminals are indeed like us. They will respond to experience as their non-criminal counterparts would respond. Given no alternative to satisfaction but a career in crime, losers will choose crime, as many of us would. Given the incentives to follow law-abiding careers, they will usually choose such careers. The evidence for this encouraging and hopeful conclusion is not wishful thinking. It is buried in the superficially dismal statistics of programme failures. There is no other explanation of the successes which accompanied the failures. The Director's question is answered. They are like us. If treated accordingly, losers can be winners.

16. A Prisoner's Perspective

HANUS HERMANN

THE transition from a civilian into a prisoner may come about either unexpectedly or after lengthy preparations. These preparations may be dominated by an intensive fear of the unknown or by the more realistic anticipation of the consequences of loss of liberty and social stigma experienced in the past. In exceptional cases imprisonment may even be desired in order to escape from the adversities of the free life outside. The transition itself may be performed in a 'civilized' way or with vindictive brutality. Whatever the circumstances, however, the transition is always effected in a very brief space of time: a few words are spoken, and before their sound dies the prisoner's entire perspective of life, of society, of himself has changed.

The magnitude of the shock brought about by this sudden change of perspective depends very much on whether it is experienced for the first time or not. Only a person who has experienced the transition in the past can prepare emotionally for its impact. Those who experience it for the first time seldom possess the imagination necessary to anticipate the change. The writings of penologists will hardly help, though some novelists—Fielding, for example; and, of course, the great Russian writers from Pushkin to Solzhenitsyn—do convey to the perceptive reader the ethos of imprisonment.

Nothing short of actual incarceration, however, can communicate the total impact of life in prison. Prison visits are deceptive. It was part of my assignment in 1946 to see whether Greek prisoners benefited from UNRRA supplies. Only after having spent many years in prison myself did I realize how false was the picture of prison life and conditions formed as a visitor. Those who spend their working days in prisons as custodians could probably perceive more were they not involved themselves: for to indulge even partly in perceiving the prisoner's predicament would hamper them in the performance of their duties.

If the magnitude of the shock brought about by the sudden change in perspective depends primarily on the state of mental preparedness, its nature differs according to what type of person the prisoner is.

Almost every prisoner looks back in the first hours and days, and views with anguish the empty space which he used to fill in the 'outer world'. It makes little difference whether the prisoner was in a position of command or working according to a predetermined routine: he will always find it difficult to accept that life outside can go on without him. There is a painful loss of identity. By the act of imprisonment the subject is often stripped of all his civilian clothing, but always of all his civilian functions. As a breadwinner or a lover, as a skilled worker, manager of a factory, or member of a criminal gang, his identity was always defined in the context of a social group. Now, and often for the first time, he is 'socially naked'; he is what he is—at least until he finds a new place in the captive society of prison.

This sudden stripping of all adornments and supports, of all constraints to one's behaviour and of all props to one's personality is, I think, the main reason why the prisoner's features are suddenly accentuated to the onlookers. In his inner music the dominant themes are amplified, while the weaker and secondary melodies are further attenuated. A few months after my imprisonment I found myself sharing a cell with Professor Zdenek Stejskal, Professor of Applied Psychology at Charles University in Prague. When I asked him what, in his opinion, is the main effect of prison on the prisoner's personality, he said that everything that is good or bad in the prisoner is accentuated while he is in prison. My subsequent experience amply confirmed this dictum.

Speaking about 'good' and 'bad' may be a misleading exercise. Prisoners quickly learn to distinguish between the real elements of personality and the results, achievements, or failures by which these elements can be obscured. Thus one learns with more or less surprise that military courage and bearing are made up essentially of weakness, submission, and obedience to command: army officers, even high-ranking ones, are ready to spring to attention whenever a guard enters a room and can easily be reduced to tears if exposed to petty persecution. Those who accord to respect for rules and order, intellect and reasoning, a higher place than to a simple belief in a moral code, are likely to be more submissive. Thus teachers and university professors, lawyers and doctors tend to crumble, while 'simple' people of strong beliefs, whether fitters, agricultural labourers, or innkeepers, prove often to be a rock of friendship and security for their fellow prisoners. A man who became a university professor, because he was an intellectual exhibitionist and paraded fashionable theories, will have less to offer in prison than a man of much less education. The latter will express views sincerely held, resulting not from bookish knowledge but from a life of experience. A priest, a notary (commissioner for oaths), a colonel in the army, and other people trusted in civilian life by virtue of their profession, will not necessarily prove trustworthy also in the darkness of the coalmine. There was only one man to whom I was ready to entrust my safety and life when exploring shifting ballast and sand in a blocked tunnel in the uranium mine: he was a gipsy, sentenced to a long term in prison for having murdered his wife—out of jealousy, as he used to say.

It may be that personalities become more transparent in prison, and that the impact of fundamental features of character are more directly felt both because of the greater urgency of everything that has to be done and because of the absence of social routines and conventions cushioning their impact. It would, however, be quite wrong to assume that this temporary change in personality appreciation and behaviour has the same intensity and same slant in every prison. There is no such thing as *a* prison. Prisons differ widely, and from the prisoner's point of view the difference between two prisons may be sometimes greater than that between civilian life and prison. The differences between prisons are not only a product of prison rules but also of prison atmospheres which are inherited and perpetuated in a given institution, however rapid the turnover of prisoners. Only an almost complete change of the prison population can achieve a change in the institutional climate. There are prison camps with identical command and identical rules from which prisoners go to work in the same mines or on the same building sites, but still the life in one can be hell, while life in the other is as good as one could expect under the circumstances. Prison camps produce their own moral standards, their own 'camp law' which is observed and enforced by prisoners, and can destroy people who are not ready to submit.

Apart from this ideological element—which often can be traced to the particular circumstances in which a camp evolved—there are conditions of work, supply, and prison regime which have an important effect on prisoners' well-being and behaviour to each other. It goes without saying that starving people and deprived smokers are on edge most of the time, but when hunger can be satisfied and the barracks are warm everybody is much more friendly. Also the prisoner's outlook, his assessment of the future, is a product of the prison atmosphere and standard of life. The biblical story of Joseph could not be more true in that part where he was asked by fellow prisoners in Egypt about their future. The future is, of course, the overriding interest of every prisoner. The answers given by Joseph confirm that he was no ordinary prisoner, but that he enjoyed in prison a comfortable standard of living which enabled him to differentiate his answers according to what he knew about the political profile of the individuals who asked him.

Most prison predictions are based less on facts and more on the need for hope. Hell is the place where there is no hope, as we know from Dante. Short-term prisoners cling to the knowledge of their date of release; the absence of hope would make prison unendurable and those who serve long or indeterminate sentences have to manufacture some other kind of hope. The time which they believe they will still have to spend in prison can be found to be almost exactly in inverse ratio to the severity of the prison. The same political prisoner, who in a relatively well supplied and easy-going prison camp will believe that he will spend another two or three years in prison, will convince himself that amnesty will come in a couple of weeks when moved into a strict regime, closed prison where he lives without contact with other human beings, without fresh air, without ever seeing the sky. This rule is so reliable that one can very well judge prison conditions by asking the prisoners the simple question 'When do you expect to get home?'

The appreciation of hardships of different kinds, and the ability to survive them differs with the personality of the prisoner. It is easy to understand that for a man who found self-expression in life by manual work, the opportunity of using his manual skills in prison is of very great importance, while an intellectual will have the same need for books, writing, and intelligent conversation. People whose life interest is not centred on their work but on caring for others, will soon form little families if they can, and will suffer very badly if they cannot. In this way the problem of enduring imprisonment and of assessing its degree of severity has much to do with the ability to substitute for work done in the 'former life', and to substitute for the relationships enjoyed or hoped for in that life.

There are, of course, also new problems. Solitude can be endured much more easily by a man or woman of lively imagination who can fill in the empty space of time with a programme of imaginary occupations. Such a person can for years endure solitary confinement which would drive crazy, within a few short weeks, a gregarious man depending on companionship and small talk. Indeed an imaginative man can use the elements of sensory distortions and creeping madness for building up a new and interesting life within the bare walls of a permanently closed call. There are imaginary affairs to settle, languages to learn by evocation of knowledge long forgotten, mathematical studies to be pursued (even with closed eyes and without either paper or pen), houses to be built in one's mind, furnished and peopled when completed. When the prisoner opens his eyes and sees the cracks in the wall transformed into caravans and processions of wild animals the prisoner can, according to his temperament, despair of his hallucinations or enjoy them, trying to remember whatever his delusions bring him.

The decisive deprivation of prison is not, however, a matter of food, warmth, and physical exercise in the open air. It is the social rejection of one's existence and the deprivation of love and sympathy. To this one can distinguish two basic categories of reaction. Either the prisoner shares the social rejection of himself, because he accepts with the society that punishes him that he has done something wrong; and in that case he is bound in time to crumble and he will hardly ever be what he was before. He cannot bear the continued 'first' rejection from the community of which he feels a part. The other type of prisoner is the one who rejects the society's values, or the viewpoint of the court which sentenced him, or that of the prison authorities, or even sometimes of his fellow prisoners. Such a prisoner has a chance to avoid disintegration of his personality so long as he will go on resisting the moral pressure, and accept hardships which result from being a 'recalcitrant prisoner'. If he will retain pride in what he is, remain true to himself and not do things *he* believes to be wrong, he may survive as a moral personality—always assuming that he will be lucky enough to survive physically.

This problem of not adopting the interrogators', the judges', or the prison authorities' view of oneself is, of course, primarily the problem of the political prisoner, but it may also be the fate of a sexual offender, a drug addict, or a person who has 'opted out'. This may be the case of an anarchist, of a person from another ethnic group with a different code of behaviour. Strong feelings of personal hate, which prompted the criminal action, are sometimes a substitute for a more general ideological framework. A Communist in a Greek prison, or a non-Communist in an Eastern European prison, a Jehovah's Witness almost anywhere, a gipsy who believes that it is his duty to fulfil obligations resulting from a family vendetta or to commit a crime of passion—all these may survive if they are strong enough to resist the established order's view of themselves.

The non-acceptance of the view which the prison's incarcerators have of him is not a matter restricted to political and ideological attitudes. The less tangible and elusive qualities of a personality, which it is difficult to define, are probably more important for survival. In prison, to remain true to oneself means war, but there is the peace which 'is not absence of war but which comes from the strength of a courageous soul', as Spinoza said.

There is of course, nothing more galling to the prison authorities than a man who can suffer the extremes of adversity and remain undaunted. To retain his personal dignity may be fraught with danger to the prisoner's physical comfort, and even to survival. The hardships which it brings can be viewed as premiums against an insurance policy, the only one a prisoner can take out: that if he survives, he will come out of prison unbroken. There is, however, one danger on this path, and that is that the mental resistance to the hostile forces which put him in prison and keep him there will gradually erode the prisoner's capacity for tolerance and will teach him to hate. As often as not such alteration will be functional, because people often need to hate to be able to resist. This can well have serious consequences for the prisoner both while still inside and when he comes out. Even an essentially peaceful man who never handled firearms or other weapons can develop a compulsive reflex movement, as if he were brandishing a gun, but which provides an outlet for his feeling of hate for his guards and other persecutors.

The development of such regrettable but necessary defence mechanism is of relatively lesser consequence if it concerns political divisions, and is directed against a small well-defined group of oppressors. It can, however, assume much more tragic dimensions if the prisoner has to fight for his moral survival across a barrier which divides people according to their origin, colour of their skin, or sex. It is sad to think of the damage done to the individual and society by institutions which people can leave unbroken, only if they have learnt in the process to hate the other half of mankind.

For the prisoner the story does not end when he leaves prison.

Everyone tends to treat him as a special creature, some by being particularly hostile or particularly helpful; most by avoiding him. More important still, the released prisoner carries the prison within himself. For a long time he will be speaking about 'how we do things', and 'we' is the prison community of which he became a part. The change of perspective, which took place so quickly on his imprisonment, is reversed after his release only by a very slow process. Two explanations can be offered for this retardation in adjustment to changed circumstances. One is that on coming home the prisoner feels inadequate to the tasks facing him or to the expectations springing from a different 'civilian' set of values. For this reason he falls back on the support of the spirits which he left. Another reason may be that the released prisoner is suffering by an irrational guilt feeling for having left his comrades behind. He is free, and they are still there. For this reason, perhaps, he also must see the brighter side of the life in prison and to refer proudly to the routines and to the achievements which it makes possible.

The post-prison attitudes and behaviour must be, to some degree, determined by the tremendous effort which the prisoner had to make in order to establish a new social existence within the prison community. This process of individual integration proceeds along widely different, and sometimes contradictory, patterns which I will attempt to describe but cannot explain. For most people who worked hard before they came to prison, it is again hard work by which they re-establish themselves in the esteem of the prison community and keep their self-esteem intact. The object of the work done is either totally ignored or justified by means of reasoning processes, sometimes highly implausible. Thus a manual worker, who is most actively conscious of his hostility towards the regime which put him behind barbed wire, will use all his skill when made to repair or erect barbed-wire fences, and will improve on the instructions he received and go to the length of telling the guards how the work should be done more efficiently. Prisoners without hesitation build prison bunkers into which sooner or later they will be thrown themselves.

Made to dig uranium for the Soviet Union, the Czech anti-Communist farmers, sentenced to long terms in the course of collectivization, invented a myth justifying their display of hard work, of ingenuity and skill in getting radioactive material for their enemy, without pay and at a grave risk to their health. The myth was that the Soviet Union did not have the technology necessary for processing uranium ore and that, as a result, the ore supplied from Czech mines was being stockpiled in the Soviet Union and would fall into American hands after the Americans had defeated the Soviet Union. This sub-myth was thus fitted into the general myth of liberation by an East–West war, and these farmers believed that 'after the war' they would be paid by the Americans for the stockpiles of uranium ore which they prepared for them in the Soviet Union.

This prison myth combined perfectly the satisfaction of two emotional requirements. The Czech farmers hated the Soviet domination of their country, and they hated to work without being paid for it. They simply had to invent a mythology which would enable them to work for the enemy by providing an illusion that they were helping themselves. It is, however, much more difficult to explain the behaviour of people who were shy or incapable of work in their civilian existence. Very often one encountered 'asocial' individuals, who had either led a parasitic existence or lived off petty crime, but in prison turned into pioneer workers. The explanation may be that, once deprived of the possibilities of other types of aggression or of self-distinction, they had to resort to work as the last medium for putting their excellence across.

A special but frequent case is that of an ordinary offender who has been deprived of parental care or who grew up without an effective father. Such a person will often accept the prison authority as a parent substitute, and will try to please. Stronger than this, in most cases, and much more general, however, is the desire to secure the approval of fellow prisoners and to identify with them into a family or into a community. It is a well-known fact that professional thieves rarely steal from their fellow prisoners. One could speculate that this reveals that their stealing was a form of social revenge for having been in one or another way disadvantaged, and that their social acceptance by the prison community put an end to it.

For the prisoner who comes home or returns to civilian life the crucial question is whether he will have to rely on the prison image which he carries in his heart. In most cases this will not only be a memory of hardships, torture, or adversities; it will also be a somewhat rose-tinted picture of solidarity, fellowship, and community. This *aurea aetas* is invented on leaving the prison as a shield against the hostile outer world.

At this stage of his passage, the ex-prisoner is prone to view all prisoners as essentially good, and all people who somehow manage

to stay out of prison as wicked and certainly guilty of his imprisonment and of all the misery of society in general. It *may* be of vital
importance, depending on the length of his sentence, for a man
landing in prison to find a new social structure to which he can fit,
within which he can continue a human, that is, social existence in
prison. But it is *always* important for the released prisoner, and for
society, that he should find a community which needs him and to
which he can belong by contributing to it, be it skills or love. The
prisoner who leaves prison unbroken may be less obviously in need
of help than the diffident, broken ex-prisoner who accepted the
society's ostracism of him. Because of the process of moral resistance
which enabled him to survive unbroken, such an ex-prisoner will be
prone to identify the entire outer world with his oppressors, and
though he may be well equipped to fend for himself, he may need
help to break out of this pattern.

I have dwelt at some length on the negative influences and dangers
to the prisoner's personality and to society resulting from imprisonment. But prison has certain positive aspects, apart from keeping
dangerous individuals under lock and key and supposedly serving as a
deterrent to others. Prisoners realize these positive aspects to the
degree that you often hear them saying among themselves that
everyone should spend at least some time in prison, that it is a
university of life, and they have learned much they could not
have learned anywhere else. What then are the positive effects of
imprisonment? The first thing, and one not particularly desirable
from the social point of view, is that it will free the prisoner of a good
deal of the terror with which he may have viewed imprisonment
before he first experienced it. The unknown is always feared more,
and the fear of imprisonment reappears in smaller doses whenever
the prisoner is moved from one prison to another where he has not
been before. The important lesson here seems to be that to make the
most of any deterrent effect of imprisonment one should postpone
sending offenders to prison as much as possible. Once experienced,
prison loses much, if not all, of its terror.

The second important effect of prison is an expansion of the prisoner's personality by his meeting people he would not have met
under his ordinary circumstances of life. This is of great importance,
even in societies which are much less socially stratified than the
British. The advantage of meeting people from different backgrounds,
with different life experiences, different levels of education, and

different habits, is further enhanced by the fact that they meet in a transparent state, when the hardships of prison existence obliged them to shed most of the conventional defences and pretences.

The expansion of personality by meeting people under circumstances facilitating sincere contact may be accompanied, depending on the type of prison, by expansion of knowledge and skills as a result of the employment in prison or prison camps. The usefulness of this for the unskilled or illiterate is obvious, but intellectuals may also benefit by being obliged to employ their muscles and to realize the capacity of their bodies. After some years the bookish man may return home broad-shouldered and with greater confidence, not only in his moral resistance but also in his physical strength and endurance. The process of breaking is all too depressingly familiar. It is less widely acknowledged, however, that by the mere fact of not having been broken, a prisoner can gain the self-confidence which he lacked. Thus prison can make the man who survives.

This should not obscure the fact that the prisoner, who comes out apparently strengthened by not having been broken, faces a very great danger in the first period of his freedom. It is at this time that many people collapse and die from one cause or another. There seems to be a very great danger in allowing oneself to feel that one is out of danger, and in this way an excess of kindness and care, and of removing obstacles out of the ex-prisoner's way, will be often counter-productive, and may even be lethal.

At this point it is unavoidable to bring into the picture the family to which the prisoner returns, and in the first instance the marriage partner or lover to whom he or she returns, or hopes to return. This aspect may be of less crucial importance for a short-term prisoner, but anyone who spends years in prison tries almost constantly to lead a double life by continuing a sort of imaginary presence in the other world by keeping the link with his family alive. He may suffer by a feeling of guilt that he made them unhappy: he may suffer, if prone to jealousy, by imagining that his family is happy while he is in prison; he will contemplate the possibility that they form other relationships which compete, and will compete in the future even more, with the relationship that the prisoner himself tried to keep alive. Even if he is a generous person and takes comfort in the fact that those he (or she) loves have probably found a substitute, this will not eliminate anxiety at the thought that he will lose them. The degree to which the emotional link with the family can be maintained is highly important for the degree of separation that develops in the prisoner's mind between the inner and the outer world. It is less easy to reject the outer world totally if the prisoner's family—and by this term I mean the nuclear family or close friends—are part of this outer world. They have a redeeming effect.

The prisoner may think that people outside prison cannot all be entirely bad if those he loves are among them, but some are not ready to accept such reasoning. They will feel that the entire outside world is bad, including those they love. Even so, for most prisoners the way back is to the family which is the vital link between the prisoner and society. Hence the devastating effect which the prison systems practising complete separation—with no visits and few letters, or with visits of no practical importance, say, once a year and lasting a few minutes—have on the prisoner, and to a lesser degree on his family. This may come to light only when the prison gates open and the spatial separation comes to an end. The prisoner returns, he thinks that he is back, the family thinks he has come back. In fact all that has happened is that they are all again in the same place, but they do not live in the same time.

The Shangri-la effect of the prison is seldom readily appreciated by the prisoner or by those to whom he returns. Still, its explanation is simple. The length of time is not measured by the passage of the moon or by the revolutions of the earth. It is measured by the number of events that have happened. Looking back, the prisoner sees a series of identical days and identical weeks, so that a year that passed seems to be but a week, but the year to come seems an eternity. Only a prisoner can know the horror of an empty future. For the prisoner the past year almost did not happen and the coming year has no end.

There is a pervasive difference in time appreciation between those who meet on a prisoner's release. The years which have passed seem short to the returning prisoner, and very long to those left behind. For the man inside, the future was a burden impossible to bear without hope lightening it. Those outside viewed the future more realistically; the year that passed seemed long, filled with work and events.

One of the important distortions of the prisoner's perspective is thus brought about by his own appreciation of himself in the space of time. Those who welcome him back see him aged by the years that they perceived as long. The returning prisoner, however, sees himself hardly a day older than when he was put away, in a place where the days hang heavily and little of note happens.

On leaving this Shangri-la, the ex-prisoner will age in a few hours the full number of years he spent in prison. This is the third transition and change in perspective imposed by prison. It is probably the most difficult to cope with and to survive in good health. The shock of rapid ageing is hardly less for those to whom the prisoner returns. It may in fact have more tragic consequences even than his initial loss of liberty.

17. CAUTION: Some Thoughts on the Penal Involvement Rate

NIGEL WALKER

A feature of the penal system which has received remarkably little attention—considering its importance—is the extent to which members of our society have been involved in the system at what can be called the receiving end of it—that is, as persons suspected, accused, and perhaps convicted of criminal offences.

I call this 'penal involvement', and I had better begin by emphasizing what I am *not* talking about. I am not talking about '*criminal* involvement'—that is, the number of people in a society who have committed serious crimes or trivial offences, irrespective of whether they have been detected or not. This too is a fascinating subject, about which we know far too little. But what seems to me even more important than either the unreported crimes or the untraced offenders are the *traced* offenders, who have experienced interviews with the police, followed in many cases by trial, conviction, and sentence. These are the people who have become involved in the penal system at its receiving end. The *penal* involvement rate of a society is the percentage of its members who have experienced this process, in all or some of its stages. Why the penal-involvement rate is so important is a question which I shall be discussing in a moment. The point that must be made first is that we are much too ignorant about the penal-involvement rate of our own, or any other, society.

It might be imagined that we could make quite an accurate estimate of the percentage of our population which has ever been officially identified as the perpetrators of any sort of offence, whether indictable, or non-indictable. After all, findings of guilt are recorded by police forces, and should be countable.

In practice we have no hope at present of actually making a count. The machinery for the central recording of convictions ignores convictions for most non-indictable offences, and for nearly all motoring offences. The most, therefore, that the central recording system could be expected to tell us is the total number of living people in this country who have been convicted of any indictable offence, and one or two of the more serious non-indictable offences. In fact, it cannot do even this, since it has no routine method of ascertaining when a centrally recorded offender has died or emigrated. This is not a criticism of the Criminal Record Office, which after all does not exist for the benefit of criminologists. It means, however, that for the moment and for some time to come we shall have to rely on estimates made from samples, and I know of only two samples which provide really worthwhile information on this subject.

Mr. Michael Wadsworth, working with Dr. Douglas and his Medical Research Council team, has been following up all the males who were legitimately born in the first week of March 1946 and has traced their court appearances up to their twenty-first birthdays. Some of them of course have died or emigrated, and some were untraceable. But Mr. Wadsworth has been kind enough to allow me to quote his not-yet-published figures, which, when adjustments were made for uneven representation of social classes, suggest that something like 15 per cent of males aged twenty-one in 1967—that is, about 1 in 7—had been found guilty at least once of a standard list offence—that is, of an offence serious enough to be centrally recorded—in other words not a mere drunk and disorderly or speeding or TV licence offence. This percentage might well be slightly higher if it had been possible to include illegitimate males in the sample; but we do not know.

It is true that a lot of these findings of guilt occurred in juvenile courts, and while the boys were at school. But about a quarter occurred after their seventeenth birthdays, and over half after their fifteenth birthdays, when most of them had left school. Moreover, we can expect another 2 per cent or so to incur their first conviction by their middle twenties, and it will be interesting when this stage of the follow-up has been completed. My guess is that it will bring the percentage up to about 17 per cent. What is more, if these are fairly good estimates for the male population as a whole, what must the percentages be like in urban areas and social classes which have higher-than-average penal-involvement rates? Over a decade ago, Michael Schofield's team interviewed 456 boys between their seventeenth and nineteenth birthdays in three London areas and two northern and two southern provincial areas of England. Nearly one in four admitted to having appeared in court for an offence, and nearly a half—47 per cent—said they had been in trouble with the police. These very high figures may well be due to over-representation of delinquency-prone areas and social classes.[1]

It is worth pointing out, too, that the estimate for young males in general does not include any but the most serious motoring offences, although it does include taking motor vehicles without the owner's consent. At the moment we have no basis on which to estimate the enormous numbers of men and women who have been convicted— let alone cautioned—for misbehaving with a motor vehicle. From the purely numerical point of view—as Lady Wootton has aptly remarked—the most important contribution to our rising crime rate is attributable to the internal combustion engine. No doubt this ignores important differences between the serious and the trivial, the intentional and the negligent: but, for the purpose of my argument, what matters is that, like crimes of violence, sex or dishonesty, traffic offences bring people into conflict with the law and the police. From this—and other—points of view, I welcome recent predictions that there may soon be a worldwide petrol shortage.*

What I want to do now is to speculate about the consequences, present and future, of this high level of penal involvement, which is probably a fairly recent phenomenon. Not only is widespread motor-car ownership a recent development, but so is the sharp rise in convictions for serious crimes.

Not all of what I want to say is speculation. In one or two ways we have already been brought face to face with some very practical consequences. For example, the Morris Committee on Jury Service[2] were told that when the names of thirty-eight jurors at the Old Bailey were checked in the middle 1960s it was found that four definitely had convictions serious enough to be in the Criminal Record Office files, and nine others appeared to have records: so that as much as a third might have had experiences of being tried which would prejudice them. Although the Committee were assured that the juries in question seemed to have returned reasonable verdicts (presumably in favour of the prosecution), they took the situation seriously enough to recommend the changes in the law which now

---

[1] See pp. 33 and 149–51 of Schofield's book *The Sexual Behaviour of Young People* (Longman's, 1965); references are to the 1968 Pelican edition.

[2] Cmnd. 2627 (1965), para. 132, pp. 41–2.

* This was written in the summer of 1973.

disqualify certain ex-prisoners from jury service.[3] Even so, in the course of an Old Bailey trial in the summer of 1973 it was found that out of 220 jurymen called for service on three successive days no less than thirty-three—15 per cent—had previous convictions serious enough to be recorded by Criminal Record Office.

The problem of the criminal juryman sounds easy enough to deal with, at least on paper. But there are other aspects of the increasing level of penal involvement which are less easy to measure or deal with. One of these aspects is the attitude of the public to its agencies of law enforcement—and especially to the police and the courts. An increasing percentage of us have personal experience of being detected, questioned, and finally prosecuted, and it is an experience which has an understandable effect. Every minor inconvenience caused by the process seems to become an injustice; every remark on the part of the police seems to be a target for suspicion and resentment.

From this point of view the difference between respectable conduct—such as endangering life by one's driving—and what we regard as disreputable offences—such as drug abuse—is less important than usual. No doubt one's alarm and resentment are greater if one sees one's reputation or one's liberty in real danger; but even if all that is at stake is a fine and an endorsement of one's licence one is still on the wrong side of the law, and seen from the wrong side it presents an ugly face, no matter how courteous its officers may be. Even well-meant precautions, such as the removal of a drunk driver's tie, are seen as unnecessary indignities.

Indeed, from the point of view of the social phenomenon I am discussing, the bad driver is one of the most important types of offender. Not because of the harm which he may do—although this is often as great as the harm done by murder—but because he is so numerous and so influential. The middle-class private motorist is the only group of criminals with its own organized and financially solvent pressure group—or rather, two of them. Stiffer penalties for motorists are always more strongly opposed in Parliament than stiffer penalties for drug use, or weapon-carrying.

Nevertheless, although acquisitive criminals—thieves, robbers, confidence men—are less well represented in Parliament, and

[3] For some reason they seemed to assume that someone who had merely been convicted of an offence, without being imprisoned for it, was unlikely to be a prejudiced juryman.

although they are generally less influential, this disadvantage is decreasing. Not only is the property-offender better educated than he used to be—and therefore more articulate—but he has more opportunities for being articulate. Publishers have found that there is a market for autobiographical books by criminals. It is true that books by criminals are not entirely new; but they are more numerous, and read more seriously than they ever were in previous eras.

I do not want to suggest that they should not be read seriously. Many of them contain a lot of genuine information, not only about the working of the machinery of justice but also about the psychology of the author. Particularly valuable are biographical books such as those written by Tony Parker, using tape-recorded conversations with offenders; they are a valuable compromise between sympathetic understanding of the offender himself and an objective description of the ways in which he defeats efforts to help him.

What all these books have in common, however, is a critical attitude to the agencies of law enforcement. The point is not the question whether this is justifiable, but simply the fact that this is what they are selling, and that it has an effect upon the reader, especially upon the reader who does not have any objective information by which to judge the fairness of the criticisms.

The same is true of other mass media, and especially television. Sunday newspapers long ago realized the market value of murderers' life stories; but it is only recently that the interest of documentaries about petty offenders has been discovered. This discovery was probably made by television producers; and certainly more people have learnt more about our penal system from television in the last ten years than was ever learned from any other source.

The effect of the sudden opening of this new channel of communication between the typical criminal and the public is so recent that we have not yet begun to see its importance. In the past there have been waves of concern about the treatment of prisoners—one in the 1890s as a result of agitation by a prison chaplain, one in Edwardian days when middle-class suffragettes found themselves in prison, one after the First World War when the conscientious objectors were able to write about their experiences in prison. In the 1960s the imprisonment of some of the Campaigners for Nuclear Disarmament led to the founding of the Prison Reform Council. But in all those cases it was respectable, middle-class people who were speaking; and they were listened to because they themselves were not criminals in the colloquial sense and therefore could presumably be believed. Now we are able to listen at first-hand to 'real criminals' and rightly or wrongly we believe at least some of what they say.

What is the effect of all these communications? I have already mentioned the antagonism which can be aroused by personal experience of law enforcement, and it is likely that this can be communicated by a vivid account of someone else's experiences. Sometimes, of course, the account is so obviously biased that it alienate's one's sympathy instead of enlisting it. It is quite irrelevant, however, from the point of view of my argument whether the offender's account of his experiences is biased or even inaccurate. The question is 'What effect does it have?' Even if the audience does suspect exaggeration—as any sensible person is bound to—this does not protect it entirely against the point of view which is being put across; and this point of view is always to the discredit of the agencies of law enforcement.

Another effect is the decline in the importance of stigma. The stigma of public conviction is a stronger deterrent—at least for some people—than the penalty or measure which the court is likely to order. Women—and not only middle-class women—have committed suicide while awaiting a court appearance for shoplifting which would have led to a fine at most. No doubt most potential offenders—who tend to be young males rather than middle-aged women—are less sensitive to public exposure. Nevertheless, a survey of teenage males—by the Government Social Survey—found that the deterrent that they ranked highest was the opinion of their family. Next was the loss of their job; third was the general shame of appearing in court; and the probable penalty was fourth.

I cannot give you any evidence to show that the stigma of conviction *is* losing power as a restraint upon conduct. All I can say is that this is a likely effect of our increasing familiarity with people who have been convicted. What can be observed, however, is a phenomenon that might be called 'inverted stigma'. Some respectable citizens take pains to emphasize their friendship or acquaintanceship with criminals. It is as if respectability had become something slightly contemptible, which had to be excused, like being middle-class.

LABELLING

There are one or two other speculative points which I want to make before going on to consider what might be done about our increasing penal involvement rate. There is, for example, a school of sociologists who believe that by labelling someone as a criminal you increase the probability that he will repeat whatever form of misbehaviour caused him to be labelled. Various ways in which this can happen have been described. If he is labelled a thief he may find it difficult to get a legitimate job, and be driven to commit more dishonesties. Ostracism may drive him into the company of people who have been similarly ostracized, and these associations may lead to new law-breaking. It is even suggested that by labelling a young person as, say, a thief you may cause him to believe that he is more or less bound to thieve, just as telling a heavy drinker that he is an alcoholic may perhaps reduce his confidence in his ability to cut down his drinking. I must emphasize that the evidence in support of what is called labelling theory is not at the moment very impressive, and while I have an open mind about it I am not resting my case on it.

VICTIMOLOGY

What one cannot deny, however, is a tendency to reverse the process of moral condemnation, and aim it at the victim. One or two criminologists—notably von Hentig and Wolfgang in the U.S.A.—have drawn attention to the extent to which the victims of offences of violence, fraud, sexual molestation, and so on had behaved in such a way as to invite the crime. Others have pointed out that shoplifting seems to be most frequent in the shops which do the most to encourage customers to help themselves. Hire-purchase firms—which suffer from a considerable amount of dishonesty on the part of their customers—have been accused in effect of inducing a state of diminished responsibility by their sales methods. Again the point is not the moral question whether the victim *should* share the blame—although in some cases it would be more realistic to make him do so. The point is that we seem to be taking up a point of view which is a little closer to the offender's.

I am not suggesting that these developments are altogether harmful; a little more understanding of the offender's point of view, for example, must make us more realistic and less retributive. But there are other features of these developments which are bound to worry agents of law enforcement; and what I now want to discuss is what might be done about them. There are several kinds of solutions, some unrealistic and some not entirely unrealistic.

First, one might simply suggest that police be even more selective in deciding to track down offenders. Already, of course, the economics of manpower and other resources make it impossible not to exercise some degree of selection, based on some sort of priorities. A murder receives more attention than the theft of a handbag from an unlocked car. Is there a case for being more selective still?

There may well be: but I don't think that it is the right solution to the problem which I am concerned with, which is how to enforce the law without convicting too many people. With certain exceptions, which I shall mention later, I don't want to see fewer offenders detected: I want to see fewer convicted. Nor do I mean that I want to see more acquitted. An acquittal means either that an innocent person has been prosecuted or that a guilty person has got away with something: both are eventualities which we want to keep to the minimum.

Nor would it meet my point to adopt the Scottish expedient, which has recently been elaborated in a report by Justice, the Howard League, and NACRO,[4] that an offender's conviction should be ignored for certain purposes after a certain period. The details of the idea do not matter for my purpose. It has its merits, but is not really relevant to the problem I am talking about. For not only must the offender put up with the formal and informal consequences of conviction for whatever time is allowed by the scheme: the scheme cannot protect him from people's memories and gossip. Even more important, it cannot prevent him from being convicted in the first place; and if I am right in suggesting that once convicted he is to some extent hostile to law enforcement and the agents of law enforcement, that is something which will not be remedied by officially forgetting his conviction a certain number of years later.

How much could be achieved by narrowing the scope of our criminal law? This is no longer as unthinkable as it was, since we have abolished the crime of attempted suicide, and greatly narrowed the definitions of illegal abortion and criminal homosexual acts. Attempted suicide, in particular, is a good example of conduct which nobody wants to encourage, but which we now see as a matter for the doctors rather than for the courts. It is not generally known, by the way, that as far back as the beginning of this century the Liverpool Police had an unpublished instruction which discouraged the prosecution of attempted suicides,[5] and that they were followed

[4] *Living it Down: the Problem of Old Convictions* (Stevens, 1972); and see the Rehabilitation of Offenders Act 1974, first introduced by Lord Gardiner in 1973.

[5] See Sir Leonard Dunning's article 'Discretion in Prosecuting', in the *Police Journal* (1928), 1, 39 ff.

about the time of the First World War by the Metropolitan Police.

It is easier of course to get rid of a prohibition if some highly respected profession—such as medicine—will assume responsibility for dealing with the type of behaviour in question. That is what happened with attempted suicide; and we may be in sight of it where chronic drunkenness is concerned. I doubt whether any profession is going to take the Litter Act off our hands; but it is worth pointing out that this Act was not really a governmental response to widespread horror, but the result of a private member's Bill.

What cannot be ignored in this context, however, is the prohibition on the use of cannabis. Before I tell you what I *am* saying I had better tell you what I am *not* saying; and what I am not saying amounts to a good deal more than what I am saying:

1. I am not saying anything about the abuse of other drugs,

2. I am not saying that cannabis is harmless. It may well be as harmful as alcohol or tobacco, although the evidence concerning these is overwhelming, and the evidence about cannabis is so far scanty.

3. I am not suggesting that we encourage anyone to use it in preference to alcohol or tobacco. I have no quarrel with the people who wish to publicize its possible dangers,

4. I am *not* denying that a very real danger is the driving of motor vehicles under the influence of cannabis.

What I *am* saying is:

5. That our penal anti-cannabis legislation is the result not of an informed decision on our part, but of our obedience to international conventions based on even less information than we have now;

and this is what I am really leading up to—

6. It is the worst thing for police–public relations that has happened since the invention of the motor car. It has created a large group of young men and women, who see the sense in strict control of heroin, LSD, amphetamines and barbiturates, and who are pretty law-abiding, but who as far as cannabis is concerned see the police as the enforcers of an unjustifiable law.

If so, the police have been manoeuvered into a very unfortunate position. Nor do I see any clear-cut solution which any government could take without being misunderstood. In the U.S.A. one or two police forces are simply adopting the typical American solution, which is non-enforcement without repeal, but they are naturally keeping quiet about it.

Again, however, it is doubtful whether the deletion of a few—or even quite a number of—offences from the statute-book is going to solve the problem I have drawn your attention to. Something more than that is needed. One possibility is an interesting development in several jurisdictions of the U.S.A. which goes by the name of 'diversion' or 'diversionary procedure'. In effect, although the details of the procedure varies, it consists of suspending prosecution for a definite period, usually after a court appearance, and usually on an undertaking by some organization to see that the accused receives some supervision and is helped to find employment or treatment for his addiction or mental disorder, as the case may be. If by the end of this period he has not got into trouble, the case is dismissed by the court or the prosecutor enters a *nolle prosequi*. The point is that the offender is not convicted. The idea is finding favour for two reasons. First, it saves time and trouble for the overworked public prosecutors' offices, although it is said that many cases which are diverted are cases of a kind which they might well have dropped anyway, either because the offender seemed a harmless person of good character, or because they were by no means likely to secure a conviction. Second, it avoids the unintended effects of a conviction, which in the U.S.A. can be even more serious than here.

Nobody has yet published the results of any properly controlled investigation which would show whether, in terms of reconvictions or other criteria, diversion is more effective or less effective than disposal by the court. For all we know it may make no difference: but that is not quite the point.

In fact, diversion—which seems to have originated in the juvenile courts—has something in common with our juvenile liaison schemes. The main difference is that in the U.S.A. the police forces do not have the same discretion to abandon prosecution as ours do. This being so, what I want to discuss is the idea that the solution to my problem so far as this country is concerned may well be an extension of the existing police practice of cautioning or warning an offender instead of prosecuting him. I realize that it is already well developed where motoring offences and offences by juveniles are concerned. I also realize that it is by no means unheard of for adults to be cautioned for an indictable offence—and in fact the first empirical study of this practice was the work of a Research Officer in the Penal Research Unit in Oxford, Mr. Steer.[6] According to the Criminal Statistics, well over 12,000 adults are dealt with in this way every year, a figure which represents just under 4 per cent of indictable males and just under 10 per cent of indictable females.

The very high cautioning rate for women in comparison with the men's is almost entirely accounted for by shoplifting.[7] One woman is cautioned for this for every two women successfully prosecuted. If shoplifting is disregarded for both sexes, the cautioning rate for both sexes is not very different; about $3\frac{1}{2}$ per cent for men and $4\frac{1}{2}$ per cent for women in 1971. But there is an unusual feature of the men's cautions, too; a disproportionately large number of them are cautions administered to young men in their late teens or early twenties for unlawful sexual intercourse with girls under sixteen. Nearly five young men are cautioned on this account for every one who is brought to trial. The reason may be partly the degree of tolerance which most people nowadays feel towards this offence; but two other reasons have been suggested. First, the girl and her parents may prefer the case to be disposed of without the publicity of a Crown Court trial. Second, young men under the age of twenty-four are provided by statute with a very easy defence: that they believed, with reasonable cause, that the girl was over the age of consent, and that they have not previously been convicted of a like offence.

Such cases apart, however, there are at least three more or less official rules which govern cautioning, although with exceptions. The case must be strong enough to take to court;[8] the offender must accept the caution as justified[9] and the complainant, if any, must agree that a caution is sufficient. What I want to suggest is that without breaching the first two of these rules a considerable extension of cautioning is possible and desirable, especially where first offenders are concerned.

[6] See David Steer's *Police Cautions: A Study in the Exercise of Police Discretion* (Blackwell's, 1970).

[7] The cautioning rate for the non-indictable offence of soliciting by prostitutes is also very high—but that is because for the first and second offence a caution is the officially approved course.

[8] As we have seen, however, cautions for unlawful sexual intercourse with girls between the ages of thirteen and sixteen may be an exception to this rule because of the statutory defence.

[9] Although it is worth noting that the Street Offences Act of 1959 clearly contemplates that a prostitute may be cautioned for soliciting even if she objects to the caution, since the Act provides for an appeal against the caution.

The advantages of this procedure are obvious. The offender is detected, but not publicly prosecuted or convicted. He thus learns that detection is probable or at least a possibility to be reckoned with—depending on the number of occasions on which he has not been detected; but he is not publicly branded. His attitude towards the police is bound to be somewhat more favourable than if he had been prosecuted, however lenient the sentence he might expect from the court. No injustice is done so long as the police observe the rules—do not caution unless you have a case good enough to go to court and unless the offender is prepared to accept a caution as justified.

There is obviously plenty of scope for using this expedient more often. But if police forces are to be encouraged to do so, I think that courts and Parliament must face one or two issues. First, the courts at the moment refuse to take official notice of a caution. With the exception of a few juvenile courts, they will not let a previous caution be mentioned when the police are asked whether the accused has a criminal record. Only a finding of guilt in a criminal court can be mentioned. This must sometimes tip the balance in favour of prosecution, especially if the police think that the person may well repeat his offence; for if he has merely been cautioned he will appear to the court to be a 'first offender'. Is there any sound reason why a caution should not be reported to the court if a person is later convicted, in the same way as a previous conviction?

Lawyers may argue, I suppose, that the accused might accept a caution in cases in which he might, without realizing it, have a good defence. No doubt this is quite often the case when a young man under twenty-four is cautioned for the offence of unlawful sexual intercourse. If you are attracted by my suggestion that cautions should be recorded, and, where relevant, taken into account by a court if the offender has to be sentenced on a later occasion, I think you must concede that he should be warned that this may be the result of accepting a caution, and allowed to consult a lawyer if he wishes to do so. It also follows that if he decides to accept a caution— as he surely will in most cases—his acceptance should be officially recorded in a document signed by him, which indicates that he is aware of its possible consequences, and aware of his right to legal advice.

But what about the complainant? As I have said, the senior officers who decide between cautioning and prosecuting nearly always[10] take

10 Except, I believe, in motoring cases, for reasons which I do not know.

into account the attitude of the complainant, whether this is for or against prosecution. This is understandable: the police want to satisfy the law-abiding members of the public that they are enforcing the law. What is more, there is sometimes the question of restitution. If the complainant has suffered loss or damage of a kind for which the accused might reasonably be required to make restitution, a caution would prevent this from being ordered by a criminal court.

I can see two solutions, either or both of which might be adopted. Might not the police, when deciding between cautioning and prosecuting, take into account whether the offender has made restitution? This will no doubt shock some people, and I can almost hear phrases such as 'blackmail' and 'bargain justice'. Yet one often hears convicted offenders or their counsel pleading in mitigation that complete or partial restitution has been made, and courts sometimes seem to be impressed by this. I see nothing wrong with a bargain which not only saves public money and manpower but also results in quicker compensation for the victim than a delayed conviction would do. A stronger objection is that the offender who has the means to offer immediate compensation would have a better chance of being cautioned than the offender who could not do so or could do so only by instalments. For this reason I would prefer my second solution, which is to allow a magistrates' court to make a restitution or compensation order on the evidence of a caution. And, since one of the advantages of a caution from my point of view is that it does not publicly stigmatize the offender, the press should be restricted from publishing identifying particulars in such cases, just as they are in proceedings against juveniles.

These may seem minor problems: but I want to show that they can be solved, and therefore that it is not absolutely essential that the police should be so strongly guided by the complainant's attitude when deciding whether to caution. I am thinking especially of the numerous shoplifting cases, in which the shop seems to have more or less the final say in the matter.

It follows of course from my objective in making this suggestion—which is to keep down the numbers of people who have been publicly convicted—that it applies particularly to adult *first offenders*. I am not so naïve as to imagine that every so-called first offender is really being dealt with for his first offence. Not only do many first offenders ask for several similar offences to be taken into account; but there are also cases—even shoplifting cases—in which the method or other

features of the case suggest professional experience. Again, professional receivers of stolen goods are notoriously difficult to convict,
and I do not suggest that a caution would be an adequate way of
dealing with one of them. At the other extreme, however, let me
point out that there is already an official rule that a first and even a
second offence of soliciting for prostitution should be dealt with by a
caution. But I am not suggesting that there should be a hard and
fast rule for the generality of offences.

In case I sound to you like an arm-chair penologist, let me say that
with the help of the Home Office's Statistical Division—whom I
should like to thank at this point—I have been doing a little home-
work on adult first offenders. We took a sample of men and women
convicted in 1970 of one of a number of fairly common offences;
woundings, burglary, robbery, indecent assault, shoplifting, certain
other kinds of theft, taking away motor vehicles without the owner's
consent, and handling stolen goods. We then calculated what percentage of these people were first offenders. But instead of simply
calling someone a 'first offender' if he had no previous convictions
in the records, we insisted that he also had no other offences 'taken
into consideration' (which reduced the percentages a little) and also
that he was not convicted of more than one offence on the occasion
of his first unsuccessful appearance in court (which reduced the
percentages more substantially). The results can be studied in the final
column of the table on p. 235. Let me just point out that some of them
were low: for example, only about 1 in every 8 men who burgled
dwellings had no previous convictions, no t.i.c.s and no multiple
convictions. The percentages were also fairly low for other burglaries,
and for serious woundings by men.

At the other extreme, however, the percentages were high for
shoplifting. Nearly half the men and two-thirds of the women were
first offenders even by our more realistic standard. This is remarkable
when you remember how large a percentage of detected women
shoplifters are cautioned already. I suspect that some of these so-
called 'first offenders' had been cautioned before being prosecuted:
but we cannot confirm this. The percentages were also substantial
for women convicted of thefts in dwellings, or as employees, for
women involved in taking away cars, and even for men who had
stolen as employees. Now as I have said I am not so naïve as to
assume that none of these people had done any of these things before.
No doubt some had; and no doubt a few had been detected and

cautioned. All I am using these figures to suggest is that there is probably considerable scope for extending the police practice of warning first offenders.

TABLE 1

Persons aged seventeen or older convicted during 1970 of certain selected offences.

Type of offence (with Home Office group no. in brackets)	Number in sample†	ESTIMATED PERCENTAGES* OF OFFENDERS WITH		
		No previous convictions for standard list offences‡	No previous convictions or offences‡ taken into consideration	No previous convictions, offences taken into consideration or additional‡ convictions at time of first conviction
By males	N	percentage	percentage	percentage
Serious woundings (5)	174	23–35	23–35	15–25
Other woundings (8)	2,154	41–5	41–5	33–7
Indecent assaults (20)	429	49–58	46–55	37–46
Intercourse with girl aged 13, 14, or 15 (22)	126	33–48	31–47	21–35
Burglary of dwelling (28)	1,769	21–4	16–19	11–14
Other burglaries (34)	2,863	26–9	20–3	14–16
Robbery (34)	295	19–27	15–23	8–14
Thefts in dwellings (40)	510	28–34	24–31	19–25
by employees (41)	1,724	63–7	57–61	44–8
from vehicles (45)	1,849	49–53	43–7	34–8
by shoplifting (46)	1,944	53–7	50–4	45–9
Taking motor vehicles without owner's consent (48)	1,972	38–42	36–40	28–32
Handling stolen goods (54)	1,941	44–8	41–4	33–7

Nigel Walker

TABLE 1 *(continued)*

Type of offence (with Home Office group no. in brackets)	Number in sample†	ESTIMATED PERCENTAGES* OF OFFENDERS WITH		
		No previous convictions for standard list offences‡	No previous convictions or offences‡ taken into consideration	No previous convictions, offences taken into consideration or additional‡ convictions at time of first conviction
By females	N	percentage	percentage	percentage
Woundings (8)	167	67–79	67–79	55–68
Burglary (dwellings) (28)	104	58–74	40–58	25–41
Burglary (other) (30)	81	46–66	33–53	19–37
Thefts in dwellings (40)	127	55–70	49–64	36–51
by employees (41)	295	79–87	56–66	37–47
by shoplifting (46)	2,086	78–81	72–6	65–9
Taking motor vehicles without owner's consent (48)	65	62–82	57–78	52–74
Handling stolen goods (54)	367	66–75	60–9	49–58

* Because of the size of the sample examined, which varied for each offence group, it is not possible to base a precise estimate on the sample, and there is a 1 in 20 chance that the true percentage lies outside the range quoted. But since a small, but by no means negligible percentage of these offenders were counted on two or more occasions during 1970, the true percentage is likely to be somewhat nearer to the higher than the lower figure.

† Consisting of Home Office records of court appearances at which there was a finding of guilt for a standard list offence.

‡ Throughout this table only standard list offences are counted.

One or two features of my proposal would require legislation, either certainly or possibly. An example is the suggestion that compensation or restitution orders might be made by a summary court on the basis of a caution. On the other hand, I do not know of any strictly legal reason why courts should not begin tomorrow to hear evidence of previous cautions when sentencing an offender, although no doubt in practice they would want a clear lead from the Lord Chief

Justice or the Court of Appeal (Criminal Division) before doing so. But the idea of taking official statutory notice of police cautions is not unheard of: it is already done in the Street Offences Act of 1959, which is based on the assumption that prostitutes will be cautioned at least *twice* before being prosecuted for the first time. Such cautions are already recorded locally, and can be the subject of an appeal to a magistrates' court.

To sum up, I am suggesting

(i) that the percentage of our adult male population with non-motoring convictions is so high that since law enforcement needs the support of an overwhelming majority of the population we should be looking hard for ways of keeping this penal involvement rate down;

(ii) that we should therefore take a look at one or two offences of the kind which are frequently committed by people with otherwise clean records to see whether we really need them on the statute book;

(iii) but that we should also extend the practice of police cautioning for indictable offences, especially where offenders with clean records are concerned, although certain safeguards will be needed. If the cautioning rate for indictable adults were to rise considerably above its present rather low rate of 4 per cent, I doubt if any harm would come of this. On the contrary, I think it would do good, and not least to relations between the police and that section of the public which might be called 'more or less law-abiding'.

(This paper was originally delivered, as the James Smart Memorial Lecture, and published in the Police Journal (1973) XLVI, 4, 293 ff.)

18. Intermediate Treatment

NICHOLAS HINTON

'INTERMEDIATE treatment' is a somewhat vacuous phrase used ever since the publication of the White Paper, *Children in Trouble* (Cmnd. 3601), to describe new forms of community treatment of children and young persons brought before the juvenile court. It finds its permanent legislative form in the radical Children and Young Persons Act 1969.

Since the beginning of this century, legislation concerned with children and young persons has been the starting-point for change in the other parts of the criminal-justice system: the Probation Service itself being the most notable example of this. The 1969 Act continues this tradition. It aims first, to reduce the likelihood of a child appearing in court at all; second, to lessen the inevitable stigma attaching to criminal proceedings, and third, to encourage the development of a wide range of provisions for children at risk who may not necessarily be offenders.

Initiating change in the penal system is always a controversial matter. The 1969 Act is no exception, for it has been the object of argument since its inception. A bad beginning was made in 1965 with the publication of the White Paper, *The Child, The Family and the Young Offender*, whose more radical proposals included plans to abolish the juvenile courts. This and several other parts of the Paper were abandoned amid a storm of protest led by the Magistrates' Association. Even now the Act itself continues to arouse strong feelings, and there exists a vocal lobby by calling for its revision. Many of the difficulties in the working of the Act are undoubtedly due to the very considerable delay in implementation, and unfortunately the last major provision of the Act to be implemented is that of intermediate treatment. So even if one views intermediate treatment as an imaginative and progressive concept, it begins life with a millstone round its neck, not of its own making. At the same time no one would deny that it is a concept that has proved to be extraordinarily difficult to translate from the drawing-board into practice. It is as if the legislation is saying, 'Knowing that the majority of children benefit from a happy childhood, it is intended to extend this to the less fortunate.' The questions remain: what constitutes a happy childhood, and how can this be encapsulated and made readily available to others? So nothing as yet can be said of the effectiveness of intermediate treatment, but perhaps much can be learnt about the difficulties of translating ideas for change into the practice of the penal system.

The concept of intermediate treatment has its roots in a report of the Home Secretary's Advisory Council on the Treatment of Offenders made in 1962. It was called 'Non-residential Treatment of Offenders under Twenty-One'. There for the first time in an official report the need for a wide variety of flexible treatment situations was acknowledged. But the first attempt to further many of the aims of this report failed, in that the 1965 White Paper *The Child, The Family and the Offender* was abandoned. It was not until its successor *Children in Trouble*, appeared in 1968 that the idea of intermediate treatment was revived.

Previous forms of treatment available to the juvenile courts distinguished sharply between those involving complete removal from home and those which left the child in his home environment. This left the juvenile courts with difficult decisions to make in judging whether circumstances required the drastic step of taking a child away from his parents and his home. The provisions concerning intermediate treatment are designed to fill a gap by providing courts with an intermediate possibility. They will make available forms of treatment that allow the child to remain in his home but bring him into contact with a different environment, different interests and experiences which may be beneficial to him. An important object is to make use of facilities available to children who have not been before the courts, and so to secure the treatment of 'children in trouble' in the company of other children through the sharing of activities and experiences within the community. Broadly the purpose is to bring 'children in trouble' back into the mainstream of all social services available to children generally.

So the 1969 Act provides for a wide range of educational and recreational facilities commonly available in the community to be a resource for children in trouble. Normally such children and young persons will be under a supervision order imposed by juvenile courts, but the particular intermediate treatment resource will be entirely at the discretion of the supervising officer. The reasons for this are twofold: first, it is not possible in the majority of cases for the court to match the child's needs to the available resource at the time of the actual court appearance, and second, it is thought that intermediate treatment is likely to be most effective if it operates within the context of the relationship between the child and his supervisor. The only limitations placed upon the supervising officer by the Act are that the intermediate treatment resource should be one approved by the Secretary of State, and second, that it should fall within the time limits prescribed by the Act. Twelve Regional Planning Committees are responsible for submitting intermediate treatment plans for their areas. Once approved by the Secretary of State, these resources constitute the intermediate-treatment facilities available to the supervising officer, who may be local authority or probation officer within the region. The Regional Planning Committees have the further task of reviewing the use of the various facilities within their area, and making alterations and additions where necessary. Hopefully this will ensure that resources are kept up to date and atuned to contemporary needs.

A supervision order containing an intermediate treatment requirement can entail either of two different forms of treatment: residence at a specified place for a fixed period of not more than three months beginning in the first year of supervision, or temporary residence, attendance, or participation for a period, totalling not more than one month in each year of supervision. The White Paper and the Act stress that children required to undertake intermediate treatment may not necessarily be offenders. They may, for example, be subject to care proceedings for a variety of reasons, such as parental neglect or ill-treatment. Second, although the Act specifies time limits for intermediate treatment, it is hoped that the facilities available will sufficiently engage the child's interest as to encourage him to continue of his own free will beyond these time limits.

Despite the fact that so much has been said and written about intermediate treatment it appears to remain a curiously elusive and intangible concept. Successive government ministers and others responsible for policy-making continue to commend its virtues and imply that these will be clear to all, once intermediate treatment is available throughout the country. Yet for those charged with the responsibility of providing concrete facilities, such exhortations are unhelpful. It is so much easier to plan, build, and cost a prison, a community home, or even an adventure playground, than to develop a flexible variety of treatment facilities that bring a child into contact with a different environment, interests, and experiences which may be beneficial to him (which is not one attempt to define intermediate treatment). If 'intermediate' is a vague word—what are the two extremities within which the intermediary lies?—'treatment' too poses problems. This is a term on loan from the medical profession. Intermediate treatment should be concerned with making up a deficiency rather than healing. So naturally enough the tendency is to look for existing models; to fasten on a particular project or scheme and sense relief at having found a package deal which one can safely call intermediate treatment. Such long-standing projects as the Northorpe Hall scheme in Yorkshire or the Rainer Foundation's Hafod Meurig Centre in North Wales have been regarded in this light. The Northorpe Hall Trust has for the past ten years run a programme of residential week-end activities for children at risk in Leeds, combining this with mid-week visiting of their families at home and at school. Hafod Meurig, a converted school on Snowdonia, offers children from all over the country opportunities for canoeing, mountain climbing, and other outdoor pursuits, supervised by a staff who combine such skills with those of social work. It helps perhaps to see such schemes as specialist projects, for however appropriate they may be, one will surely never be in a position to develop such expensive resources regionally, let alone nationally. But even if one does not have a mental picture of a Hafod Meurig or a Northorpe Hall, it is very easy and convenient to institutionalize one's thinking on intermediate treatment.

It has been said quite simply that intermediate treatment is a matter of allowing disadvantaged children opportunities that others have by right. This seems a good starting-point, for it helps one to see whatever resource is provided is something which many will just take for granted as a quite usual and straightforward childhood interest or activity. Furthermore, this enables one to see the difficulties that arise in trying to formalize simple everyday activities into a plan, a building or a 'responsible person', such as is envisaged in the White Paper as being one way of activating resources. The greater the attempt to formalize intermediate treatment, the more difficult it will become for the child or young person to accept it. Intermediate treatment will achieve its object only if community activities are acceptable to the child. Nobody can fail to experience feelings of resentment and an unwillingness to co-operate, whether they be advantaged or disadvantaged, so long as plans or schemes are imposed on them. The activities themselves, be they rock-climbing, camping week-ends, or flute lessons, must be of interest and acceptable to the child concerned. So the role of the intermediate-treatment worker is all important. It is that of an enabler, a resource person, or facilitator. In the main it would seem that his job is to enable children to develop their own resources. Only as such can intermediate treatment hope to allow children to broaden their dimensions and develop a wider range of meaningful relationships.

So intermediate treatment should be a flexible resource. It should be on-going rather than consisting of disconnected week-ends or holiday events. Principally it should be community-based, in the sense that it must relate for the child to the little area to which he, his family, and peers feel they belong. Perhaps this may be summarized by saying that intermediate treatment must begin where the child is. In other words, it provides the opportunity of avoiding a major drawback of so much social work and penal practice, that of projecting a client into a world that bears little or no relation to his own.

If it is essential that intermediate treatment relates closely to the child; it is also important that others involved play their part. So much of social-work practice, and particularly the penal system, is wrapped up in a professionalism which denies any opportunity for participation by others. This only serves to isolate and stigmatize the offender. In any local authority area the magistrates, the police, the parents, the administrators, the schoolteachers, and many others besides will be involved. Unless all parties have the means for easy communication, intermediate-treatment committees which would include all the bodies involved, and indeed a representative group of parents and children, providing not only a forum for communication but also a means of testing the relevance of a particular facility at any point in time.

Perhaps the greatest obstacle in the way of implementing intermediate treatment is that of staffing and training. This is naturally of immediate concern to any agency such as a local authority which is given a new job to do. Another agency faced with similar problems is the Probation and After-Care Service, which makes a considerable and widespread use of volunteers. The Inner London Probation and After-Care Service, for example, has been using volunteers for at least five years. In the main the service is happy about the way the use of volunteers is developing. There has been no shortage of recruits from advertisements, a wide range of volunteer activities have developed, and a short evening orientation course is held for each new batch of volunteers. The courses have been run in a way that enables those who find themselves, or are thought to be, unsuitable to drop out. Some lessons have been learnt too. There is a strong tendency for the vast majority of volunteers to come from the middle classes with the disadvantage of retaining that barrier between the worker and the majority of his clients. Also clients tend to see such a volunteer as simply an extension of the professional probation officer, partly because volunteers have not succeeded in finding an identity and role distinct (yet equally valuable) from that of the officer. Local authorities should have no difficulty in developing similar schemes, and intermediate treatment provides ample scope for volunteer involvement.

The use of volunteers may well provide additional manpower resources and an opportunity for involving a wide section of the community, but intermediate treatment enables one to take this further. Effective intermediate treatment will in the main operate within the little communities where the children concerned live. Considerable potential lies within these communities which can be readily tapped. Within this culture, of which the children are a part, it is often their older brothers or other young adults who possess effective leadership qualities. They share a common life-style and experiences which enable them to communicate in a way that both parties understand. Among these people lies perhaps the most hopeful and relevant potential available for the professional social worker as resources to be tapped and trained. The concept of using indigenous workers, particularly in preventive work, is widespread and successful in America. Apart from the advantages in communication, the traditional barriers between the 'helped' and the 'helper' are broken down, and frequently for the helper, such an opportunity provides a meaningful alternative to his previous life-style. One use that might be made of the ninety-day residential intermediate-treatment provision is that of a training course for older children in the basic skills necessary for them to act in the role of aides or ancilliaries to professional social workers responsible for intermediate treatment. Above all else the involvement of older children in meeting the problem of their own community is a certain way of ensuring that intermediate treatment remains relevant.

It will be another ten years before there is any available evidence as to the effectiveness of intermediate treatment. The five years of discussion that have passed since the White Paper, *Children in Trouble,* have illustrated above all, our tendency as a society to define and isolate problems and those suffering those problems. The 1969 legislation simply sees the court as providing the necessary mechanism to enable those many children whose delinquency involves breaking the law to benefit from intermediate-treatment resources, despite the fact that it is hoped they share them with many others who have never been near a court. If the police or a social worker can avoid for the children in question a court appearance and yet still involve the child in an intermediate-treatment programme, it would seem that, without the need for compulsion, a valuable community resource has been properly utilized.

If intermediate treatment, at its outset or later in its development, becomes an institution, it is doomed. In common with many more social-work activities, in order to realize its aims, it must be community-based. That is, it must have its roots, look for its ideas, its ability to change and keep up to date, and its very identity in the local community, rather than in the social service department of a local authority, a voluntary organization, or a government office. The converse is a rigid and irrelevant service which will allow not only intermediate treatment but also our social services generally, or the police, or schools, or the health services to become remote and detached, and therefore relatively incapable of helping people. If, on the other hand, intermediate treatment can operate effectively as a community-based service, it will have a considerable impact not only on the children of today, but also on the system of tomorrow, which they as adults should determine.

19. The Community Service Order

JEF SMITH

LIKE most recent initiatives in the field of penal reform, the idea of
the Community Service Order owes its origin to the overcrowding
of Britain's prisons and the seemingly eternal search for alternative
penalties to imprisonment as a means of dealing with crime. In
recent years offenders have been committed to gaol in such numbers
that the Prison Service has reached a point of crisis, and the therapeutic possibilities of confinement all but totally eliminated. Together with the other innovations of the 1972 Criminal Justice Act,
the new order will be judged in many eyes quite simply by its ability
to reduce the numbers of men in prison.

Consensus on the objectives of the Community Service Order ends
at that point. Indeed the strength of the idea in terms of practical
politics has been its capacity to meet the requirements demanded of
a treatment technique from a wide and divergent range of penological points of view. The punitive case is well taken with the fact
that the work demanded of offenders can be hard, manual, and
disciplined, and that the regime through which the necessary hours
are completed will cause some inconvenience, will make inroads on
leisure hours, and could even carry a certain social stigma. All this
will be accomplished, it is argued, at small expense to the public
purse and without the inconvenience to the authorities of providing
residential accommodation or elaborate security. A man placed on a
Community Service Order, in short, suffers a substantial invasion
of his liberty without the community providing him with free
lodgings.

Marginally more positively, the work done by those on orders is
seen by some as having an at least symbolically retributive value.
The man who has robbed society pays back in some measure through
his labour, learning perhaps in the process some of the blessed
satisfaction to be gained from making a creative, rather than a
destructive contribution. This argument comes close to more liberal
views of the therapeutic value of the proposal. The radical reformers
who have welcomed the introduction of the scheme outline the

positive psychological effect on any offender of his being valued for something useful that he can contribute, a first crude move perhaps towards the rebuilding of ego strength, a quality others would prefer to describe as worth, confidence, or self-esteem.

The notion of community service appeals, in fact, to much the same coalition of penal theorists as does intermediate treatment, an innovation which in many ways it parallels. Both schemes are aimed at that middle ground of intervention on deviancy between, on the one hand, residential care, and, on the other, the bare conversational contact of a casework relationship. Occasional discussion towards the development of a trusting advisory pseudo-friendship has been shown to be quite inappropriate for some delinquents, perhaps because they have difficulty in developing relationships of any kind, perhaps through difficulty in handling the largely verbal currency of casework; until recent, however, probation supervision offered little else. On the other hand, to pluck a child or adult from his home can often disastrously disrupt many positively supportive structures, and the institutions in which offenders are clustered seem inescapably to develop norms far from helpful to the individual's successful reintegration into society outside. Was it not possible, reformers had begun to ask, to remove the delinquent rather more selectively from his home background for shorter periods, to specific projects, under controlled supervision, with defined objectives?

Whatever its mixed antecedents, the idea of community service was given a thoroughly liberal welcome when formally launched by the Wootton Committee. The Report was published in June 1970, the product of a seven-member subcommittee of the Advisory Council on the Penal System on Non-Custodial and Semi-Custodial Penalties. Chaired by Baroness Wootton of Abinger, the subcommittee described the Community Service Order as its most ambitious proposal and argued strongly that schemes should be seen as offering 'the opportunity . . . for constructive activity in the form of personal service to the community . . . and not as wholly negative and punitive'. The idea was, of course, not altogether new, and Lady Wootton and her colleagues paid tribute to three strands of experience on which they particularly drew—the British tradition of voluntary service, some limited experiments overseas, and the well-established practice of employing prisoners and Borstal inmates on extra-mural work.

Experience from outside the United Kingdom was briefly reviewed by the Committee, but can hardly have played an important role in its thinking. State and municipal courts in the United States of America, for example, can order traffic offenders to carry out work in hospitals, and in West Germany juvenile courts can issue directives which offer scope for such imaginative, if risky, linking of punishment to crime as sending young drunks to help in homes for inebriates. Gimmickry of this sort, however, was wisely, if somewhat aloofly, dismissed by Lady Wootton, the value of the work done being ranked as more important than its apparent appropriateness to any particular offence.

Earlier British experience in the involvement of offenders in work of value to the community has usually been linked with custodial treatment, from which it provided, as it were, some slight extramural relief. The inmates of some Borstals and probation hostels have participated in voluntary schemes outside their institutions, and over recent years, selected prisoners have been allowed to work alongside volunteers on weekend projects. These experiments, though interesting in their own right, have rarely been at all systematically evaluated and their relevance to the new orders is in any case doubtful. Participation has always been voluntary, but is usually made attractive to those involved by the fact that it includes a temporary escape from the confines of the institution, a situation quite contrasted to that of an offender carrying out a stipulated programme of work as the sole constituent of his sentence.

The Wootton Committee did feel it important, however, to relate its proposal to the well-established national tradition of volunteering to undertake tasks of social usefulness. Again the parallels are arguable. Organized voluntary service is a largely middle-class concept in our society. It depends on a surplus of leisure, a normative framework which rewards service with heightened prestige or respect, and generally at least a small capacity to bear some incidental, if minor expenses. It is not too cynical to suggest that no one gives anything for nothing; volunteers need rewards as much as paid workers, though these may well not be expressed in monetary terms. Traditionally volunteers have been middle-aged, the women attracted by the opportunity to use otherwise excessive free time, the men perceiving the benefits to be obtained from a reputation for involvement in activities not directly remunerative. The rapid expansion of further and higher education has added an army of school children and students to the ranks of volunteers, and a whole new range of organizations, specially equipped to cater for the particular contribution of the young. Again it has proved important to recognize the need for projects to offer young people more than merely the satisfaction of doing useful work. Significantly the best-publicized of schemes over the last twenty-five years have provided participants with the chance to travel abroad, with, of course, the very proper additional objective of spreading international understanding or aiding developing countries. Organizations with programmes limited to this country invariably find it easier to recruit to projects offering strong human contact and high immediate job satisfaction. Where manual work has to be carried out, it is generally made more palatable by being organized through groups, often in short residential work-camps which provide the young participants with the opportunity for social contact.

In practice, it has to be admitted, the offender placed on a community service order is unlikely to see his service quite as positively as would a volunteer. His participation will be voluntary only in the sense that, as with a probation order, his consent in court will be required (and usually given for fear of a less attractive sentence). Manual work is unlikely to be a refreshing break from a weekday sedentary job, from too much leisure, or from relaxed study, projects will rarely offer offenders the opportunity of travel, and service will hardly bring social prestige, honours, or business advantage. Indeed, it would be easy to see the work demanded under a Community Service Order as little more than forced labour, and it is wise to remember that it may well be so perceived by many of those sentenced. This is, of course, little different from acknowledging the fact that some offenders placed on probation experience supervision as a tiresome chore rather than as the helpful and positive relationship intended.

A good deal of thought was given during the formulation of the proposal to the question, whether the work that an offender placed on a Community Service Order would be required to perform could be reckoned to be forced labour within the meaning of various international agreements. The European Convention for the Protection of Human Rights and Fundamental Freedoms forbids forced or compulsory labour, excepting only work done in the course of detention or during conditional release.[1] The 1930 International

[1] Article 4 (2) provides that no one shall be required to perform 'forced or compulsory labour'. The only relevant exception is paragraph (a) of that Article

Labour Office Convention for the Suppression of Forced or Compulsory Labour more broadly permits work exacted as the result of a court conviction, but specifically excludes the placing of an offender at the disposal of private associations.[2] Compliance with the I.L.O. rule would of course have debarred the participation of voluntary organizations in the supervision of offenders. These considerations may well have contributed to the adoption of the formula for consent which was eventually provided in the legislation. It seems likely that a British government would be willing to introduce a similar sort of order without the consent provision only if it were first able to promote an amendment to the Conventions.

The liberal standpoint of the Wootton Committee ensured one other critical characteristic for the scheme—its being administered by probation officers. A very different tone would have been set if the projects had been placed under the prison service, though the possibility was considered; the main objections were the geographically awkward siting of prisons and the need to root the order firmly in the community with a direct link to the court. But there are other advantages to probation auspices, some of them to the service itself.

Probation has remained loyal to the casework relationship as a technique of helping its clients to achieve change, through a period in which social workers in other settings have begun to experiment widely if not yet with very conclusive results in the fields of group and community work. Ways of working, directed less exclusively to achieving modification of the individual and increasingly to factors in this wider environment—indeed to the society in which he lives—are consistent both with the more overtly radical political positions adoped by many social workers of late and with recent developments in sociological theories of deviancy. Though the clients of the penal services, by their very status as clients, are fairly clearly identified as out of step with the norms of society, many probation officers feel that appropriate therapy should help to relate a man to his fellows rather than to stress the exclusive need for him to adjust personally.

which states: 'Any work required to be done in the ordinary course of detention imposed according the provision of Article 5 of the Convention or during conditional release from such detention.'

 2 Article 2 (2) provides: 'Any work or service exacted from any person as a consequence of a conviction in a court of law, provided that the said work or service is carried out under the supervision and control of a public authority and the said person is not moved to or placed at the disposal of private individuals, companies or associations . . .'

The effects of these facets of theory and practice on the probation service itself have not yet been felt significantly, but they could, in time, herald major changes. Probation officers have prided themselves on the individual responsibility they exercise over their cases —a degree of professional automomy they mark as particularly contrasted to the relatively bureaucratic stance of local authority social workers. Such a mode of work depends, however, on its practitioners operating within a wider organization. The effect of the introduction of schemes of work other than the personal case-load will inevitably lead to a more developed teamwork approach, and, in the nature of organizations, to a lessening of the freedom of front-line operators as a hierachy of resource control develops. The Community Service Order is not the only innovation pointing the service to a more structured future; over the next few years it looks like taking its place beside a whole battery of resources controlled by probation officers—hostels, day centres, week-end schemes, groups of all descriptions—which in due course could present almost a full range of social services for the isolated and delinquent.

The need for voluntary organization to maintain the sort of positive image that attracts good public relations and continuing financial support somewhat undermines their wholehearted participation in a scheme such as the administration of Community Service Orders. By contrast the Probation Service must be, and is prepared occasionally to weather criticism. The distinction neatly demonstrates the falsity of the statement that statutory bodies in the social services are necessarily conservative because of their public funding, and voluntary organizations inherently innovatory, thanks to their financial independence.

The working out of practical details for the implementation of Community Service Orders, following the welcome given to the Wootton Report, fell to a Home Office working party chaired by Mr. E. N. Kent, presently an Assistant Secretary in the Probation and After-Care Department of the Home Office. On only one major point did the Kent working group disagree with its predecessor. Wootton had argued for the option to be open to courts to combine a Community Service Order with a probation order, but Kent preferred to contrast the two types of treatment by keeping them quite separate. The distinction frees a supervising probation officer of the controlling role required in the administration of a Community Service Order, gives the new Order a status of its own, and arguably will make evaluation simpler. Provision is retained for an offender under a Community Service Order to seek voluntarily the help of a probation officer, or for a court or courts to impose both orders on the same man for separate offences. For these good reasons, the Act follows the Kent formula closely.

On most other fronts, however, the Kent Committee took Wootton's thinking one stage nearer to practical operation. In particular it began the important job of consulting with the voluntary organizations whose work was again seen as an appropriate model and whose co-operation was hoped for. A senior staff member of the National Council for Social Service was a member of the group and seven local councils were drawn into consultations. It has been an important part of the plan throughout that offenders should have the opportunity, wherever possible, of working alongside normally recruited volunteers; one obvious technique of achieving this desirably therapeutic objective is for those on orders to be grafted into existing schemes of service run by well-established voluntary bodies. The voluntary movement, however, has always been sensitive to any suggestion that pressure is brought on its workers in any way that would undermine their genuinely voluntary status. Doubts have been expressed in the past, for example, over schoolchildren undertaking work as an item in their curriculum, and as offenders will in no real sense of the work be volunteers for service, a number of organizations wished to be quite clear on this point.

The ambivalence of the voluntary bodies is most acutely expressed on the question of taking back to court offenders who breach the conditions of their orders—by failing to turn up without an excuse, by repeatedly arriving late, and in some cases presumably, by not working hard enough. Almost unanimously, the bodies consulted felt that their image and activities would be harmed if they were required to furnish in court evidence of a breach, though it had to be pointed out that it would be impossible to prevent the defence in any proceedings mentioning the name of an organization with which the offender had been involved.

It would be dangerous to assume therefore that Community Service Orders, by being administered by probation officers, will automatically escape the adverse image of the law as it is perceived by most offenders. Rather the reverse process could be occurring; with the acceptance of the running of the scheme by the Probation Service a further step is taken towards the bureaucratization of a once highly professional operation. Large bodies which value good relations with their clients may succeed in personalizing contact for a while through a structure that encourages the development of long-term relationships with individual workers; but the scale and complexity of organizations makes such arrangements difficult to perpetuate. It would be naïve not to note that the closeness of the officer–offender relationship, the aspect of probation that has traditionally been regarded as its greatest strength, is not present in the concept of community service, though that is not to concede that the plan may not have compensatory strengths in other directions.

This problem contributed to an important development in the plans for the running of actual schemes as they were worked out in more detail. It now seems likely that probation services will organize some projects in which they retain full responsibility for the supervision of participants. Other schemes, in which the day-to-day work is more under the control of a voluntary body, or indeed of another statutory agency, will be able to pass unsatisfactory workers to a probation-run project. If necessary, breach proceedings can later be taken by probation officers running their own projects. From the participant's point of view then, there will be the best possible chance to make a success of the Order.

The Kent Group included as members several people who were later to be involved with the detailed running of pilot projects. Five experimental areas—Inner London, Nottingham, Durham, Kent, and South-West Lancashire—were selected during 1972 and a sixth—Shropshire—added towards the end of the year. In each area a senior or assistant principal probation officer was assigned or specially appointed to run the local scheme and additional administrative staff gradually allocated. The detailed work of liaison with voluntary groups naturally passed to a local level and a clearer idea of the sort of projects that might be available began to emerge. It was apparent from an early stage that a broad distinction could be drawn between work involving fairly personalized contact with people and service not necessarily less valuable but perhaps less demanding in terms of relationships. The former would be mostly auxiliary social work, the latter largely manual. It was hoped that even the manual work would have a clear community usefulness about it. Organizers of volunteers know the dangers of projects of which the worth is in doubt and the regrettable ease with which quite useless work can be suggested by those who are able to get free labour. From an offender's standpoint, a project without obvious value would, of course, be seen as either a condescending attempt to keep him busy, or worse, stone breaking under a new guise.

The danger that offenders would be seen to be in competition with paid labour was recognized at an early stage, particularly as 1972 was a year of generally high unemployment and of particularly bad conditions in the two pilot areas situated in the north of England. A general assurance was given that projects would not be undertaken if it was at all possible that they might be carried out professionally—though this makes it even more difficult to make sure that work is useful and relevant—and following national consultation with the Trade Union Congress local representatives and consultants were appointed to each of the Probation Committees involved in the pilot scheme.

It seemed likely as the scheme was formally made available to selected courts at the start of January 1973 that manual projects would predominate in the fields of improving leisure and recreational facilities and helping the aged with decorating and gardening. Auxiliary social work outlets for service could include assisting at Cheshire Homes and community settlements, helping with pony riding for the disabled, and even serving as Assistant Scout Masters. The narrow line between the two sorts of work and the fact that building a playground, for example, might lead on to helping with play leadership was seen as offering desirable flexibility, perhaps too the chance for an individual offender to progress naturally to new types of service, or even remain involved in a project after the formal end of his Order. Almost predictably the scheme which attracted a great deal of press attention in Inner London—the clearing of the Thames foreshore—is unlikely to be operative for some time on account of the large number of local authorities that would have to be involved.

As planning and consultations were in progress in the selected pilot areas, the Criminal Justice Bill was making its way through Parliament to receive the Royal Assent in October 1972. The aspect of Community Service Orders that proved most controversial in the debates was their length, amendments being moved at various stages to revert from the Bill's maximum of 240 hours to the limit of half that length proposed originally in the Wootton Report. The longer term, it was suggested, could lead to service lasting as long as nine months with work on every Saturday, but the Government, while admitting that neither proposal had any very scientific basis, argued that it would be easier to lower the maximum if courts were found habitually to impose strong sentences than to increase a figure found to be too low. It is probable too that the Home Office firmness on this point owes something to the need to satisfy more conservative elements in Parliament and among magistrates that the new Act was not to be seen as being soft on the criminal.

Inevitably the operation of the scheme will depend a good deal on how it is used by the courts. An explanation of what is involved must be given to an offender in court before he consents, and the way in which judges and chairmen express the nature of the order will clearly play a major part in how its imposition is perceived. There is certainly a great deal of goodwill towards the schemes, and the evaluation of its operation in the pilot areas will be awaited eagerly. A Home Office research team will monitor progress and aims to produce a first report, which can hardly be more than a descriptive survey, by mid-1974. The sections outlining the order have been described as the showpiece of the Act, and certainly a great deal is expected of them. The fact that the recommendations of the Wootton Committee were embodied in a statute within two years of having been published is evidence of the hope being placed on the new measures. If they fail, the crisis of the prisons will deepen; but if they achieve even a modest success the whole field of alternative sentences to incarceration could open up a new future for penology.

20. Non-custodial Supervision

PETER McNEAL

THE Probation Service has lived through its promising youth. It has yet to reach its prime, although perhaps in the late 1950s some observers felt that it had finally come of age. Certainly by that time it was beginning to play an increasingly important role in the assessment and treatment of a wide range of offenders, and it was in 1958 that Sir Leon Radzinowicz wrote: 'If I were asked what was the most significant contribution made by this country to the new penological theory and practice which struck root in the twentieth century—the measure which would endure . . . my answer would be probation.'[1]

It was in 1907 with the Probation of Offenders Act that the supervision of an offender in the community, instead of a prison sentence, became a possibility. With this measure the courts could withhold punishment, and a breakthrough was made into the system of an automatic punitive reaction to crime.

Change was gradual. The Probation Service slowly expanded and established itself within the court setting, but even in the 1940s and possibly the early 1950s it still retained an almost rural character, with a confidence and certainty of identity that is so often associated with a small community. Its role was to provide a unique casework service for the courts, and that was how it was seen. The two main areas of work were the supervision of probationers and the preparation of social-inquiry reports. In retrospect that period now seems one of comparative calm.

The report of the Streatfeild Committee in 1961[2] represented a watershed for the service by recognizing the skill and competence of the court social worker. Not only was the content of our work to be extended by providing the higher courts with pre-trial social-inquiry reports, but the service was also encouraged to make positive recommendations in these reports as to an offender's suitability

[1] *The Results of Probation* (Macmillan & Co. Ltd., 1958). A report of the Cambridge Department of Criminal Science.
[2] Report of the Departmental Committee on the Business of the Criminal Courts (Cmnd. 1289), Feb. 1961.

for treatment, and not just suitability for probation. Since that Report successive Acts of Parliament and Statutory Regulations, directly or indirectly, have widely affected the work of the service. It has acquired a multitude of assorted duties, numbering now more than thirty, which prevent any narrow definition of the work undertaken. Since 1964 the service has accepted responsibility for voluntary and statutory after-care, prison welfare, parole, and, in addition, a variety of work with hostels, divorce-court welfare, voluntary organizations, other social agencies, and individual volunteers. It was in 1967 that it was aptly renamed the Probation and After-Care Service.

Martin Davies argues in a recent article that the Probation Service has 'good reason to be pleased with itself' as a result of the way in which new work has been absorbed during the 1960s with less disruption than might have been anticipated:

> ... with regard to staff morale, with regard to the way the service satisfies the demands of the local courts for diagnostic advice, and with regard to the way the service fulfils its statutory and other requirements in respect of its clients, organizational directives are being achieved day by day, week by week, as a result of careful planning and continuous effort on the part of central government, probation committees and the administrative grades of the service.[3]

Looked at from inside the service, this assessment seems very optimistic, particularly at the present time of unrest. If the organizational aims have been achieved, it has often been at the cost of a serious loss in morale, and a dilution of professional standards in the care and treatment of offenders. In my view, too much has been expected of a young profession; it has expanded too quickly without sufficient preparation for newly allotted tasks, or adequate resources being made available.[4] The recent implementation of the main recommendations of the Butterworth Committee,[5] in particular the two-tier salary scheme for main-grade officers doing the same job, has resulted in widespread discontent in many areas, and is seen as threatening the basic roots and spirit of the service.

---

[3] Martin Davies, 'The Objectives of the Probation Service', *British Journal of Social Work* (Autumn 1972), p. 314.

[4] See David Fowler, 'Probation Problems', *New Society*, 30 Nov. 1972: 'Scarcity of resources has long been an issue in the service. The credibility gap between the words and deeds of policy-makers has fostered a mood of cynicism'.

[5] Report of the Butterworth Enquiry into the work and pay of probation officers and social workers (H.M.S.O., London, 1972).

Following the implementation of the new Criminal Justice Act 1972 the immediate need for the Probation and After-Care Service is for a period of consolidation. The first and overriding requirement is the recruitment and training of more probation officers.[6] The recent report of the House of Commons Expenditure Committee[7] stated quite clearly that the estimate of 4,700 (since increased to 5,000) probation officers by 1975 is only likely to relieve existing pressure and will not meet the full requirements of a service already committed to important new experimental areas of work.

Historically the Probation Service has played a vital part in the administration of criminal justice and has brought to the criminal-court setting a much needed concern for the individual offender. Although our involvement in the juvenile courts, as a result of the Children and Young Persons Act 1969, will be significantly reduced in the future, I believe that our primary role is still as social workers to the courts, and as a recent paper by the National Association of Probation Officers (N.A.P.O.) made clear, there is a wide measure of agreement among officers that the 'future service should include in its programme any work which "emanates" from the courts, and the scope of its activities should be regulated by this concept'.[8] It seems to me that this is a useful formula and provides a logical justification for involvement in the new areas of prison welfare, parole and after-care, as well as the work of matrimonial reconciliation and, in particular, the staffing of the proposed new family courts.

At this point is it is useful to consider what kind of organizational and administrative structure would be best able to meet our primary task. The Seebohm Committee was precluded (by choice of the Probation and After-Care Service?) from examining the possible inclusion of the Probation Service with the local-authority social-work services, but integration has been implemented in Scotland following the Social Work (Scotland) Act 1968. The arguments advanced in favour of this absorption rest mainly on the social-welfare nature of probation, and the essential unity of social-work theory and practice. The permanent isolation of probation means

[6] Fowler, op. cit., 'On average the service is 7·5% understaffed and in some areas, 26%.'

[7] *First Report from the Expenditure Committee, Probation and After-Care 1971/72* (H.M.S.O., London) para. 46.

[8] *The Future Development of the Probation and After-Care Service*, National Association of Probation Officers, 1970.

that it is excluded, at least organizationally if not professionally, from the mainstream of social work, and the continued existence of a separate social service for offenders suggests that they are quite different from other people. In fact offenders share common needs with many others in social distress, and in being treated separately are in danger of being 'labelled'. It is important to look beyond the immediate symptoms of breakdown to the underlying problems of family and community. A family-based social-work service which excludes responsibility for the deviant and delinquent is seen as being illogical, impractical and also uneconomic in terms of manpower. In addition, while local authorities share in the financing of the service, they have little control over its management.

Another view of future development is that the service should become a national one, controlled by a central government department under, say, a Ministry of Justice, and become a correctional service. Many officers feel that in any case the service has already moved a long way towards such a position with its increasing involvement in the penal system, with greater concentration on work with adult offenders, and more particularly with our commitment to prison welfare. In this view the service would become a specialist agency concerned exclusively with the care and treatment of the adult offender, closely associated or even amalgamated with the prison service, losing most, if not all, of its links with courts. The case is made that the Probation Service now has developed a body of knowledge and built up a professional expertise that makes it uniquely equipped to fulfil this new role. It is argued that criminality is not just another symptom of underlying social malaise, but that it represents specific behaviour patterns which are *sui generis* and need concentrated specialist treatment. The criminal is seen as having a particular problem about authority, and the probation officer, in his capacity as an agent of social control backed by the authority of the penal system is well placed both to meet the special needs of the offender and to supply the element of coercion that public disquiet about crime demands.

It is further argued, and on the whole by those outside the Probation Service, that because of the rapid increase in the number of offenders before the courts and the additional responsibilities placed on the service, the only viable structure is a national one. Such a service would be financed and administered by central government, recruitment and training would be rationalized, and professional standards could be raised. Further, as with the Prison Service, such an organization could possibly expand more quickly, and would be in a stronger position *vis-à-vis* the Treasury for allocation of resources.

The Probation Service has rejected both these views of its future. Maybe the present administrative structure is deficient in many respects, but it is preferred to the known alternatives. The service wishes to remain independent for reasons which seem to me very convincing. At the moment the organization in England and Wales is based on a tripartite combination of responsibility which provides for the involvement of central government, local government, and the courts (largely the magistracy) in the running of the service. The expenditure committee described it as 'an untidy picture of divided responsibility and divided control', and yet welcomed the view of the Home Office that the service might continue to be run 'separately but not centrally'. An earlier Report by the Morison Committee in 1962 had also found that the administrative arrangements work well 'in spite of their theoretically insupportable structure'.[9]

The independence of the service ensures that it is free both from local political pressure and from control by the Executive—it must be free of sectional interests, and be seen to be free of such interests. Administered largely by committees of magistrates, and additional co-opted members, who on the whole have an understanding of the needs of the service, and who work closely with probation officers in the court setting, a degree of mutual trust and respect has developed. A local authority, with all the demands made on its limited resources, might understandably consider that the needs of children, the sick, and the aged were paramount, and those of offenders secondary. In addition, if a merger took place, the responsibility for the service would pass to the Secretary of State for Social Services, and if the penal system is to be seen as a whole the Home Secretary must retain some control over the resources provided.

At the same time we do not want to be a specialist crime-treatment service. For a start it would make our casework task more difficult than it is already, with offenders seeing us as controllers rather than enablers, simply an extension of the long arm of the law. However sophisticated our terminology may be, we still continue 'to advise, assist, and befriend', words which have been in use ever since the

[9] *Report of the Departmental Committee on the Probation Service* (H.M.S.O., London, 1962), para. 171.

Probation of Offenders Act 1907. A correctional service, as Mervyn Murch foresees when writing about the dilemma facing probation, would inevitably mean that we should cease to be a broadly based social-work service for the courts, and 'by making the treatment of offenders its primary task . . . more general social work activities in the court setting would increasingly be seen as of secondary importance'.[10] There would be the danger that diagnosis and treatment would be seen as separate and divorced from one another. It thus seems vital that when the new family courts are established, the probation service should provide the welfare officers, and be intimately involved, so that the balance between the undoubted correctional element in our work should be matched by the caring and befriending element.[11]

We want to preserve our links and involvement with the local community. This stems from a tradition which is seen by probation officers to be of great importance, that the service is essentially a local service, serving a local community and a local court. The very roots of the service sprang from the local community with the police-court missionaries, who were indigenous members of a community concerned about their neighbours, and who developed close relationships with the courts. From that tradition a strong principle of autonomy has developed. The freedom that the present structure has allowed individual probations officers in their ways of working, the responsibility that they have been encouraged to accept in the management of their casework, have been the main reason for the undoubted high level of job satisfaction felt by a majority of probation officers. The fear is that the dead hand of a centrally administered system, among other things, would seriously impinge on this freedom of action and stifle initiative and experiment, as we became absorbed by the civil service. Already there has been a gradual and rather insidious extension of control as the service has grown and the hierarchy has expanded. It is important that the extension of the hierarchy results in greater support and encouragement for the

[10] Mervyn Murch, 'Seebohm: A Painful Dilemma for Probation', *Probation* (Mar. 1969).

[11] See for example, 'Evidence to the Law Commission Working Party on Family Courts', *Conference of Principal Probation Officers 1972*: 'Many probation officers are motivated by a vocational urge to work in the preventive field and with younger persons. To entirely remove from the Service this aspect of its work would, in our view, considerably weaken its capacity to provide for its staff a social work experience throughout the whole range of social mal-adjustment.'

officer working at grass-roots level, and not a concentration of power at the top.

The need for imaginative leadership at all levels in the probation service was never greater than at present, when there is a real danger that the administration of the service will become more and more alienated from the basic-grade probation officer. The evidence submitted by N.A.P.O. to the Expenditure Committee dealt at some length with this matter, stressing in particular that the kind of bureaucratic structure associated with commerce and industry was inappropriate in probation.

Much has been heard of late about changes in government policy with respect to the future role and development of the probation service. Gradually it has dawned on administrators that not only does imprisonment have a deleterious effect on many prisoners, but also that many more offenders could be dealt with in the community without undue risks to public safety being taken. For some years now there has been much talk about alternative methods to imprisonment; although it seems likely that a desire to expand non-custodial means of dealing with offenders stems as much from the fact of overcrowded prisons and the need for economy as from a turning away from more punitive measures.

Many estimates have been given of the number of offenders who might be dealt with by non-custodial methods. We imprison a higher proportion of offenders than many western-European countries,[12] and sentences tend to be longer. The average length of sentences in 1971 was 28 per cent higher than ten years earlier.[13]

Many offenders are immature personalities who rapidly become institutionalized, finding personal relationships more and more difficult. Many of them are extremely inefficient people who desperately need help to develop a greater measure of self-determination. Their crimes reflect their inefficiency; punitive measures are so often counter-productive in dealing with them. It is thought to be true that, if many of these men are not locked up, there will be an increase in minor crime, but this may be the price society will have to pay for a new strategy. On the other hand, without being alarmist, or over-persuaded by current American experience, it seems that, judging by the last two decades, major indictable crime

---

[12] See Bishop, 'Aspects of European Penal System', above, p. 5 and fn. 6.
[13] See Report on the Work of the Prison Department, 1971, Cmnd. 5037, see Table, para. 7, pp. 2–3.

will increase in this country over the next decade. If therefore the prison system were to concentrate largely on the hard core of professional criminals, and particularly those who are violent, it might be possible to be more ambitious in the treatment of the army of petty recidivists who comprise so much of our present prison population. The Probation Service will undoubtedly be called upon to play a central role in this campaign.

Allowing for cultural differences we can gain some idea of the possible range of treatment programmes that might be developed from the penal policies already adopted in certain other countries, particularly where the emphasis has been on the greater use of supervision in the community. In both California and Holland (which have very different penal philosophies) major changes in policy have been effected, bringing about a reduction in the prison population, curbing the rate of recidivism, and making substantial economic savings.

In 1964 the California legislature commissioned a research study into future trends in the prison population and the forecast was that new admissions would double in a decade. A vast new prison-building programme would have to be undertaken at the cost of over $100 m.; in the event it was decided to expand the Probation Service instead and so the probation subsidy programme was started. Research findings had already shown that at least 25 per cent of new admissions to penal institutions could be safely and effectively supervised in the community. So a plan was devised, of some financial complexity, whereby an expanded Probation Service was subsidized in proportion to the extent that it was able to reduce the number committed to state institutions.

Since July 1966 forty-seven counties, covering 96 per cent of the population of California have so far joined the scheme. The total number of adults and youths in state penitentiaries and institutions has dropped by 8,000 and there are now 200,000 people on probation compared with 50,000 in state and county gaols. It cannot be claimed that the crime rate has fallen, but the rate of recidivism has declined.[14]

For a state of about 20,000,000 inhabitants there are more than 5,000 probation officers. Compare this with 3,687 officers in June 1972 for a population in England and Wales of 48,000,000. Treatment methods vary considerably and a number of experiments in differential treatment have been introduced. Before the scheme

[14] See Malcolm Stuart, *Guardian*, 7 Oct. 1972.

started caseloads were as high as 200 per officer, which only allowed for minimal supervision. Now caseloads may be as low as twenty, and some clients are seen daily. A beginning has been made at devising a typology of offenders, matching treatment to needs.

During the last ten years the Dutch have cut their prison population by half, and the crime rate has risen by 10 per cent. Britain, with over four times the population of Holland, has more than fifteen times as many people in prison, and our recorded crime rate has doubled in ten years.

The Dutch judiciary at the instigation of the Public Prosecutor's Office has gradually introduced a new sentencing policy with an emphasis on keeping people out of prison as long as possible, and in sending people to prison for shorter periods. The extent to which many prisoners become dependent on the institutional life seems to be widely recognized in the Netherlands. David Cohen describes 'the attempt to maintain deterrent value by making prison more of a mystery—a last resort you send a persistent offender to, rather than one of your first solutions. It is the final punitive step.'[15]

Probation is used extensively throughout Holland. Details of the probation organization need not concern us here, other than to stress the remarkable combination of private voluntary effort together with financing from public funds that make up the system. Two of the most striking features of the Dutch system of an alternative to prison are firstly, the extent to which the community is involved—for example many agencies are set up for young people by young people, and secondly, the variety and range of different treatment programmes available within the community for delinquents or people in crisis situations.

We are faced in this country today with a real crisis in our prison system. Since 1950 the prison population has doubled in England and Wales, and trebled in Scotland, and a recent forecast estimated that the present number of 36,000 (two years ago it was 40,000) in custodial care could rise to between 55,000 and 60,000 at the beginning of the 1980s.

Already the Government has announced a new prison-building programme—urgently necessary in the light of the conditions in some of our early-Victorian penal establishments, which are still housing thousands of prisoners. The danger is that new prisons will be immediately filled up, rather like new motorways, with an overflow

[15] David Cohen, 'Out of Jail', *New Society*, 4 May 1972.

from existing structures, and the result will be that more and more people will be committed to custody. At the same time as we build new prisons and improve conditions in them to allow for more rehabilitative methods, the over-all population can and should be reduced as the older prisons are pulled down.

The next decade could be a time for bold experiment. Already a start has been made with the introduction of parole, and with the important new developments in the Criminal Justice Act of community-service orders and day-training centres. An experimental bail hostel in London has recently opened. A research project in differential treatment is under way, and certain areas are to be involved in an experiment in intensive supervision. But if these various schemes are to be developed and expanded, if a real impact is to be made on the prison population, and intensive treatment in the community is to become a reality, the present level of recruitment to the Probation Service will have to be sharply increased. Hugh Klare talks in terms of 10,000 probation officers being required in the 1980s,[16] an increase of over 100 per cent on the present number. In 1971 there was a growth rate of 5·4 per cent. How can it be done? An intensive recruitment drive must be linked with the provision of adequate resources. The probation officer has a demanding and difficult job, requiring a wide range of skills and considerable personal resilience. If more offenders are to be dealt with in the community, many of whom are socially inadequate, some suffering from personality disorder, others aggressive, many very demanding in terms of time and patience, standards required of potential entrants to the service will have to remain high. The immense satisfaction and the absorbing interest of the work should appeal to many, especially those contemplating, or indeed already in, careers which are neither fully stretching nor personally rewarding.

With a new recruitment drive there are, of course, serious implications for training, both at the initial stage and, equally important, as an officer's career develops. In-service training and frequent refresher courses become more important and relevant as the demands upon officers increase and knowledge develops. In an expanded and invigorated service there would be room for a much wider range of treatment methods and new techniques. However, individual casework is likely, in my view, to remain predominant. In a society in danger of becoming more impersonal the help and

[16] Evidence to the Expenditure Committee, Report, op. cit., p. 81.

support in a close relationship with a sympathetic and understanding adult can, in part, counteract the sense of alienation that many of our clients feel. Some people will need the most intensive individual attention, others may best be helped in a group situation. Officers will clearly need to be trained for both.

In the future it is likely that there will be a greater emphasis on community work. There will certainly be an extensive use of hostels of different types for many of those people who are homeless, lonely, perhaps with a serious drink problem, who need the support of a small community. Already a number of probation hostels for adults have been opened, and many more are planned. Residential provision is the first requirement for many offenders, and there is currently an acute crisis as one lodging house after another closes down. The common experience of probation officers in dealing with many prisoners on release is that there is simply nowhere for them to go, and this total lack of adequate provision is seen as a major factor in persistent crime. A wide range of facilities is needed, half-way houses, hostels catering for homeless single people (and not exclusively ex-prisoners), and non-residential centres such as the Circle Club, a meeting place for ex-prisoners and voluntary associates, where food, companionship, and social activities are provided. The problem of homelessness is not solved by just providing accommodation. Friendship in a caring community is a primary need.

Traditional ways of working will have to be supplemented by new approaches together with the use of additional resources. One such development may well be the provision of community-care and day-treatment centres. In London a pilot experiment is about to start with such a centre, where the more damaged and deprived clients, with whom traditional casework methods achieve little or no success, may be referred for immediate basic needs in the first instance, with a longer-term aim of bridging the gap between institutional living and the community. A wide range of facilities will be provided; work projects, group therapy, remedial teaching, medical and psychiatric services, to name a few. The aim is to provide a supportive community for the rootless and homeless, who live at or near permanent crisis level. The Probation Service is dealing with an increasing number of such men, mostly in the field of after-care, and some kind of residential provision where on-going and regular daily support are available, has now become imperative.

One important new development is in the recruitment and training of ex-offenders to undertake social work. A start is about to be made in Bristol where the Home Office has agreed in principle to an experiment in which young people found guilty of serious offences can be offered social work careers as an alternative to custodial sentences. In Chino, California, such a scheme has been in operation for some years, and the results are encouraging. The Manhattan Court Employment Project, launched by the Vera Institute of Justice, employs counsellors who are ex-offenders, all of whom come from some of the toughest ghetto areas.

There are many volunteers working together with probation officers in the field of after-care at the moment, and this has certainly been one of the most important and significant developments in the last few years. There would now seem to be the opportunity, based on experience and knowledge, to widen the scope of this voluntary effort, recruiting support from wider sections of the community, and using associates in other areas of work. The Expenditure Committee suggested using volunteers to a greater extent in the probation field; I think a strong case can be made for certain experimental projects using volunteers, especially as new developments in community work are started.

The need for continuous assessment and research into both traditional and experimental methods of working is axiomatic. In the next few years it is important that we should develop a clearer understanding of what it is we are doing and, together with administrators and policy makers, we will need to be more concerned about questions of effectiveness of different treatment methods. The fact must be faced that we do not know what type of treatment is most appropriate for different categories of offenders, and perhaps it will be many years before a typology of offenders is available.

Many probation officers, and particularly those who have joined the service in the last few years, have a strong sociological orientation. Many of them bring a radical new thinking to our problems and they are not slow to question the conventional wisdom. Influenced by the writings of criminologists in America and in this country, crime and its causes are seen as being deeply rooted in the social structure. Psychological theories of aetiology are not readily accepted. Many clients are seen as the economic casualties of the social system. A corrective was needed to the concept of agency function that dominated probation, as well as the social-work profession as a whole, during the 1950s. This sanctioned the emphasis on the one-to-one relationship, often to the exclusion of the total family and environment from which the client came. But however strong the case is for substantial social and economic change, the contribution that we can make as social workers can only be marginal. What we are able to do is to be forceful in articulating the needs of many of the socially deprived with whom we have close contact. We are more aware than most professional groups in our society that reality of life for many people is intolerable, and we should, in my opinion, be particularly concerned about the problems of the low-paid worker, employment and training opportunities, leisure facilities for the young, housing. The recent Halsey Report, concerned with the education of socially disadvantaged children, argues that 'education is about housing, jobs, incomes, and all the accompanying social features'.[17] Home and neighbourhood are, for good or ill, the most forceful educational influences.

The same is true of crime. If the Probation Service is to be an instigator or agent of social change, equally it will be the catalyst for new treatments of offenders. To perform both these functions the service will need to rely even more on the philosophy of advising, assisting, and befriending those socially disadvantaged and deprived.

[17] A. H. Halsey, *Educational Priority: E. P. A. Problems and Policies* (H. M. S. O. 1972).

Biographical Notes

NORMAN BISHOP: Joined the Prison Service in 1948 and served as a Housemaster at Camp Hill and Portland Borstals, Deputy-Governor at Prescoed Camp, Governor of Pollington, and Principal of H.M. Prison Service Staff College. Joined the Council of Europe's Division of Crime Problems in 1963 and became Head of Division in 1964. Became Head of the Swedish Correctional Administration's Research and Development Unit in 1971.

LOUIS BLOM-COOPER, Q.C., LL.B (London); Dr. Jur. (Amsterdam). Chairman of the Howard League for Penal Reform; member of the Home Secretary's Advisory Council on the Penal System, 1966–73. Justice of the Peace for Inner London, 1966–9, and for City of London, 1969– .

JOHN P. CONRAD: A.B. from the University of California. A.M. from the University of Chicago. Career correctional administrator of the California Department of Corrections, 1947–67. Chief of Research, United States Bureau of Prisons, 1967–9. Chief, Center for Crime Prevention and Rehabilitation, United States Department of Justice, 1969–72. Senior Fellow, The Academy for Contemporary Problems, 1972–Present. Senior Fulbright Fellow in Criminology, London School of Economics, 1958–9. Associate Director, International Survey of Corrections, 1960–2. Author of *Crime and its Correction* (Berkeley, University of Calfornia Press, 1965). Various articles and publications dealing with correctional administration, 1956–73.

GAVIN DREWRY: Lecturer in Government, Bedford College, University of London. Born 1944; graduated (politics and law), Southampton, 1966. Research interests include the legislative process, law reporting in England, the functions of appellate courts; co-author (with Louis Blom-Cooper) of *Final Appeal* (1972) and co-editor (also with Louis Blom-Cooper of *Law and Morality* (1974); regular contributor of articles in legal and political science journals; a member of the Study of Parliament Group.

GORDON HAWKINS: Associate Professor of Criminology, University of Sydney, Australia, since 1961: also engaged as a Research Fellow at the Center for Studies in Criminal Justice, University of Chicago, in 1967–8, 1969–70, 1971, 1972, and 1973.

Born in 1919. Educated at University College, Cardiff, and Balliol College, Oxford. Served with the 1st, 8th, and 14th Armies in North Africa, Italy, and Burma during World War II. Police Officer and Magistrate in Assam, 1945–6.

Fellow of the University of Wales, 1952–4. U.K. Prison Governor, 1954–9; Assistant Principal U.K. Prison Staff College, 1959–61.

Co-author with Norval Morris of *The Honest Politician's Guide to Crime Control* (1970) and with Franklin Zimring of *Deterrence: The Legal Threat in Crime Control* (1973).

HANUS HERMANN, LL.D., was educated in Prague and graduated from Charles University. Lived in Britain during the war and then returned to Czechoslovakia. Arrested by the Czechoslovak State Security, mainly for being a non-conformist and having the wrong sort of background. Sentenced to 12 years' prison for 'high treason', was released after six years in the wave of 'de-Stalinization', and later rehabilitated. After the Soviet invasion in 1968, moved to London, where he still works in the field of international business law.

NICHOLAS HINTON: born 1942; read law at University of Cambridge; worked for four years as Assistant Director of the Northorpe Hall Trust, an experimental project for delinquents in Leeds. Joined N.A.C.R.O. in 1969 to initiate staff training programme; Director, N.A.C.R.O., May 1973.

SIR ARTHUR JAMES: born 1916; educated Caterham School and Jesus College, Oxford—read jurisprudence and then B.C.L., double first. Middle Temple, Hamsworth Law Scholar, Barstow Scholar, Council of Legal Education; Recorder of Great Grimsby and of Derby, and Deputy Chairman Warwick Q.S. Took silk in 1960, Member, Criminal Law Revision Committee. Appointed one of Her Majesty's Judges in 1965 and to Court of Appeal in 1973. Member of Parole Board, 1967–70 (Vice-Chairman 1970); Chairman, V. and G. Tribunal of Inquiry. Chairman of Home Secretary's Committee on Distribution of Business between Crown Court and Magistrates' Courts.

SIR BRIAN MacKENNA: called to the Bar in 1932; became Queen's Counsel in 1950 and appointed one of Her Majesty's judges in 1961.

NOEL McLACHLAN: Reader in History and Member of Board of Studies in Criminology, University of Melbourne, and Editor of *Historical Studies* and *The Memoirs of James Hardy Vaux* (London, 1964). Ph.D. at L.S.E. On the staff of *The Times*, 1956–63, the last three years as a leader writer in the field of social services and problems, including crime.

PETER McNEAL: Senior Probation Officer Inner London Probation and After-Care Service. Worked as a Research Assistant to Dr. H. Mannheim, and then joined the Prison Service as a Borstal Housemaster until 1964, before coming a Probation Officer.

PETER NOKES: born 1932; read History and Social Anthropology at Cambridge 1950–4; research sociologist, Belmont Hospital S.R.U. (the Henderson Hospital) 1954–6; Certificate in Education, University of Bristol 1956–7, followed by four years teaching in approved, secondary modern, and grammar schools. Lecturer in Communication, University of Leeds 1962, and subsequently in Applied Social Studies. Attached first to Nuffield Centre for Hospital and Health Service Studies, University of Leeds, later to Division of Applied Social Studies, Department of Adult Education and Extra-Mural Studies. Visiting lecturer, Department of Psychiatry, University of Leeds, 1967–71; and H.M. Prison Service Staff College, Wakefield, since 1962. Member sub-committee XIV (Group and Community methods in the treatment of offenders), European Committee on Crime Problems, Council of Europe 1970–3. Member Royal Institute of Philosophy.

Publications in *Human Relations, British Journal of Criminology, Adult Education, Prison Service Journal, Universities Quarterly. The Professional Task in Welfare Practice*, 1967: *The Management of Information*, is forthcoming.

RICHARD R. PREWER, V.R.D., LL.B.(Lond.), M.R.C.S., L.R.C.P., M.R.C.Psych., D.P.M.; medical training at Barts; qualified 1936. Joined Prison Service, 1938, and seconded to Broadmoor; called up for Naval service at outbreak of war; later served as a neuro-psychiatric specialist, and in medical charge of Kielder Camp (a special unit for psychopaths and others) 1943–5; returned to Prison Service 1946; Medical Officer at Parkhurst 1946; Camp Hill Borstal Institution 1946–8; and at Lincoln Prison 1948–55; Honorary Psychiatric Consultant, Louth County Infirmary, Lincs., 1950–5; Senior Medical Officer, Parkhurst Prison 1955–73; Principal Medical Officer, Isle of Wight prisons 1973; member (and co-founder) of an inter-disciplinary study group on the causes and treatment of crime, meeting at Newark, Notts., 1949–55; Chairman of the Isle of Wight Branch of the Historical Association 1970–   ; special interest in the history of English prisons.

ANN D. SMITH, B.A. (Oxon), 1939; Ph.D. (Edin), 1960; Member of the Parole Board for Scotland, 1968–71; Ellis Committee on Remand Homes; Russell Committee on Succession of Illegitimate Children. Lecturer, Dept of Criminology and Criminal Law, 1967–   . Author of *Women in Prison* (1962); and various articles in journals.

JEF SMITH. Group Controller, Research and Development, Social Services Department of the London Borough of Tower Hamlets. Previously Deputy Secretary-General, International Voluntary Service. Member of the Aves Committee on the Use of Volunteers. Is a freelance writer on social policy and social services. Appointed Director of Social Services for the City of London 1974.

RAY STIRLING: Principal, Bingley College of Education 1974–   ; formerly headmaster of a Comprehensive School in Harlow; Field officer with the Schools Council 1971–3. Justice of the Peace and Member of the Advisory Council on the Penal System, 1970–3.

J. E. (TEDDY) THOMAS. University of Hull. Spent seven years in the English prison service as an assistant governor, including a period training staff at the Staff College, Wakefield. Before that, administered local prisons in Central Africa. Has visited and studied prison systems in Europe, Africa, Asia, Australasia, and North America, frequently lecturing and holding discussions with staff and policy makers. Author of several articles on prisons, and of *The English Prison Officer since 1850*.

GORDON TRASLER: One-time prison psychologist (at Wandsworth and Winchester) and now Professor of Psychology in the University of Southampton. Member of the Advisory Council on the

Penal System, 1968–73; interested in the theory of criminality and the effects of imprisonment.

NIGEL WALKER: Wolfson Professor of Criminology and Director of the Institute of Criminology, Cambridge. Chairman of the Home Secretary's Advisory Council on Probation and After-Care; Member of the Advisory Council on the Penal System 1968–73, and the Committee on Mentally Abnormal Offenders and editorial boards of the *British Journal of Criminology and Criminal Law Review,* Author of *Crime and Insanity in England, Sentencing in a Rational Society, Crimes, Courts and Figures, Crime and Punishment in Britain, A Short History of Psychotherapy,* etc.

Select Bibliography

Advisory Council on the Penal System 1966:
  Detention Centres, H.M.S.O. 1970.
  Detention of Girls in a Detention Centre, H.M.S.O. 1968.
  Non-custodial and semi-custodial penalties and disabilities, H.M.S.O. 1970.
  Regime for Long-term Prisoners in Conditions of Maximum Security, H.M.S.O. 1968.
  Reparation, H.M.S.O. 1971.
  Young Adult Offender, H.M.S.O. 1974.

Advisory Council on the Treatment of Offenders 1945–64:
  After-Care and Supervision of Discharged Prisoners, H.M.S.O. 1958.
  Alternatives to Short Terms of Imprisonment, H.M.S.O. 1957.
  Corporal Punishment, Cmnd. 1213, H.M.S.O. 1960.
  Non-Residential Treatment of Offenders under 21, H.M.S.O. 1962.
  Organisation of After-Care, H.M.S.O. 1963.
  Preventive Detention, H.M.S.O. 1963.
  Treatment of Young Offenders, H.M.S.O. 1959.

ALPER, B. S., and BOREN, J. F. *Crime: International Agenda*, Lexington Books, 1972.

American President's Commission on Law Enforcement and Administration of Justice: *The Challenge of Crime in a Free Society*, U.S. Printing Office, 1967.

ANCEL, M. *La Défense social nouvelle: un mouvement de politique criminelle humaniste*, Editions Cujas, 1966.

ANDRY, R. G. *The Short-term Prisoner*, Stevens & Sons, 1963.

ARROWSMITH, P. *Somewhere like this*, Allen, 1970.

BABINGTON, A. *The English Bastille*, Macdonald, 1971.

BARNES. H. E., and TEETERS, N. K. *New Horizons in Criminology* 3rd edn., Prentice Hall, 1959.

BARRY, Sir John. *Alexander Maconochie of Norfolk Island*. Univ. of Melbourne Press, 1958.

—— *Death of John Price*, Univ. of Melbourne Press, 1964.

BARTON, R. *Institutional Neurosis*, Wright, 1959.

BECCARIA, C. *Of Crimes and Punishments*, anonymous English translation, J. Almon, London, 1767.

BENTHAM, J. *Principles of Penal Law*, *Works*, Vol. I, W. Tait, Edinburgh, 1837.

BOTTOMS, A. E., and McCLINTOCK, F. H. *Criminals Coming of Age*, Heinemann, 1973.

BURT, C. *Young Delinquent*, Univ. of London Press, 1944.

Cadogan Committee on Corporal Punishment, Cmd. 5684, H.M.S.O. 1938.

CLAY, W. L. *The Prison Chaplain*, Macmillan, 1861.

CLEMMER, D. *The Prison Community*, Holt, Rinehart & Winston, 1966.

CLOWARD, R. A., and OHLIN, L. E. *Delinquency and Opportunity*, Glencoe Free Press, 1964.

COHEN, A. K. *Delinquent Boys*, Glencoe Free Press, 1956.

COHEN, S., and TAYLOR, L. *Psychological Survival*, Pelican Books, 1972.

COOK, T., GATH, D., and HENSMAN, E. *The Drunkenness Offence*, Pergamon, 1969.

COOK, T., and GUNN, J. *Penal Reform*, Liberal Publication Department, 1974.

CRESSEY, D. R. *Criminal Organisation*, Heineman, 1972.

— — (Ed.). *The Prison*, Holt, 1960.

CROSS, Sir Rupert. *Punishment, Prison and the Public*, Stevens, 1971.

DEVLIN, Lord. *The Enforcement of Morals*, O.U.P. 1959.

DEVON, Dr. J. *The Criminal and the Community*, John Lane, 1911.

DU CANE, Sir Edward. *The Punishment and Prevention of Crime*, 1885.

EAST, Sir Norwood, and HUBERT, W. H. De B. *The Psychological Treatment of Crime*, Home Office, 1939.

ELKIN, W. *The English Juvenile Courts*, Kegan Paul, 1938.

EMERY, F. E. *Freedom and Justice within Walls*, Tavistock, 1970.

ETZIONI, A. *The Active Society*, The Free Press, 1968.

— — *The Theory of Complex Organisation*, The Free Press, 1961.

FIELD, X. *Under Lock and Key*, Max Parrish, 1963.

FLEW, A. *Crime or Disease*, Macmillan, 1973.

FOX, Sir Lionel. *The English Prison and Borstal System*, Routledge & Kegan Paul, 1952.

GIALLOMBARDO, R. *Society of Women*, Wiley, 1964.

GIBBENS, T. C. N., and PRINCE, J. *Shoplifting*. I.S.T.D. 1962.

GIBSON, E., and KLEIN S. *Murder 1957 to 1968*, Home Office, 1969.

Gladstone Committee on Prisons, Cmnd. 7702, H.M.S.O. 1895.

GLASER, D. *The Effectiveness of a Prison and Parole System*, Bobbs-Merrill, 1964.

GLOVER, E. R. *Probation and Re-Education*, Routledge & Kegan Paul, 1956.

— — *Roots of Crime*, Imago, 1969.

GOFFMAN, Ervin. *Asylums*, Penguin, 1968.

GORING, Dr. C. *The English Convict, A statistical study*, H.M.S.O. 1913.

GRIFFITHS, A. *Memorials of Millbank*, 1875.

GRÜNHUT, M. *Probation and Mental Treatment*, Tavistock, 1963.

— — *Penal Reform*, O.U.P. 1948.

HAMMOND, W. H., and CHAYEN, E. *Persistent Criminals*, H.M.S.O. 1963.

HART, H. L. A. *Punishment and Responsibility*, O.U.P. 1968.

HINDE, R. S. E. *The British Penal System 1773–1950*, Duckworth, 1951.

HOBHOUSE, L. T., and BROCKWAY, A. F. *English Prisons To-day*, Longmans, Green & Co., 1922.

HOGARTH, J. *Sentencing as a Human Process*, Univ. of Toronto Press, 1971.

Home Office: *The Adult Offender*, Cmnd, 2852, H.M.S.O. 1965.

The Child, the Family and the Young Offender, Cmnd. 2742, H.M.S.O. 1965.

Children in Trouble, Cmnd. 3601, H.M.S.O. 1968.

Compensation for Victims of Crimes of Violence, Cmnd. 1406, H.M.S.O. 1961.

Ditto, Cmnd, 2323, H.M.S.O. 1964.

Criminal Statistics, H.M.S.O. (annually).

Habitual Drunken Offenders, H.M.S.O. 1972.

Penal Practice in a Changing Society: Aspects of future development (England and Wales), Cmnd. 645, H.M.S.O. 1959.

People in Prison, Cmnd. 4214, H.M.S.O. 1969.

Prison Department Report, 1972, Cmnd. 5375, H.M.S.O. 1971.

The Sentence of the Court—A handbook for courts on the treatment of offenders, H.M.S.O. 1969.

The War against Crime in England and Wales, Cmnd. 2296, H.M.S.O. 1964.

Treatment of Young Offenders, Cmnd. 2831, H.M.S.O. 1927.

HOOD, R. *Borstal Re-assessed*, Heinemann, 1965.
— — *Sentencing in Magistrates' Courts*, Stevens & Sons, 1962.
— — *Sentencing the Motoring Offender*, Heinemann, 1973.
— — and SPARKS, R. *Key Issues in Criminology*. World University Library, 1970.
HOWARD, D. L. *The English Prisons*, Methuen, 1960.
Ingleby Committee on Children and Young Persons, Cmnd. 1191, H.M.S.O. 1960.
IVES, G. *A History of Penal Methods*, Stanley Paul & Co., 1914.
JACKSON, R. M. *Enforcing the Law*, rev. edn., Pelican Books, 1972.
— — *The Machinery of Justice*, 5th edn., Cambridge Univ. Press, 1967.
JOHNSTON, N., SAVITZ, L., and WOLFGANG, M. *The Sociology of Punishment and Correction*, 2nd edn., Wiley, 1970.
KASSEBAUM, G., WARD, D. A., and WILNER, D. M. *Prison Treatment and Parole Survival*, Wiley, 1971.
Kilbrandon Committee on Children and Young Persons (Scotland), Cmnd. 2306, H.M.S.O. 1964.
KLARE, H. J. *Anatomy of Prison*, Hutchinson, 1960.
— — (Ed.). *Changing Concepts of Crime and its Treatment*, Pergamon, 1966.
LE MESURIER, L. *Boys in Trouble*, John Murray, 1931.
McCLINTOCK, F. H. *Attendance Centres*, Macmillan, 1961.
— — and AVISON, N. H. *Crime in England and Wales*, Heinemann, 1968.
— — and GIBSON, E. *Robbery in London*, Macmillan, 1961.
McCORKLE, L. W., *et al. The Highfields Story*, Holt, 1958.
MANNHEIM, H. *Comparative Criminology*, Routledge & Kegan Paul, 1965.
— — *Criminal Justice and Social Reconstruction*, Routledge & Kegan Paul, 1946.
— — *The Dilemma of Penal Reform*, Allen & Unwin, 1939.
— — *Group Problems in Crime and Punishment*, Routledge & Kegan Paul, 1955.
— — *Social Aspects of Crime in England between the Wars*, Allen & Unwin, 1940.
— — (Ed.). *Pioneers in Criminology*, Stevens, 1960.
— — and WILKINS, L. T. *Prediction Methods in Relation to Borstal Training*, H.M.S.O. 1955.
MARTIN, J. P. *Offenders as Employees*, Macmillan, 1962.

MATHIESEN, T. *Defences of the Weak*, Tavistock, 1965.

MAYHEW, H., and BINNEY, J. *The Criminal Prisons of London*, new edn., F. Cass & Co., 1968.

Morison Committee on the Probation Service, Cmnd. 1650 and Cmnd. 1800, H.M.S.O. 1962.

MORRIS, N. *The Habitual Criminal*, Longmans, 1951.

— — and HAWKINS, G. *The Honest Politician's Guide to Crime Control*, Univ. of Chicago Press, 1969.

MORRIS, P. *Prisoners and their Families*, Allen & Unwin, 1965.

MORRIS, T. P. *The Criminal Area*, Routledge & Kegan Paul, 1957.

MORRIS, T. P., and MORRIS, P. *Pentonville*, Routledge & Kegan Paul, 1963.

MORRISON, W. D. *Crime and its Causes*, Sonnenschein & Co., 1891.

Mountbatten Commission, *Report of the Enquiry into Prison Escapes and Security*, Cmnd. 3175, H.M.S.O. 1966.

NITSCHE, Dr. P., and WILMANNS, K. *The History of the Prison Psychoses*, Journal of Nervous and Mental Disease Publishing Co., 1912.

PARKER, T. *Five Women*, Hutchinson, 1965.

— — *The Twisting Lane*, Hutchinson, 1969.

— — *The Unknown Citizen*, Hutchinson, 1963.

— — and ALLERTON, R. *The Courage of his Convictions*, Hutchinson, 1961.

PATERSON, A. *The Principles of the Borstal System*, Prison Commission, Home Office, 1932.

POLLAK, O. *The Criminality of Women*, A. S. Barnes, 1961.

POLSKY, H. *Cottage Six*, Russell Sage, 1962.

RADZINOWICZ, Sir Leon. *History of English Criminal Law and its Administration from 1750*, Cambridge Univ. Press, 1948–68.

ROSENBERG, A. M. *The Unwilling Patient*, I.S.T.D. 1966.

— — and WOLFGANG, M. *Crime and Justice*, Basic Books, 1971.

ROSE, G. *Schools for Young Offenders*, Tavistock, 1967.

— — *The Struggle for Penal Reform*, Stevens, 1960.

Royal Commission on Capital Punishment, 1949–1953, Cmnd. 8932, 1953.

RUCK, S. K. (Ed.). *Paterson on Prisons*, Frederick Muller, 1951.

SAVITZ, L. See JOHNSTON, N.

SERGE, V. *Men in Prison*, Penguin, 1972.

SHAW, A. G. L. *Convicts and the Colonies*, Faber, 1966.

SOOTHILL, K. *The Prisoner's Release*, Allen & Unwin, 1974.

SMITH, Ann D. *Women in Prison*, Stevens & Sons, 1962.

SPARKS, R. F. *Local Prisons: The Crisis in the English Penal System*, Heinemann, 1971.

— — See also HOOD, R.

State of New York—Attica 1972.

STEER, D. *Police Cautions: a study in the exercise of the discretion*, Blackwell, 1970.

STEPHEN, Sir James FitzJames. *History of the Criminal Law*, Macmillan, 1883.

STRATTA, E. *The Education of Borstal Boys*, Routledge & Kegan Paul, 1970.

Streatfeild Committee on the Business of the Criminal Courts, Cmnd. 1289, H.M.S.O. 1961.

STREET, D., WINTER, R., and PERROW, C. *Organisation for Treatment*, Glencoe Free Press, 1966.

STÜRRUP, G. *Treating the Unbreakable: chronic criminals at Herstedvester*, Johns Hopkins Univ. Press, 1968.

SUTHERLAND, E. H. *Principles of Criminology*, Univ. of Chicago Press, 1955.

SYKES, G. M. *The Society of Captives*, Univ. of Princeton Press, 1958.

TEETERS, N. K. See BARNES, H. E.

THOMAS, D. A. *Principles of Sentencing*, Heinemann, 1970.

THOMAS, J. E. *The English Prison Officer since 1850*, Routledge & Kegan Paul, 1972.

TOBIAS, J. J. *Crime and the Industrial Society in the 19th Century*, Batsford, 1967.

— — *Against the Peace*, Ginn, 1970.

TRASLER, G. B. *The Explanation of Delinquency*, Routledge & Keegan Paul, 1962.

TURNER, M. L. *Safe Lodging*, Hutchinson, 1961.

WALKER, N. D. *Crime and Insanity in England* (Historical Perspective), Vol. I, Univ. of Edinburgh Press, 1968.

— — *Crime and Punishment in Britain*, 2nd edn., Univ. of Edinburgh Press, 1968.

— — *Crime, Courts and Figures*, Penguin, 1971.

— — *Sentencing in a Rational Society*, Penguin, 1971.

— — and McCABE, Sarah. *Crime and Insanity in England*, Vol. II, Univ. of Edinburgh Press, 1973.

WALKER, P. N. *Punishment: An illustrated history*, David & Charles, 1972.

WALMSLEY, R. *Steps from Prison*, Inner London Probation and After-care Service, 1972.

WARD, D., and KASSEBAUM, G. *Women's Prison*, Weidenfeld, 1966.

WEBB, S., and WEBB, B. *English Prisons under Local Government*, Longmans, Green, & Co., 1922.

WEEKS, H. Ashley. *Youthful Offenders at Highfields*, Univ. of Michigan Press, 1958.

WEST, D. J. *The Habitual Prisoner*, Macmillan, 1963.

— — *Present Conduct and Future Deliquency*, Heinemann, 1969.

— — *The Young Offender*, Pelican, 1967.

— — (Ed.). *The Future of Parole*, Duckworth, 1972.

WILKINS, L. T. *Evaluating Penal Measures*, Random House, 1969.

— — See MANNHEIM, H.

WILLINK, H. *Royal Commission on the Police*, Cmnd. 1728, H.M.S.O. 1962.

WILLS, W. D. *Spare the Child*, Penguin, 1971.

Wolfenden Homosexual Offences and Prostitution, Cmnd. 247, H.M.S.O. 1957.

WOLFGANG, M. See JOHNSTON, N.

WOOTTON, B. *Social Science and Social Pathology*, Allen & Unwin, 1959.

WRIGHT, M. *Use of Criminology Literature*, Butterworths, 1974.

ZIMRING, F. and HAWKINS, G., *Deterrence: the legal threat in crime control*, Univ. of Chicago Press, 1973.

'ZENO', *Life*, Macmillan, 1968.

LEGISLATION

Prison Act 1877
Prison Act 1898
Prevention of Crime Act 1908
Criminal Justice Administration
    Act 1914
Criminal Justice Act 1925
Criminal Justice Act 1947

Criminal Justice Act 1948
Prison Act 1952
Criminal Justice Act 1961
Prison Rules 1964
Criminal Justice Act 1967
Criminal Justice Act 1972

Index

Acts
— Children and Young Persons Act, 1933, 26n
— Children and Young Persons Act, 1963, 45
— Children and Young Persons Act, 1969, 28, 31, 45, 153, 238–40, 244, 247
— Criminal Damage Act, 1971, 45
— Criminal Justice Act, 1948, 7n, 28n, 42, 45, 58, 59, 102, 108, 165
— Criminal Justice Act, 1961, 27n, 28n, 29n, 45, 165
— Criminal Justice Act, 1967, 30n, 33, 45, 165, 168
— Criminal Justice Act, 1972, 6, 27n, 28n, 29, 30, 33, 39, 45, 124, 153, 165, 168, 172, 245, 253, 254, 257, 264
— Criminal Justice Administration Act, 1956, 45
— Criminal Justice Administration Act, 1962, 45
— European Communities Act, 1972, 27
— Firearms Act, 1968, 45
— First Offenders Act, 1958, 28n, 45
— Homicide Act, 1957, 44
— Industrial Training Act, 1964, 151
— Litter Act, 1958, 229
— Mental Health Act, 1959, 126
— Misuse of Drugs Act, 1971, 45
— Murder (Abolition of the Death Penalty) Act, 1965, 42
— Peel's Gaol Act, 1823, 2
— Penal Reform Act, 1898, 7
— Preserving the Health of Prisoners in Gaol Act, 1774, 116
— Preventive Detention Act, 1908, 2
— Prison Ministers Act, 1863, 9
— Prisons Act, 1862, 11n
— Prisons Act, 1865, 4
— Prisons Act, 1877, 55
— Prisons Act, 1952, 45
— Probation Act, 1887, 2
— Probation Act, 1907, 2, 255, 260
— Social Work (Scotland) Act, 1968, 257
— Street Offences Act, 1959, 231n, 235
— Theft Act, 1968, 45
— Transportation and Penal Servitude Act, 1853, 13–15
— Transportation and Penal Servitude Act, 1857, 14
Adams, S., 199
Advisory Council on the Penal System, viii, 28, 29, 38, 53, 57, 62, 72, 86n, 139n, 246, 247, 249, 253, 254
Advisory Council on the Treatment of Offenders, 61, 72, 239
Alcohol, 94, 122, 123, 163, 171, 183, 229, 247, 265
Allen, H. C., 21n
Alper, B. S., 83
America – see UNITED STATES OF AMERICA
American Friends' Service Committee, 105–12
Amygaloid nucleus, 123
Ancel, M., 97
Andenaes, J., 186n 188n, 189, 191, 194
Approved schools, 2
Ashford Remand Centre, 50
Ashworth, Mr. Justice, 188n
Atkinson, Mr. Justice Fenton, 26n
Attendance centres, 6, 48
Attica Prison, 103
Austin, P., 161n
Australia, 14, 15
Austria, 86
Avison, N. H., 16n, 19n, 186, 191

Babington, A., 116n
Bagehot, W., 37
Bail, 50
Bailey, W. C., 198

Barnes, H. E., 12n
Barry, Sir John, 23n
Barton, R., 5n
Behan, B., 56
Belgium, 84, 91
Bentham, J., 12, 23, 189
Bentley, D., 50
Bethlem Royal Hospital, 118
Beutel, F. K., 192
Biles, D., 1n
Binny, J., 9n
Birmingham Prison, 55
Bishop, N., 25n, 89, 176n 261n
Blake, G., 26n, 56
Blissen, E., 146
Blom-Cooper, L., 58, 133
Blundeston Prison, 5n
Board of Visitors, 55, 65, 66
Bordua, D. J., 21n
Boren, J. F., 83
Börjeson, B., 89
Borstal, 65, 120, 129, 134–6, 142, 148,
    149, 191, 246, 247
— future of, 57, 58, 199
— origins of, 2, 56, 107, 145
— structure of, 23, 57, 145, 147
— training, 27, 28, 32n, 39n, 98, 130,
    167, 170, 179
Bowen, D., 10n
Brixton Prison, 50, 51
Broadmoor Hospital, 49, 50, 118, 130
Brougham, Lord, 13
Browne, Sir Thomas, 127
Buehler, E. P., 137n
Butler, Lord, 127
Butterworth Committee, 256

California, 109, 144, 197, 199–204, 262
Cambridge Institute of Criminology, 1,
    189
Campaign for Nuclear Disarmament,
    225
Canning, G., 102
Capital punishment, vii, 3, 4, 12, 16, 27,
    32, 35n, 36, 39, 41–4, 48, 53,
    61, 107, 108, 190
— Royal Commission on, 42, 190,
    191
Carnarvon Committee, 4
Chadwick, O., 10n
Chesterton, G. K., 110, 111n
Christoph, J. B., 41–3
City and Guilds Examinations, 146

Clark, G. Kitson, 21
Clark, Sir Frederick, 144
Classification – see PRISONERS
Clay, Revd. J., 10
Clay, W. L., 10n
Clemmer, D., 131n
Clockwork Orange, A, 10
Cloward, R. A., 204
Cohen, D., 263
Cohen, S., 22n, 131n, 136n
Collins, P. 15n
Colville, Viscount of Culross, 46
Comenius, 152n
Commons, House of, 37, 43, 45, 46,
    48–56
— Select Committee, 1837, 13
— Select Committee on Expendi-
    ture, 1972, 257
— Select Committee on Gaols, 1835,
    9n
— Select Committee on Persistent
    Offenders, 1932, 105, 108, 119
— Select Committee on Prison
    Discipline, 1850, 4n, 7n, 12n, 15n
— Select Committee on Prison
    Ministers Acts, 1870, 9n
Community Service, 27, 139, 153, 180,
    184, 246, 247, 265
Community Service Orders, 39, 45,
    180, 245, 248, 250, 251, 253,
    254, 624
Compensation – see RESTITUTION
Conrad, J. P., viii, 135, 136
Cooper, B. D., 122n
Cornish, W. R., 35n
Corporal punishment, 16, 39, 66, 108,
    121
Council of Europe, 86n, 90n, 91n
Court
— of Appeal, 26, 30, 187, 195, 235
— Crown, 31, 231
— Divisional, 31n
— High, 174n
— Juvenile, 238, 239
— Magistrates', 27, 31, 233
— Supreme, 107n
Cranworth, Lord, 13, 14
Crime
— decrease in, 16, 18, 19, 190, 194,
    203, 205
— detection of, 21, 22
— increase in, 16, 19, 21, 22, 24, 188,
    194, 197, 206, 223

Crime (*cont.*)
— moral aspects of, 11
— normality of, 20, 22, 97, 98
— poverty-based, 18
— prevention of, 19, 166, 206, 207
— property, 18, 19, 88, 98, 224, 225
— prosperity-based, 18
— statistics of, 16, 17, 21, 22, 85, 88, 93, 109, 155, 159, 186, 190–4, 197, 235, 236, 262
Criminal Injuries Compensation, 50
Criminal Record Office, 222–4
Cross, Sir Rupert, 2n, 5, 6n, 8, 57n, 103–10, 112–14, 179, 199, 200

Dante, 213
Dartmoor Prison, 59, 117, 119, 121
Davies, J., 156n
Davies, M., 256
Day training centres, 153, 180, 264
Death penalty – see CAPITAL PUNISHMENT
Delinquency – see YOUNG OFFENDERS
Dell, Mr. Edmund, M.P., 28n
Detention Centre Orders, 32n, 167, 170
Devlin, Lord, 35
Dicey, A. V., 24
Diminished responsibility, 87
Diversionary procedure, 230
Donald, J. V. J., 138n
Donaldson, Lord of Kingsbridge, 46
d'Orban, T. P., 161n
Douglas, J. W. B., 222
Drewry, G., 40n, 66n
Drugs, 40, 90, 93, 122, 123, 161, 163, 167, 183, 205, 213, 224, 229
Dubreuil, H., 95n
Du Cane, Sir Edmund, 4n, 6, 7, 16, 55
Dunning, Sir Leonard, 228
Du Parcq, Mr. Justice, 59

East, W. N., 119, 120
Education and Science, Department of, 142
Ehrlich, 193n
Elder, P. D., 163n
Ellis, D., 161n
Emery, F. E., 113
Ericsson, C-H., 95n
Etzioni, A., 200
European Convention for the Protection of Human Rights, 248

Evans, T., 40
Eysenck, H. J., 16n, 19n

Fairlie, H., 37n
Fairn, R. D., 8
Faulkner, D. E. R., 160n, 161n
Felice, M., 161n
Female criminality – see WOMEN OFFENDERS
Ferri, E., 192
Fielding, H., 210
Fines, 32n, 48, 85–9, 99
— day-fine, 86
First offenders, 28, 207, 233–6
Fitch, J. H., 138n, 140n
Foote, C., 105
Fowler, D., 256n, 257n
Fox, Sir Lionel, 4n, 7, 10n, 23, 101–3, 112–14, 142, 149
France, 84, 91, 192
Freud, S., 119
Fry, E., 8, 9n, 11

Gardiner, Lord, 45n, 228n
Gatrell, V. A. C., 16n, 18, 21
Germany – see WEST GERMANY
Giallombrada, R., 156n
Gibbs, 193
Gibbs, C., 162n
Gilbert, Jane, 161n
Gilbert, Jim, 147
Glacier Institute of Management, 72
Gladstone Committee, 1895, 3, 7
— Report of, viii, 8, 55, 56, 59, 109, 143, 154
Gladstone H, 7
Glaser, D., 199
Glover, E. R., 11n
Goddard, Lord Chief Justice, 43, 44
Goodman, N., 156n
Goodman, P., 149
Gorer, G., 10n
Gowers Commission – see CAPITAL PUNISHMENT
Great train robbers, 51, 62
Grendon Psychiatric Prison, 120, 122, 124, 126, 183
Grey, Earl, 13, 14
Griffiths, A., 9
Grünhut, M., 1–3, 6, 10–13, 23
Gunn, J., 120n

Hadden, T. B., 16n, 18, 21
Haford Meurig Centre, 241
Haley, Sir William, 22n
Halsey, A. H., 267
Hamlyn Lectures, 179
Hammond, W. H., 190
Hanratty, J., 40, 50
Hart, H. L. A., 114
Hartell, 17n
Hawkins, G., 20, 57n, 187n, 192, 193
Heath, N., 56
Henriques, U. R. Q., 9n
Herman, V., 47n
Hinde, R. S. E., 2n
Hindley, M., 50
Hobsbawm, E. J., 17n, 21n
Holland, 143
Holland, 25n, 75, 84, 86–8, 143, 191, 262, 263
Hollesley Bay Colony, 56
Holloway Prison, 48, 50
Home Office, 5, 6, 8, 15, 30, 32, 38, 42, 48–53, 60, 150, 234, 236, 250, 254, 259, 266
— Research Unit, 140, 156n, 161, 199
Home Secretary, 26, 30n, 32n, 33, 40, 43, 53, 64, 119, 239, 259
Homosexuality, 5n, 228
Hood, R., 2n, 18n, 20, 22n, 199
Horstkotte, H., 84n
Howard, D. L., 4n, 5
Howard, J., 11, 116
Howard League for Penal Reform, xii, 6, 12, 24, 38, 66, 70, 228
Hubert, W. H. de B., 119, 120
Hulks at Woolwich, 116
Humble, J. W., 72, 74n
Huntercombe Scheme, 58

Ilich, 149
Immigrants, illegal, 50
Imprisonment
— cost of, 90
— effect of, 210
— justification for, 115
— negative effects of, vii–ix, 90, 114, 131, 134, 137, 138, 211–17, 219, 220
— positive aspects of, 217–18
— progressive stages of, 2–3
Incapacitation, 176
Industrial Training Board, 146, 147

Inglis, K. S., 10n
Intermediate treatment, 238–44, 246
International Labour Office, 249
Iremonger, J., 21n
Ireland, 191
— Northern, 45, 50
Irwin, J., 105
Italy, 84, 91, 97
Ives, G., 9n

Jackson, R. M., vii
Janner, G., 50
Jebb, Lt.-Col. J., 4, 6, 7n, 12n
Johnston, N., 199n
Jones, H., 19n
Jones, K., 82
Jones, P., 26n, 50, 51
Judge, A., 21n
'Justice', 228
Juvenile delinquency – see YOUNG OFFENDER

Karl Holton School, 137, 144
Kassebaum, G., 68, 156n, 199
Keith, Lord of Avonholm, 44
Kemp, T., 186n
Kennedy Youth Centre, 137, 138n, 199
Kent, E. N., 250, 251
— Committee, 251, 252
Khaled, L., 159
Kircheimer, O., 192
Klare, H. J., 8n, 20n, 264

Leonard, D., 47n
Lerman, P., 198
Letters, 93, 219
Life imprisonment, 16, 26, 27, 39n, 48
Llewellin, W. W., 199
Lord Chancellor, 170
Lord Chief Justice, 170, 235
Lords, House of, 37, 42–6, 48–51
— Select Committee on the present state of the gaols, 9n
Lowdham Grange, 56
Luvaglio, M., 40
Luxembourg, 84

McCabe, S., 162n
McClintock, F. H., 16n, 19n, 186, 191
MacDonagh, O., 23n
McIntosh, M., 22n
MacIver, R., 78
McKay Commission Report, 103

Mackintosh, Sir James, 42
McLachlan, N., xi, 83, 112
Macnab, K. K., 17, 18
Maconochie, Capt. A., 4n, 15, 23
Magistrates, 30, 46, 170, 242 – see also
   COURT
— Association, 28, 170, 238
Mannheim, H., 1, 2n, 6, 19, 22
Maritain, J., 142, 144
Martinson, B., 93n, 198
Mather, F. C., 21n
Mathieson, T., 93n
Mayhew, H., 9n
Mayo, E., 77
Medical Research Council, 222
Merritt, J., 21n
Merton, R. K., 74
Midlands Women's Remand Centre,
   51
Mill, J. S., 35
Millbank Prison, 5, 8, 9, 116, 119
Miller, H., 112
Molesworth, Sir William, 13n
Molesworth Committee, 13
Morison Committee, 259
Morris Committee, 223
Morris of Borth-y-Gest, Lord, 46
Morris, N., 13n, 20, 189, 195
Morris, T. P., 20
Morris, T. P. and P., 5n, 11, 16n, 136n
Morrison, R. L., 129
Morrison, W. D., 11, 16, 17
Motoring offences, 224
Mountbatten Enquiry, 56, 62
— Report, 59, 62, 64, 65, 67, 72,
   115n, 149
Murch, M., 260

N.A.C.R.O., xii, 25n, 32n, 37n, 38, 46,
   228
National Council for Social Service,
   251
National Health Service, 124, 126, 127
Newcastle, Duke of, 13
Newgate Prison, 116
Newsam, Sir Frank, 38n
Nicholson, N., 43n
Nihil, Revd. D., 9
Nisbet, R. A., 79
Nokes, P. L., 74n
Norfolk Island Penal Settlement, 15n
Norman, F., 112
North Sea Camp, 56

Northope Hall Scheme, 241
Nycander, S., 99, 100n

O'Brien, Capt. D., 9n
Offord, D., 161n
Ohlin, L. E., 204
Old Bailey, 224
Orwell, G., 112
Osborne, G., 21n

Paley, Archdeacon, 23
Parker, T., 135n, 136n, 160n, 225
Parkhurst
— Asylum, 118
— Prison, 117, 119, 121, 122, 124–6
— Youth Prison, 2
Parker, Lord Chief Justice, 30, 32, 44
Parliament, 6, 26–8, 31, 32, 36–47,
   51–3, 66, 116, 165, 224, 232
Parliamentary Commissioner for
   Administration, 181
Parole, 6, 25, 32, 34, 40, 57, 83, 99, 109,
   139, 167, 172, 173, 196–9, 203,
   256, 257, 264
— Board, 30, 32, 123, 180, 181
— origins of, 15n
Parris, H., 6n, 23n
Paterson, Sir Alexander, 9, 56, 57n,
   59, 101, 105–8, 145, 199
Pearson, A. J., 122n
Pelling, H., 10n
Penal servitude, 8
Pentonville Prison, 4, 11, 117
Perkin, H., 18n
Perlman, M., 13n
Philips, D. J., 18n
Plato, 144, 148
Point Puer Boys' Prison, 15n
Police Court Mission, 11
Poor Law, 5, 16
Portland Prison, 117
Preservation of the rights of prisoners,
   67
Preston Gaol, 10
Pre-trial reports – see SOCIAL ENQUIRY
   REPORTS
Preventive detention, 29n
Prewer, R. R., 98n, 183n
Price, J. B., 161n
Prison
— after-care, 49, 51, 83, 91, 99 127,
   215, 242, 256, 257

Prison (*cont.*)
— alternatives to, 58, 83, 84, 88–9, 156, 254, 263
— as a community, 79, 80, 149
— autonomy within, 90, 95, 96, 110, 213
— buildings, 4n, 5, 6, 40, 49, 63
— chaplains, 8–10
— Commission, 2, 6–8, 55, 64, 142
— Commission, abolition of, 8, 60, 61
— Department, 10, 11, 142, 146–8, 154
— discipline, 2–4, 7n, 15n, 32
— disturbances, 50, 59, 78, 91, 93, 103
— education in, 49, 92, 104, 111, 142–54
— home leave from, 58, 91–3, 95
— hostel schemes, 26, 58, 91, 94, 127, 134, 139, 180
— inspectorate, 2, 65, 66
— Medical Service, 116–19, 127
— nurses, 126
— overcrowding in, 5, 33n, 58, 59, 165
— population, 25, 33, 59, 63, 86, 87, 89, 94, 124, 155, 162, 180, 201, 263
— Psychiatric Service, 119–26
— Psychological Service, 130, 138, 140
— psychologists, 10, 129, 130, 132–5, 138–41
— Reform Council, 225
— religion in, 10, 11, 22, 92
— Rules, 1899, 7
— Rules, 1933, 7n
— Rules, 1949, 58, 102
— Rules, 1964, vii, x, 7, 31, 102, 132
— staff, 8, 16, 49, 54, 55, 59, 60, 63, 65, 70, 71, 96, 111, 121, 200
— telephones, 92, 93
— work in, 49, 92, 94–6, 150, 151, 157, 162
Prisoners
— classification of, 2, 7, 12, 111, 129, 130
— payment of, 2, 83, 91, 92, 94, 95, 151
— rehabilitation of, 198, 200, 203
— rights, xi, 97

Prisons
— and the class war, 105–7
— and the community. x, xi, 64, 65, 67
— Inspector-General of, 64
— local, 6, 24n, 25, 55, 94
— maximum security, 40, 62, 63
— open, 6, 40, 56, 58, 83, 92–4, 96
Probation, 6, 49, 51, 83, 84, 85n, 139, 170, 180, 183, 197, 199, 203, 246, 247, 249, 252, 260
— Committees, 253
— Officers, 50, 52, 168, 243, 249–52, 257, 260, 264–6
— Officers, National Association of, 257, 261
— Orders, 184
— origins of, 2, 15n
— Service, 61, 238, 242, 251, 255–9, 262, 265, 267
— subsidy, 200
Punishment
— aims of
— — containment, vii, 36, 69, 75, 82, 104, 109, 143, 154, 166, 167, 170, 172, 174, 176, 183, 184, 217
— — general deterrence, viii, 3, 6, 7, 18, 36, 55, 56, 59, 85, 99, 101, 104, 109, 113, 143, 144, 154, 166, 170, 176, 182, 184–9, 192–5, 217, 226, 263
— — individual deterrence, viii, 6, 7, 55, 56, 59, 69, 76, 82, 101, 102, 104, 106, 109, 110, 113–115, 132, 143, 144, 154, 166, 167, 170, 176, 177, 179, 182–5
— — retribution, 36, 43, 113, 143, 158, 182, 183, 185, 194, 245
— and individual liberty, 131, 174–6
— appropriateness of, 166, 176, 182, 185, 247
Punitive supervision, 99
Pushkin, 209

Radical alternatives to prison, 153
Radzinowicz, Sir Leon, 1, 20–2, 131n, 255
Rainer Foundation, 241
Rampton Hospital, 49, 118, 130
Rawls, J., xi

Recidivism, 1, 68, 97, 98, 108, 109, 117, 118, 120, 122, 123, 127, 131, 132, 184, 195, 197, 199, 207, 262
Referrals, 203, 207
Regional Planning Committee, 240
Remission, 31–4, 57, 91
Reparation, 85
Restitution, 233, 235
Reynolds, G. W., 21n
Rice, A. K., 73, 74
Richards, P. G., 41n
Richardson, H., 161n
Ridley, Sir M. W., 7n
Robin, G. D., 11n
Robson, L. L., 13n
Rochester, Bishop of, 46
Romilly, Sir Samuel, 42
Rose, G., 2n, 6n, 11n, 12n, 15n
Rostow, W. W., 17
Rousseau, J. J., 35
Royal Commission on the Penal System, 46, 53
Ruck, S. K., 10n, 100n
Rudé, G., 13n, 21n
Ruggles-Brise, Sir Evelyn, 2, 9
Rusche, G., 192

St. Bartholomew's Hospital, 116
Sandford, D. A., 137n
Savitz, L., 199n
Scandinavia, 84, 86, 88–99, 130, 156, 191, 192n
Schofield, M., 222
Schwartz, R. D., 193n
Scotland, 160–2, 191, 228, 257, 263
Scott, C. P., 111
Secretary of State: see also HOME SECRETARY, 26, 240, 259
Seebohm Committee, 257
Select Committees – see COMMONS, HOUSE OF or LORDS, HOUSE OF
Sentences
— conditional, 87–9
— decrease in length of, 89, 189, 190
— deferred, 171–2, 177
— enforcement of, 84, 91, 92
— immutable nature of, 25, 169, 175, 178
— increase in length of, 104, 165, 186, 188, 261
— indeterminate, 28, 83, 98, 178

— suspended, 6, 28, 33, 39, 45, 47, 48, 85, 98, 99, 124, 168
Sereny, G., 160n
Sewell, R. V., 130n
Sexual offenders, 122, 123, 128, 213, 231, 232, 235
Shaw, A. G. L., 13, 14n, 15n
Silver, A., 21n
Skinner, 137, 143
Slater, 161n
Smart, J., 235
Smith, A. D., 159n
Smith, R. L., 200n
Social Enquiry Reports, 30, 168, 169, 171, 255
Solitary confinement, 3, 9, 91, 213
Solzhenitsyn, A., 209
Sparks, R., 2n, 18n, 20, 22n, 113, 199
Spinoza, 214
Stafford, D., 40
Steer, D., 231
Stejskal, Z., 210
Stephens, Sir James Fitzjames, 34
Stevenson, J., 18n
Stirling, W. R., 80
Straker, A., 129
Stratta, E., 142, 147
Streatfeild Committee, 255
Stretton, H., 14
Stuart, M., 262n
Studt, E., 198
Sykes, M., 131n

Tallack, W., 12
Tavistock Institute, 73
Taylor, L., 131n, 136n
Teeters, N. K., 12n
Templeton, J., 21n
Thomas, D. A., 27n
Thomas, J. E., 4n, 6n, 7n, 8n, 16, 23n, 59n, 111n, 113, 114
Tittle, 193
Tobias, J. J., 15n, 17, 23n
Toffler, A., 146, 151
Tolstoy, L., 154
Trades Union Congress, 253
Transportation, 2, 3, 12–14
Trasler, G. B., 131n
Treatment ideology, 71, 75–7, 81, 97, 98, 104, 106, 111, 119, 123, 129, 131, 133, 143, 156, 157, 177, 198, 207, 241
Turkey, 84

United States of America, viii, 1n, 2, 15, 102, 105, 113, 130, 156, 191–3, 227, 230, 243, 247, 261, 266 – see also CALIFORNIA

Venn, G., 150
Vera Institute of Justice, 266
Visits, 56, 92, 93, 219
Voluntary Service, 247, 248
Volunteers, 242, 243, 248, 251, 256
Von Hentig, H., 227

Wadsworth, M., 222
Wakefield, E. G., 13n
Wakefield Prison, 2, 56, 122, 147
Wakefieldians, 13, 14
Walker, N. D., 16n, 22n, 36, 162n, 182, 190
Walkland, S. A., 38
Ward, D., 156n, 199
Ward, D. A., 68, 131n
Warren, M. Q., 198
Webb, B. and S., 2n, 4n
Wellington, Duke of, 116
Wells, J., 9n
Wells-Pestell, Lord, 46
Wessex Neurological Centre, 123
West Germany, 84, 85, 87, 92, 94, 192, 247
Whately, Archbishop, 13n, 14, 23

Whitehead, A. N., 147, 148, 152
Wilkins, L. T., 19n
Willcock, H. D., 190
Williams, M., 130n
Wilner, D. M., 68, 199
Wisconsin Citizens' Study Commission on Offenders' Rehabilitation, viii
Woking Prison, 119
Wolfgang, M. E., 131n, 199n, 227
Women offenders, 48, 50, 92, 155–64, 226, 234
Wootton, Baroness of Abinger, 1, 46, 162n, 223, 246, 247, 250, 251
— Committee – see ADVISORY COUNCIL ON THE PENAL SYSTEM
Wormwood Scrubs, 5n, 56, 119, 122, 126
Wrigley, E. A., 16n

Young, G., 50, 51
Young offenders, 18, 19, 57, 83, 204, 205, 222, 223, 250
— classification of, 130
— 'intermediate treatment' of, 238–244, 246
— punishment of, 26n, 28, 29, 58, 85, 98, 168, 169, 172

Zimring, F., 187n, 192, 193